Intro
Ch. 1-4

Integration Interrupted

KAROLYN TYSON

Integration Interrupted

Tracking, Black Students, and

Acting White after Brown

OXFORD
UNIVERSITY PRESS

2011

OXFORD
UNIVERSITY PRESS

Oxford University Press, Inc., publishes works that further
Oxford University's objective of excellence
in research, scholarship, and education.

Oxford   New York
Auckland   Cape Town   Dar es Salaam   Hong Kong   Karachi
Kuala Lumpur   Madrid   Melbourne   Mexico City   Nairobi
New Delhi   Shanghai   Taipei   Toronto

With offices in
Argentina   Austria   Brazil   Chile   Czech Republic   France   Greece
Guatemala   Hungary   Italy   Japan   Poland   Portugal   Singapore
South Korea   Switzerland   Thailand   Turkey   Ukraine   Vietnam

Published by Oxford University Press, Inc.
198 Madison Avenue, New York, New York 10016

www.oup.com

Oxford is a registered trademark of Oxford University Press

Library of Congress Cataloging-in-Publication Data
Tyson, Karolyn.
Integration interrupted : tracking, black students, and acting White
after Brown / Karolyn Tyson.
p.   cm.
Includes bibliographical references and index.
ISBN 978-0-19-973644-7 (cloth : alk. paper)   ISBN 978-0-19-973645-4 (pbk. : alk. paper)
1. African Americans—Education.   2. African Americans—Education—Social aspects.
3. African American students—Social conditions.   4. African American students—Ethnic
identity.   5. School integration—United States.   6. Track system (Education)—United
States.   7. Academic achievement—United States.   I. Title.
LC2771.T97 2011
371.829'96073—dc22   2010017252

Printed in the United States of America
on acid-free paper

CONTENTS

F OR MORE THAN TEN years, motivated by debate on the black-white achievement gap, I have been conducting research in schools, observing mainly black students in their daily activities and listening to their stories about their schooling experiences, their successes and disappointments, and goals and aspirations. I was moved and inspired by the students' innocence, their faith in the promise of education, and the candor with which they spoke about their lives at school and at home, and their hopes for the future. Having read so many reports describing disengagement, pessimism, and hopelessness among black youth, I was somewhat surprised by how much the students I encountered seemed to believe in the idea that education is the key to success and, therefore, strived to do well in school.

I derived many insights from the classroom observations, and the students' disclosures and the stories they told, but many of those insights came only with further research and much reflection. Initially, I was puzzled. What I saw and heard seemed to contradict both some of the more consistent research findings reported by others and media portrayals of black and low-income students. For example, I was struck by the exuberance and excitement about learning that the young black students I observed displayed in their elementary school classrooms. Their attitudes and behaviors were not consistent with the idea that black students are "culturally disinclined" to do well in school.

In this book, I take a close look at life in school for students in the post-*Brown* era. I use data gathered from 250 students in more than thirty elementary and secondary schools drawn from four studies (see table P.1). The studies focus on local samples of students within select schools, primarily in

TABLE P.1 Selected Characteristics of Studies

Study	Participating Schools[1]	Student Race and Median Household Income	Dates of Data Collection	Number of Students Interviewed
Study I				
In Their Own Words I (P.I.: K. Tyson)	Alternatives School	Black $60,000–$79,000	1996–1997	40
	Madison Elementary School	$40,000–$59,000		
Study II				
In Their Own Words II (P.I.: K. Tyson)	Linwood Elementary School	Black $6,000–$8,499	2000–2001	20
Study III				
Understanding Minority Underrepresentation (W. Darity, P.I., D. Castellino and K. Tyson, Co-P.I.s)	Avery High School	Black, Asian, white, Hispanic, Native American (income not available)	2000–2001	125
	Banaker High School[2]			
	Clearview High School			
	Dalton High School			
	East High School			
	Franklin High School			
	Georgetown Elementary School			
	Holt Elementary School			
	Ivory Elementary School			
	Jackson Middle School			
	Kilborn Middle School			

Study IV

Effective Students
(W. Darity, P.I., D. Castellino
and K. Tyson, Co-P.I.s)

Black

$50,001–$70,000

2001–2004

Anderson High School
Banaker High School
Bloomfield High School
City High School
Earnshaw School of Excellence
Everton High School
Flamingo High School
Garden Grove High School
Latham High School
Lucas Valley High School
Massey High School
Mullins High School
Parker-Berger High School
Pearce High School
Rolling Hills High School
Shoreline High School
Vanderbilt High School
Wade High School
West End High School

1. *All school names are pseudonyms.*
2. *This school participated in two of the studies listed here. The informants (e.g., students, teachers, principals) did not overlap, however.*

North Carolina. One school, Banaker High School, participated in two of the four studies. Each project uses either ethnography, in-depth interviews, surveys, or combinations of these methods to investigate the relationship between institutional structures and student outcomes, especially attitudes, behaviors, and course enrollment. My analysis relies on school and classroom observations (conducted by me or research assistants) and students' recollections and interpretations of their experiences. Allowing students to speak for themselves more clearly reveals how they perceive their experiences, their understandings of how and why they make the choices they do, and the factors that influence their decisions.

I use pseudonyms to refer to all schools and participants. As a rule, I refer to informants by name because they are real people with individual experiences and histories. I do so also for analytic purposes. By using names, I can better illustrate the range of informants expressing particular views or describing particular experiences, as well as connect the responses of individual informants to provide a fuller portrait of each.

The four studies I draw on are: (1) *In Their Own Words I* (1996–1997); (2) *In Their Own Words II: Linwood* (2000–2001); (3) *Understanding Minority Underrepresentation in Rigorous Courses and Programs* (2000–2001); and (4) *Effective Schools, Effective Students* (2001–2004). Much of my focus in this book is on the adolescents in the latter two studies, but I draw on data from the elementary schools included in *In Their Own Words* (Madison and Alternatives) and *Linwood* (Linwood) when that data contribute to a fuller understanding of particular processes.

Two studies, *In Their Own Words I* and *Linwood*, I undertook independently. Each focused on black students in all-black or predominantly black elementary schools in the Southeast. I obtained access to the schools through formal application procedures, by first submitting a proposal to the school districts, and then to principals of predominantly or all-black schools. In *In Their Own Words I* (1996–1997), I sought to explore how schooling differed for black students in black independent schools compared to black students in public schools. I selected and gained access to a black independent school and an all-black public school that were comparable in size and socioeconomic status and that were located in the same metropolitan area. Both schools served children from working-class, middle-class, and low-income families. In *Linwood* (2000–2001), I was interested in the effects of poverty and low-income status on black students' schooling. The public elementary school studied, which I call Linwood, was over 95 percent black and served primarily low-income and poor students; most students lived in the low-income housing projects surrounding the school.

In both studies, after the principals had approved the research, each suggested teachers (one third grade and one fourth grade) who might be willing to participate in an ethnographic study focused on their classrooms. The teachers I approached agreed to participate. Both studies involved daylong classroom observations for seven to eight months, and in-depth interviews with students, principals, teachers, and parents. The goal was to understand the effects of the local school environment on student outcomes. I interviewed the principal at each school, the teachers of the classrooms I observed, ten students (five boys and five girls) from each classroom, and the students' parents. I interviewed most of the students twice, once at the beginning of the study and again at the end. I spent two full days per week in each of the schools from the fall through the end of the school year. Generally, I elected to be a "pure observer"; I sat at the back of each classroom and took notes. During the day, I accompanied the classes to different subjects (e.g., art, music, physical education), lunch, recess, field trips, and assemblies, always taking notes. Research for *Linwood* was supported by a grant from the University of North Carolina at Chapel Hill, University Research Council. *In Their Own Words I* was supported by a dissertation fellowship from the Spencer Foundation.

I worked collaboratively on the two other studies, *Understanding Minority Underrepresentation* and *Effective Schools, Effective Students*, with economist William Darity Jr., and psychologist Domini Castellino. Both studies focused on North Carolina public schools. *Understanding Minority Underrepresentation*, as the title suggests, examined minority student underrepresentation in rigorous courses and programs. The study was part of a larger project commissioned by the North Carolina Department of Public Instruction (NCDPI) and included analysis of existing state data, mail-in surveys of schools' rigorous courses and programs (e.g., gifted programs, AP and honors courses), and individual interviews with principals, teachers, counselors, and a racially diverse group of students in grades one through twelve in eleven schools across the state.

The school surveys, one for high schools and one for elementary and middle schools, were designed in collaboration with NCDPI staff and distributed to all schools in the state. The surveys gathered information on the availability and structure of gifted programs, gifted screening and identification instruments and procedures, grouping practices, number and type of advanced courses offered, criteria for placement, and the race and sex of students participating in rigorous programs and courses. Response rates were 47 percent (N = 866) for the elementary/middle school survey and 52 percent (N = 231) for the high school survey. After analysis of the

survey and extant data and identification of the trends in minority representation in rigorous courses and programs across North Carolina, we selected
eleven schools to study in more detail. The schools—three elementary, two
middle, and six high schools—included some with significant minority
underrepresentation in rigorous courses and programs relative to these students' presence in the student body; some with less dramatic underrepresentation; and schools where minority students were equally or overrepresented
in rigorous courses and programs. Most of the schools fell into the first
group, and only one fell into the latter, as such public schools were rare in
North Carolina. Given the selection criteria for the schools, they may not be
representative of North Carolina high schools as a whole. We gained access
to the schools with the assistance of the NCDPI and spent one day at each
conducting interviews.

Three black female graduate students, Cheryl McDonald, Rachael
Murphey, and Alison Roberts, assisted me with the interviews. The semi-
structured interview protocol for high school students included questions
regarding course-selection decisions (e.g., "Why did you select this course of
study?"); satisfaction with decisions (e.g., "Do you like being in those
classes?"); future plans (e.g., "Do you think you might take an AP course in
the future?"); and knowledge about courses (e.g., "What do you think it
takes to be in honors English?"). These interviews lasted from thirty-five to
fifty-five minutes. Amy Mody and Ann Brewster assisted with data analysis.

More than half (62%) of the interviewed high school students are female.
The group includes a mix of students at high, average, and low levels of
achievement drawn from the six high schools. These students are not generally representative of North Carolina high school students. The majority of
informants are higher achieving; thirty-eight reported having been identified
as "gifted" in elementary or middle school. I suspect that the schools' role in
distributing consent forms to potential participants contributed to this
imbalance, although it is possible that lower-achieving students were less
likely to consent to participate.

Effective Schools, Effective Students, an investigation of the achievement gap
from the vantage point of success, had two parts, both of which included participant observation over the course of eighteen months and interviews with
students. For the analysis in this book, I focus only on the *Effective Students*
part of the study. *Effective Students* focused on sixty-five high-achieving black
adolescents in nineteen high schools within three North Carolina school districts. Through formal application procedures, we received approval from
each school district and principal to conduct the study. School counselors
identified and distributed research consent forms to eleventh-grade black

students who had been on the school's honor roll for two or more consecutive semesters. We invited all of the identified students, in most cases between two and five at each school, to participate in the study. Participation ranged from as few as one student at three schools to seven at another.

Two black graduate students, George "Jay" Murray and Valerie Rawlston, worked with me to "shadow" individual students at school approximately three to four times each during their junior and senior years. We attended a mix of their classes, and sat in during homeroom, assemblies, and lunch outings. We also attended graduations, awards ceremonies, and athletic events. At the start of each student's participation in the study, we conducted an individual interview. At the conclusion of the study, we interviewed the students again. Finally, we surveyed the parents of fifty of the participating students about their own education, income, occupation, and involvement in their children's education, among other things. We conducted the survey at the beginning of the study, at the same time that we were conducting the first set of interviews. A few parents declined to participate. Amy Mody worked as a research assistant on this project.

Effective Schools, Effective Students was supported by a grant from the Spencer Foundation to William Darity Jr., P.I., and Domini Castellino and Karolyn Tyson, Co-P.I.s.

ACKNOWLEDGMENTS

THIS BOOK WOULD NOT have been possible without the contribution of the many students who so generously invited us into their worlds at school, allowing my colleagues and me to look, listen, and learn about life in school for youth in the twenty-first century. These students candidly shared recollections of their school experiences, opening up about their trials, triumphs, hopes, and aspirations. Some even permitted us to tag along with them at school. This book is dedicated to them. They have my deep respect and admiration.

Many other people contributed to the production of this book. I am indebted to the kind colleagues, friends, and family who read drafts of chapters over the years and provided critical feedback and encouragement. Ingrid Banks, Michele Berger, Judith Blau, Simone Boyce, John Davis, Harry Edwards, Glen Elder, Caroline Hodges Persell, Michael Hout, Adrian Isles, Camille Jacobs, Tracy Johnson, Sherryl Kleinman, Charles Kurzman, Samuel Lucas, Sybil Madison-Boyd, Mignon Moore, Lisa Pearce, Nicole Roach, and Peggy Thoits unselfishly gave of their time and talents, and for that I will always be grateful. Karyn Lacy, Annette Lareau, and Karla Slocum went above and beyond the call of duty as friends and mentors and were especially giving of their time and counsel throughout the production of this book. I am forever in their debt.

Thanks also to the Spencer Foundation, whose funding provided support for much of the research I report on in this book. I am also grateful to the Russell Sage Foundation and its staff for their support of this project and the comfortable living and working spaces they provided to begin writing. The scholars at Russell Sage during my time there are also owed a debt of gratitude for their support and encouragement during our year together at the Foundation. Special thanks to Robert Barsky, Amy Binder, Charles Clotfelter, Jocelyn Crowley, Nancy Folbre, Jeff Manza, and Judith Stacey. The Institute for Arts and Humanities at the University of North Carolina also provided support for this project.

I was fortunate to work with William "Sandy" Darity Jr. and Domini Castellino on two of the projects that form the basis of my work in this book. Sandy has never wavered in his support of me or my work in the eleven years I have known him. I cannot thank him enough for that and for the many opportunities he has made available to me. He has been the consummate mentor. Many thanks are due also to the research assistants who worked on the projects: Cheryl McDonald, Rachael Murphey-Brown, George "Jay" Murray, Selina Murrell, Valerie Rawlston, Alison Roberts, Amy Mody, Ann Brewster, and Lindsay Carter.

I cannot thank M. Katherine Mooney enough for her superb and attentive editorial assistance throughout the writing of this book and for always asking tough and insightful questions. I am also indebted to my editor at Oxford University Press, James Cook, and to Carla O'Connor and Amanda Lewis and numerous anonymous reviewers who provided thoughtful and astute feedback on previous drafts of the manuscript.

Thanks also to the faculty and graduate students at the University of North Carolina at Chapel Hill, Indiana University, New York University, and the University of California at Irvine and Santa Barbara for helpful feedback on presentations of parts of the work in this book.

Finally, I thank my family and the many friends who provided unending support and encouragement as I wrote this book over and over again.

Integration Interrupted

| # Desegregation Without Integration

IN AMERICA, NOTHING MATTERS MORE for getting ahead than education. The widespread agreement on this point is perhaps why the academic underperformance of racial and ethnic minorities is the focus of so much debate and why public policy, including the No Child Left Behind Act, so often targets these students. The relatively low academic achievement of African American students, in particular, dominates a great deal of the discussion on the achievement gap. Recent figures from the National Assessment of Educational Progress (NAEP) show that, on average, seventeen-year old black students score 30 points lower than white students on reading and 28 points lower on math.[1] Few issues in the field of education have received as much attention as this one. And everyone—educators, researchers, parents, students, politicians, journalists, and celebrities—seems to have a theory about why black students are not doing better in school. What is most interesting about this chorus of voices is that many loudly repeat some version of the same argument, namely that African American youth are steeped in a culture that ridicules academic achievement because it is equated with acting white.[2]

President Barack Obama's was probably the loudest of these voices, as his remarks were made in a nationally televised speech at the 2004 National Democratic Convention. Commenting on the problems of inner-city neighborhoods, the then-senator emphasized the need to "eradicate the slander that says that a black youth with a book is acting white."[3] Arguably no other explanation of black academic underperformance has become more entrenched.

Indeed, it has become part of our commonsense understanding of why black students are underachieving. A former teacher's letter to the editor of the *New York Times* some years ago captures the gist of the public perception about the problem plaguing black students: "Many black children who are serious about their studies are subject to derision by other black students. Acting 'white' is the ultimate put-down. What is so 'white' about being a good student...?"[4]

Remarks like these initially left me confused. I had spent time conducting research in all-black elementary schools, observing classrooms and talking with students, and these remarks did not match what I had observed. I never heard any student mention acting white, in any context. The students I encountered coveted academic success. There were tears and tantrums when they did not make the honor roll or when they failed to get high marks on an assignment, or when they did not receive a gold star on the board or an invitation to the schoolwide celebration of individual achievement on the state's standardized tests, or when they were not picked for a role in a classroom play.[5] But later, as my research expanded to include adolescents, I began to hear accounts from high-achieving black students about being accused of acting white apparently because of their achievement.

Even now, however, after more than ten years conducting research in schools, what I have learned remains hard to reconcile with claims that black students are "culturally disinclined to do well in school," as linguist John McWhorter claims in his book *Losing the Race*.[6] My empirical analysis shows that explanations such as McWhorter's distort what is really going on. First, many black students do not connect race with achievement. This phenomenon is greatly exaggerated. Second, and perhaps more importantly, the idea that race and achievement are linked is not something that black youth are taught at home or in their communities. This is a connection they learn at school. The popularity of the notion that black students reject achievement as acting white and that this accounts for the black-white achievement gap has helped turn this hypothesis into an accepted fact. But using this argument anecdotally in social discourse is inaccurate and costly. We know surprisingly little about students' use of the acting white slur with respect to achievement, let alone what its empirical connection might be to the achievement gap. When did the association of race with academic achievement emerge among black students? Why have black youth come to equate school success with whiteness? This book addresses these questions by giving readers a chance to look inside of schools and listen as students talk about their everyday experiences. The students I observed, interviewed, and spent time with during the course of my research generously opened their lives to an outsider's gaze and shared their stories about life at school. They spoke frankly about their successes and disappointments, their trials and tribulations, and their goals, aspirations, and fears.

Consider Sandra, for example. We met in 2002, when she was a junior at Earnshaw School of Excellence. Sandra was one of sixty-five North Carolina public high school students participating in research my colleagues and I were conducting on high-achieving black students.[7] As we walked from one class to another on Earnshaw's sprawling campus, Sandra generally was quiet and reserved. During the interviews, however, she opened up and spoke candidly and at length. Her school, a combined middle and high school, was 49 percent white and 44 percent black. Yet Sandra described her early experiences at Earnshaw as "hell," because she had been "the only black student" in her gifted English and advanced math classes. She explained:

> Well, I—okay, because of my classes that I couldn't take with a lot of black students, so I was in, mainly made—I *had* to make friends with a lot of white students 'cause those are the only people who are in my classes. And those are the people that I tend to sit with at lunch because I had never met anyone else. I mean I had black friends, but because I don't see a lot of them, I made friends with white [students]. And because of that, [the black girls] thought that that meant I was— I didn't want to be with other black people and that I thought that I was better than them, and I was trying to "act white." . . . But that's not it, you know.

Some high-achieving black students at other schools described similar encounters with peers over the issue of acting white and particular achievement-related behaviors. For example, Juliana, a senior at Everton High School, recalled that her black friends occasionally joked that she had "turned white on [them]" after she began taking advanced courses, which they called "white people class[es]." Everton's student population was just over one-fifth black, but few advanced classes had more than one or two black students enrolled, and many had none. Another student, Lynden, a senior at City High, remembered being teased in the ninth grade by fellow blacks. They called him "White Pretty Boy" because of his friendships with the "smart" students in his advanced classes, most of whom were white. Although City High's student body was 16 percent black, black students were nearly invisible in the school's higher-level classes. In many of those classes, black students accounted for less than 5 percent of those enrolled.

Stories like these will resonate with readers who are familiar with the contemporary schooling experiences of black youth and the problem of black academic underachievement.[8] What readers may be less familiar with, however, is the unmistakable connection between this peculiar use of the acting white slur and an institutional practice common in secondary schools: tracking. This practice of separating students for instruction, ostensibly based on their ability and prior achievement, often results in segregated classrooms in predominantly white and racially diverse schools like the ones described above. The higher-level classes (gifted, honors, advanced placement) are disproportionately filled with white students, while the lower-level, standard classes are disproportionately filled with black and other minority students.[9] We call this "racialized" tracking, but it is essentially segregation.

With black and white students largely segregated within the schools they attend, racialized tracking has made it possible to have desegregation without integration. It is this school-based pattern of separation that has given rise to students associating achievement with whiteness. This association is found only in schools where racialized tracking is prevalent. In the predominantly black high schools in our study, where advanced classes were majority black, the high-achieving black students we met were not even aware that academic achievement is considered a form of acting white.[10] When we asked Sonya, a senior at Banaker High School (89% black), whether students at the school ever use the acting white slur to refer to high-achieving students in particular, she answered casually, "No, I haven't seen that. When they say you're acting white, they just do if you talk a different way."[11] Sonya and her peers at Banaker had no experience with the type of "hell" Sandra encountered across town at Earnshaw.

The marked difference in the experience of students who attend schools like Sonya's and those who attend schools like Sandra's draws attention to the importance of how schools are organized.[12] As Sandra's and many other students' experiences suggest, tracking does more than keep black and white students separated during the school day. It also produces and maintains a set of conditions in which academic success is linked with whites: Students equate achievement with whiteness because school structures do.[13] By focusing on students' equating achievement with acting white as *the* problem, without first trying to understand the cause of this phenomenon, we end up confusing cause with effect. Consequently, we attempt to treat the symptom (equating achievement with whiteness), while the disease (racialized tracking) goes unchecked. The connection between racialized tracking and students' linking of achievement-related behaviors to whiteness has received far too little attention.[14] One aim of this book is to bring that connection into sharp focus. I argue that students' linking achievement with whiteness emerged after desegregation and is a result of racialized tracking, which is part of a historical legacy of strategies used to avoid integration.[15]

In the study of high-achieving black adolescents (*Effective Students*), my research assistants and I shadowed students at school. At racially diverse and predominantly white high schools, the participants were frequently the only black students in their advanced classes. This pattern, which was especially evident in AP courses, did not escape their attention. Without prompting, many mentioned being the "only black" student in their advanced classes. Robin, for example, who attended Shoreline High School (72% white; 15% black), recalled that she did not have another black student in her advanced classes until her junior year. City High (69% white; 16% black) student Courtney called off a list of classes in which he was the only black student: honors physics, AP statistics, AP U.S. history. Jasmine made similar observations about her advanced classes at Lucas Valley High School (65% white; 24% black): "I took advanced English and I was the only black person in [the class both times]. . . . This year I'm the only black person in my physics class." Keisha, who attended Garden Grove High School (54% white; 32% black), complained about being the "only black girl in a sea" of "white people" in her advanced classes. And a student I called to arrange to shadow at school the following day warned me that she and I would be the only two black people in the room during her first class.

Observations of these high-achieving students continued over an eighteen-month period. My research assistants and I became so accustomed to the pattern of segregation in advanced classes in predominantly white and racially diverse schools that any deviation struck us as odd. Once, when I was shadowing Zorayda, a senior at Earnshaw, I was shocked as I sat down and surveyed her honors English class, made up of nineteen students, twelve of whom were black. In my field notes that day I wrote: "I've never been in a class like this here [Earnshaw] before—predominantly black."[16] Until then, I had been in classes with a racial composition of that kind only at predominantly black schools or in elective or general education classes.[17]

The participants' reports of their peers' comments indicate that other students at racially diverse and predominantly white schools also were aware of the prevailing pattern of racial segregation across classrooms. Why else would they refer to advanced classes as "white classes" or the "white-people class," or ask peers why they wanted to be in classes or programs in which there were no other black students? These types of comments reflect a general pattern. Reports of racialized ridicule (e.g., being accused of acting white, or being called an "Oreo") for high achievement and for other achievement-related behaviors (e.g., taking advanced classes) always coincide with students' experiences of racial hierarchies in tracking and achievement at the schools they attend. Thus, not all high-achieving black students are taunted for acting white because of their achievement. What I found is that those who are taunted always attend racially diverse or predominantly white schools where racialized tracking makes possible racial isolation and rejection of the kind Sandra experienced.

Today, many racially diverse schools lack true integration because of racialized tracking.[18] A number of studies emphasize this point. For example, Charles Clotfelter's research on interracial contact among students since desegregation indicates that within-school segregation increases as the percentage of blacks in the student body increases. According to Clotfelter, schools between 30 and 60 percent black show the highest rates of segregation.[19] Similarly, in their study of the correlates of tracking, Samuel Lucas and Mark Berends find that tracking is more pronounced in schools with more racial and social class diversity.[20] In stalling integration, tracking exacts enormous costs that are borne by black students such as Sandra, as well as by her schoolmates, both black and non-black. This book explores some of those costs.

Examining the Costs of Racialized Tracking

The pattern of black-white racial segregation in American public schools produced through tracking (and through gifted and magnet programs) is well documented.[21] Indeed, racialized tracking is a common feature of contemporary American secondary schools. Unfortunately, however, it gets relatively little public attention. Americans simply assume that academic placements reflect students' ability and their (and their parents') choices and attitudes toward school. These assumptions are not entirely accurate. There is more to the contemporary high school placement process than meets the eye. Yet in racially mixed schools, what does meet the eye—the image of overwhelmingly black lower-level classes and overwhelmingly white advanced classes—sends powerful messages to students about ability, race, status, and achievement. Linking achievement with whiteness is one consequence of racialized tracking, but there are others that also shape school performance and interracial relations. This book takes a look at how institutional practices such as tracking affect black and other students' schooling experiences. How do students make sense of this pattern of racialized tracking? What does it mean for students' developing sense of self and their decisions and actions at school? How does it affect black students' relationship with same-race and other peers?

In many states, schools' early placement decisions involve some form of ability grouping or the use of academic designations such as "gifted," "gifted and talented," or "advanced." Previous research has shown that these practices contribute to the initial sorting process that sets racial groups on different academic paths in elementary school.[22] Institutional sorting continues more formally and overtly in secondary school. There students are separated for instruction on the basis of a range of criteria, including perceived ability, prior achievement, and/or post-high school occupational plans and aspirations. During adolescence, as students attempt to negotiate the delicate balance between where they fit and where they feel most comfortable, both academically and socially, this sorting reinforces racial patterns and stereotypes. Thus, the schools' early placements and labels have a particularly profound and, for some adolescents, harmful effect.

This book lets us hear students' perceptions of these placements and labels and allows us to look inside some of their classrooms. Through hearing students' own perceptions of their placements and labels, this book reveals the quandary racialized tracking has created and the anguish it has wrought. During the ten-plus years I have been conducting observational and interview research on students' in-school experiences, I have found that sorting practices such as tracking and gifted programs have implications for much more than grades and test scores. These practices influence students' perceptions of the link between race and achievement, their self-perceptions of ability, how they view one another, and where they think they and others belong. As a result, in schools with racialized tracking, high-achieving black students are more likely to perceive pressure to conform to a peer culture oppositional to the norms and values of schools. However, this perception does not necessarily prevent high-achieving students from taking advanced courses. For all students, regardless of race, the most important consideration in course-selection deliberations is a desire to avoid failure and the feelings of incompetence and embarrassment that accompany that experience.

In the chapters that follow, I share more of these findings, presenting a detailed analysis of the narratives and school experiences of some of the more than two hundred students studied in twenty-eight schools. Some are like Sandra—high-achieving black students who are subject to their peers' taunts about acting white. Some are like Sonya—high-achieving black students who have not encountered this form of ridicule. Some are lower-achieving students; and some are non-black. I draw on these students' varied experiences to show how racialized tracking and the messages it conveys affect students' daily life at school, their academic self-perceptions, school-based decisions and actions, and their relationships with peers.

Racialized tracking and the belief that academic achievement is a "white thing" reflect broader social issues regarding the role of race in education. Each speaks to the continuing significance of race in America. And each also points to obstacles on the path to integration. Since desegregation, we have been witnessing a new form of educational apartheid achieved through tracking.[23] As part of a historical legacy of strategies to avoid integration, tracking has proven remarkably effective, and, in the wake of desegregation, highly consequential. Black and white adolescents often have very little meaningful contact with one another in school because they are separated for most of their core classes. Not surprisingly, these divisions are often deliberately replicated in other settings. As we observed while shadowing high-achieving black students, in elective classes, at lunch or assemblies, blacks and whites tend to sit apart from one another, occupying different sections of the room.[24] Everyday realities like these help explain why attending a desegregated school does not always provide the benefits we anticipate young people will gain from a racially diverse environment.

Tracking and Acting White after Brown

The Supreme Court's 1954 *Brown v. Board of Education* decision was supposed to eliminate school segregation.[25] More than five decades after the decision, however, black students and white students throughout much of the country still experience separate and unequal schooling. Not only have American schools been growing more segregated at the school level, they remain overwhelmingly segregated at the classroom level. Numerous scholarly and journalistic accounts detail the startling degree to which black and white students are segregated within the schools they attend.[26] Yet, within-school segregation has not engendered the same type of urgency, outrage, or national shame that segregation did before and shortly after the *Brown* ruling. There have been no marches or sit-ins, no public outcry, and very little condemnation of school officials or pressure on policy makers. But why should there be protests? Wasn't the fight for equality of educational opportunity won with the *Brown* decision? In some respects it was, if only because the ruling prohibited *de jure* segregation. But *Brown* promised more than desegregation; the decision also promised integration, as it raised hopes that black and white students would come together as equals. Instead, the movement toward integration had barely begun before it was interrupted.

The failure to achieve true integration at school is an enormous loss. No American institution other than schools brings together so many children, from so many diverse backgrounds, for so much time each day, over so many years. Not families, not churches, not neighborhoods. We might expect schools to be where children learn to see past their differences and find commonalities that would allow them to form meaningful relationships with people unlike themselves. Unfortunately, this kind of learning is rare. Instead, schools too often teach young people pecking orders, hierarchies based on status and achievement. The social divisions and animosity that exist between groups in the larger society are reinforced at school. As James Rosenbaum found in his study of tracking at a white working-class school more than three decades ago, "Tracking provides distinct categories that are highly salient."[27] When these categories (e.g., honors, remedial, college prep) mirror the racial, gender, and social class hierarchies in place outside of school, they can lead students to perceive their own and others' assigned placements as accurate and permanent. Indeed, students tend to believe that placements merely reflect racial differences in ability, work ethic, and attitudes toward school.[28] Thus, for example, some of the high-achieving black students in our study felt that in order to fit in with their peers, they had to project an attitude that downplayed school. Otherwise, they feared, they might be perceived as "acting, like, white or something if you're trying to be smart." As one student explained, this was because "it's always been [that]... the smart people are the white people."

The popularity of the belief that a fear of acting white explains black academic underachievement has obscured an important fact. It is only relatively recently that black youth have equated high academic achievement with acting white. The first published accounts of this phenomenon began emerging in the 1980s. Prior to that, there is no indication that acting white included reference to academic achievement and achievement-related behaviors. The earliest published study reporting black students' use of the term documented the students' adjustment to desegregation in a Wisconsin high school in 1969. The black students in the study raised concerns about acting white. They noted that they did not want to lose what was, as the authors put it, "a natural part of Negro behavior as it evolved in this country."[29] The students characterized acting white only as being "more inhibited," "more formal," and "lacking 'soul.'" More recent studies, however, report that among adolescents (blacks and others), acting white currently includes a host of characteristics, including taking honors and advanced placement classes, getting good grades, going to class, and doing schoolwork.[30]

This expansion in meaning of acting white indicates a cultural shift. This is in itself telling, because such shifts typically are associated with other, larger changes in the social world.[31] In other words, changes in social structure tend to bring about changes in culture. Indeed, patterns like the one Sandra described at Earnshaw suggest that the shift in the meaning of acting white was brought about largely by the change in educational policy that led to school desegregation.[32] Desegregation, and especially attempts to bypass it with tracking and gifted and magnet programs, paved the way for the emergence of distinct racial patterns in student placement and achievement in some schools.[33]

Tracking and Race in Historical Context

The practice of sorting and selecting students in order to provide them with different educational programs did not originate with desegregation, however. In the United States, this type of tracking dates back to the late nineteenth and early twentieth centuries, when the immigrant population increased and the public school system expanded.[34] During this early period, tracking helped separate students more by social class and ethnicity than by race. Racial cleavages within public schools were rare. This was because, depending on the area, non-whites were few in number, denied access to public schooling, or consigned to separate schools. In most states outside the South, neighborhood segregation ensured that blacks and whites attended different schools. In the South and some other areas (e.g., Arizona), laws enforcing segregation accomplished the same end.[35]

Thus, before desegregation, curricular differentiation in public schools reflected social class, ethnicity, immigrant status, and gender variation in the student population.[36] Not surprisingly, these also were the lines along which students often drew group boundaries and reinforced social divisions.[37] Divisions that existed outside of school undoubtedly were worsened by the disparities in tracking found inside the school. These disparities further separated and marked the haves and the have nots, those who were "expected to 'make something' of themselves" and those who were deemed unlikely to succeed.[38] Desegregation brought another line along which students within the same school could be marked and separated by the curriculum.

The path to desegregation was not smooth, however. By all accounts, it was a painfully slow and difficult process. Whites vigorously fought the federal mandate to create racially mixed schools. In Virginia, for example, officials in some counties chose to shut down the public schools rather than comply with the Supreme Court's desegregation ruling.[39] Prince Edward County officials not only closed the public schools for five years, they also used public funds to help establish private schools for whites. In other areas of the South (e.g., Mississippi), whites fled to existing private schools or established new private academies.[40] And elsewhere in the country, whites abandoned major metropolitan areas (e.g., Detroit), opting to send their children to public schools in largely white suburban districts.[41] Thus, although the Court handed down its *Brown I* and *II* decisions in 1954 and 1955, many schools, including ones outside the South, did not begin implementing desegregation plans until decades later.[42] Significant progress toward desegregation finally occurred in the 1970s, as a result of court-mandated busing in various parts of the country.[43]

Once desegregation began in earnest, the long-standing institutional practice of tracking students took on new meaning as districts faced the reality of racially mixed schools. Particularly in the South, where segregation had been mandated by law and was therefore deeply entrenched, white school officials sought to continue avoiding integration by devising legally permissible ways to separate students by race.[44] Some districts simply placed black and white students in separate classrooms. Others achieved a similar outcome by using strategies such as magnet schools, gifted programs, and other forms of curriculum differentiation.[45] Tracking became part of the arsenal of strategies used to resist school integration in the South and elsewhere. As Kenneth Meier, Joseph Stewart Jr., and Robert England have argued in their book *Race, Class and Education: The Politics of Second-Generation Discrimination*, the policy that defined equal educational opportunity as desegregated education "ignored the continued resistance to integration and permitted the development of other methods of limiting access."[46]

Eventually, legal challenges to racialized tracking emerged. In one well-documented case that landed in the courts in the early 1990s,[47] a school district in Rockford, Illinois, established predominantly white gifted programs within some of its high-minority schools as a means of complying with the state's desegregation laws.[48] Indeed, the plaintiffs' findings in the case alleged that, "These programs created virtually all-white enclaves within black schools—independent curriculums that were totally separate from the regular academic pursuits of these predominantly black schools."[49] A federal court later found the district's classroom assignment methods unconstitutional. Similar cases were brought against school districts in other states as well, often with similar outcomes.[50]

Despite these battles, racialized tracking persists—in large part because of differences in the average achievement of white and black students. School districts use whites' higher average achievement (a disparity to which tracking no doubt contributes) to justify the segregation.[51] However, a number of studies have found that even after taking students' prior achievement, socioeconomic status, and other relevant factors into account, black students still are more likely than whites to be placed into lower tracks.[52] Roslyn Mickelson's analysis of test score and track-level data collected from the Charlotte-Mecklenburg, North Carolina, schools provides an example of this. She found that among eighth-grade students scoring in the top (90–99th) percentile on the California Achievement Test, 72 percent of whites were enrolled in the top English track compared to only 19 percent of blacks. Mickelson found a similar pattern of racial disparity among twelfth-grade students as well. Findings such as these indicate that racial differences in achievement do not fully explain racialized tracking.[53]

Moreover, it is important to keep in mind that in the 1960s and 1970s, courts in a number of jurisdictions banned the use of standardized IQ and achievement tests to place students in classes because the practice produced an isolation effect, much as we find for black students today. In the District of Columbia, for example, the federal district court ruled tracking unconstitutional because of its "racially discriminatory effects."[54] In contrast, today, as the courts have determined school districts to be operating a unified system for all students, tracking that contributes to racial segregation within schools and a widening achievement gap is widespread and generally considered acceptable.[55] This is clear in a recent case brought against the City of Thomasville School District in Georgia. The plaintiffs, black parents and the local NAACP, argued that school policies and practices resulted in black students being segregated in lower-level courses. The court held that the district's system of tracking was not intentionally discriminatory and ruled in favor of the school district.[56] This reflects a significant change from the way the courts in earlier decades viewed tracking that leads to racial segregation.

For now, the court's decision leaves racial segregation within the Thomasville district's schools intact. In this city in Georgia, as in cities and towns across the country, whites and blacks will continue to experience separate and unequal schooling, and whiteness will continue to define what it means to be smart and high achieving. This book examines how this process unfolds at the school and classroom level and calls attention to its consequences for today's youth. If we are serious about achieving integration in America, this kind of analysis is critically important. We need to understand why, after more than fifty years, school desegregation has not led to true integration. The best approach is to begin by looking at what is really happening inside our schools, the place where many children have their first opportunities to interact with peers of other racial and ethnic groups.

Chapter Overview

This book investigates three core issues regarding tracking and students' schooling experiences in the post-*Brown* era. The topic of acting white has received a great deal of scholarly attention, but the process by which the link between race and academic achievement has developed among contemporary black youth remains very much under-examined. Thus chapter 1 provides a theoretical outline of the formation of this association. My argument—that students' tendency to link achievement with whiteness emerged after desegregation and is a consequence of racialized tracking—challenges some long-held views. The dominant perspective regarding black students' attitudes toward school and achievement frames the issue as largely about culture and values: Black youth learn to disparage school learning and academic success because they grow up in communities where a cultural orientation in opposition to mainstream (white) culture is widespread.[57] Chapter 1 closely examines the strengths and weaknesses of this popular idea. In explaining the limitations of the cultural explanation, the chapter shows the advantages of focusing on students' in-school experiences as the most important source of their actions and ideas regarding academic achievement.

Chapter 2 provides an empirical examination of the way in which racialized tracking creates racial distinctions among students that lead to the interpretation of academic achievement as acting white. It begins with a short discussion of two topics: the meaning and use of the broad concept of acting white among African Americans; and the issue of racial disparities in elementary school gifted programs and race talk among preadolescents. The chapter then turns to its main mission of examining the experiences of high-achieving black adolescents at nineteen public high schools in North Carolina. Finally, it investigates why some high-achieving black youth are targeted with the acting white slur while many others, including peers at the same school, are not.

Chapter 3 addresses high-achieving adolescents' vulnerability to peer cultures that are oppositional to the norms and values of schools. These include youth subcultures in which students are ridiculed for achievement-related behaviors in both racialized and nonracialized ways. Whereas chapter 2 addresses where and when taunts of acting white for achievement-related behaviors occur, chapter 3 investigates why some high-achieving black adolescents succumb to pressure to conform to oppositional aspects of the peer environment at their schools while others are able to resist and reject such pressures. My analysis reveals that there are conditions (both internal and external) that help high-achieving adolescents resist, reject, or ignore this type of negative peer influence. These include, for example, a strong sense of identity (who they are and are not) and clear post–high school goals and aspirations. My findings show, as well, that the age at which adolescents develop the characteristics and goals that keep them focused on achievement varies.

Chapter 4 examines how and why high school classrooms remain segregated even as students in the post-*Brown* era are able to select their own program of study. The chapter describes the placement processes of six North Carolina high schools and recounts how a racially mixed group of sixty-one students attending those schools went about choosing their courses. The analysis shows how students make sense of the messages about race and achievement that are communicated through institutional practices such as tracking and gifted identification and placement. The chapter also assesses the consequences of this meaning-making for students' developing sense of self, their friendship networks, and their school-based decisions. The findings reveal how schools' early sorting of students helps steer them toward particular programs of study, which also help shape their friendship networks. Students, in turn, base their course decisions on a combination of subjective criteria: their interpretation of the meaning of their prior placement and achievement experiences, and their understanding of where they fit within both the intellectual pecking order and the social networks of their school.

The conclusion summarizes the book's findings and considers what the lack of true integration in American schools means for today's youth. Reflecting on the hardships created by classroom racial isolation, the chapter offers suggestions for ways that schools might address the most damaging aspects of racialized tracking and reduce, rather than reinforce, the conditions that encourage students' casting achievement as acting white. Lastly, it suggests new directions for future research on the topic of acting white and academic achievement. In addressing these core issues, I extend my own and others' efforts to better understand the relationship between race and achievement in American schools. *Integration Interrupted* aims to help bring us closer to the still-illusive goal of educational equity for all students.

Everyday Experience, Culture, and Acting White

It's kind of like, it's not cool. I don't know how this came about, but it bothers me so much because it perpetuates the stereotype, it like, somehow it became not cool within the black community to be trying hard for yourself because it's viewed as acting uppity or trying to act white.

Shelly, *Anderson High School (59% white; 33% black)*

SHELLY'S COMMENTS REFLECT THE FRUSTRATION and bewilderment that many students feel when their peers cast academic striving and achievement as acting white.[1] How did it come about that trying hard in school is now defined as "trying to act white"? In this book, I argue that to understand this phenomenon, we must closely examine the conditions under which it occurs. When and where do we find evidence of students casting achievement as acting white? How do those settings differ from settings in which students do not link academic achievement with whiteness? Why do these differences in context matter? What consequences do they have for students' attitudes and behavior?

Approaching the issue Shelly raises with these kinds of questions leads to an understanding of students' casting academic achievement as acting white that differs from the long-standing view. For decades, the most widely accepted explanation has been one that frames academic underachievement as part of black Americans' cultural adaptation to the history of slavery, racial oppression, and discrimination in America.[2] For example, the late anthropologist John Ogbu argued that being denied access to a good education for generations has narrowed black Americans' occupational opportunities and has discouraged the black community "from developing a strong tradition of academic achievement."[3] According to Ogbu, as generations of blacks observed family and community members struggle and eventually fail to achieve upward mobility via traditional routes, their collective ambivalence about school success deepened. African Americans came to believe that education would not pay off for them as it did for whites. This belief, Ogbu asserted, led black Americans to develop a "folk theory of making it" that rejects mainstream institutions, norms, and values.[4] In short, according to Ogbu and others, black youth learn to disparage school learning and success because academic excellence is not valued in the culture of their communities.[5]

The problem with this explanation is that it ignores students' everyday schooling experiences and implies that culture is unchanging.[6] Do students' own experiences in school have no influence on how they think about their chances for success? The increases in the percentages of blacks graduating from high school and college since 1970 and the presence of a growing black professional class suggest that black Americans generally do accept that there is value in formal education.[7] Even if they are not achieving at the same level as white Americans, African Americans continue to pursue high school and college degrees at record levels. There is no hard evidence of a wholesale rejection of education as a vehicle for upward mobility among black Americans of any socioeconomic group. Likewise, evidence is lacking for the idea that this attitude has been passed down from generation to generation.[8]

In this chapter, I explain some of the theoretical reasons for arguing that black youth who link academic achievement with whiteness learn to do so in the context of their own experiences in school. I argue that racialized tracking, and other institutional displays of unequal status between blacks and whites, have a significant affect on black youth's schooling experiences and their ideas about their own abilities, achievement, race, and getting ahead. I begin with a discussion of how youth develop a sense of academic competence. I then discuss how students' achievement experiences affect their outlook on the future. Lastly, I address the role that culture plays in young people's approach to schooling and achievement.

Developing a Sense of Academic Competence

Much of the existing empirical evidence suggests that the process by which youth form an understanding of the way people achieve success in America is a complex one. It involves more than just their awareness of the history of racism, discrimination, and other injustices faced by members of their racial, ethnic, or social class group.[9] Youth rely heavily on their own experiences to judge just how open and fair American society actually is. Whether they feel that opportunities are blocked for people like them and that striving therefore would be futile, depends in large part on what happens to them in school and in the labor market.

As children progress through school, they develop a conception of themselves as students. These student identities reflect children's ideas about their academic ability, what they think they are capable of achieving, and what they believe are their strengths and weaknesses.[10] The experience of academic success inspires confidence and optimism in students. This in turn raises their expectations for continued academic achievement as well as future occupational success. Students come to see themselves as smart based on the school's evaluations—what their teachers say about them, their grades, test scores, academic awards, and so forth. They adjust their own aspirations and expectations in response to these institutional measures. Students' behavioral response to the school's evaluation may vary widely (e.g., some may work harder, some may work less hard), but the evaluations are consistently shown to affect students' academic self-concept. Indeed, we know from classic social psychological theories of the self, as well as from expectancy effects research, that children develop ideas about themselves, whether positive or negative, consistent with the evaluations of others.[11] Thus, it makes sense to pay careful attention to how the school's evaluations shape students' perceptions of their abilities and future possibilities.

Comments from participants in each of the four studies I report on in this book (see the preface) capture this interactive aspect of self-evaluation.[12] Consider Marguerite. As she describes her grades, this Vanderbilt High School junior articulates some of the process by which she has come to see herself as "smart."

> I like to keep myself above an eighty-five. I have not had a C on a report card yet. So I hold that in great esteem. If I get a C this year, I would truly cry. . . . In ninth grade, I got all A's and B's. I don't know if that was a conscious thing or if I told myself not to go below eighty-five,

but it just kind of happened. Since then, I've just held myself to that.... It's just kind of, now I think it's the expectation that I'll do well that keeps me going. But before—even the expectation began to come in middle school with [my induction into] the Junior Honor Society. After that, it was like, okay, I'm supposed to be smart.[13]

Jasmine, a Lucas Valley junior, also emphasizes the centrality of the school's evaluations in her account of coming to view herself as capable and smart.

I don't know, like, I don't know, I guess I was just smart and I just didn't know.... Like, my mom would say it, but, like, when you look at, when I took that test where I made that high score, that really, like, set my mind, you know, "She was right!" You know, I could do a whole lot better than that. I mean in fourth grade you just want to go outside and play. But after I made that high score on the test, it was like "I may be actually good at this! So why don't I put more into it?"

Massey High School senior Yvette describes a similar process of becoming more motivated to excel and developing greater confidence in her academic abilities. "But then I'm like, I have to get good grades. Like, third grade, Ms. [Olson's] class. She was a hard third-grade teacher. I thought, like 'I got to do good. I got to get'—I made all A's that year. And then after that I just started pushing myself. Because I know I can make all A's 'cause I've done it before." Most of the other students I have spoken with in the course of my research are like Marguerite, Jasmine, and Yvette. They draw on their school's rewards and evaluations to form their understandings of their own abilities and capabilities. And also like these three students, many have offered accounts that show the significance and enduring effects of early achievement experiences in this process.

It is not surprising to find that students view themselves as smart, average, or below average based on grades and other school evaluations, as well as on comparisons to other students' performance. Yet, too frequently, we overlook the significance of these school evaluations for the expectations students form of themselves and the decisions they make in school. Gifted identification provides an especially clear example of this relationship. As I explain in detail in chapter 4, statewide, North Carolina students who were identified as "gifted" in elementary or middle school were significantly more likely to enroll in Advanced Placement (AP) classes in high school than were students who had not been identified as "gifted," independent of these students' prior achievement. Among the high school students interviewed about their course-selection choices, "gifted" students believed that they were "expected" to take AP courses. They viewed themselves as being "more intelligent than [the] average person" and felt that they did not "fit" anywhere other than advanced classes. In contrast, "non-gifted" students believed that AP courses were "too challenging" for them and that they were "not smart enough" to be in those courses.

Other research, such as Reginald Clark's study of black family life and school achievement and Julie Bettie's study of race, class, and identity among girls describe similar findings.[14] Such studies show that students rely heavily on their own achievement experiences to form self-evaluations and assess their chances of success.[15] These self-assessments and self-evaluations in turn affect students' actions. Clark's description of the outlook of one low-achieving participant in his study is a poignant illustration of this process.

> Alice admits that school has been a bad experience for her. Hardly ever has she had enough success to make the experience a pleasant one. Now, she questions her own intelligence and ability (and, ultimately, her worth as a person)....Unwilling to humiliate herself time and time again in the classroom, Alice has become protective of her ego and less concerned about her ability to perform school tasks well.[16]

Given her academic experiences, Alice plans to end her formal education with a high school diploma. She has come to the conclusion that higher education is not for her, explaining to Clark, "I'm too slow for college." According to Clark, however, "she secretly wishes to attend." While other factors may have influenced Alice's aspirations and actions at school, it is apparent that her own achievement experiences have had a significant effect on her sense of academic competence and her outlook on the future.

School Achievement and Getting Ahead

The research conducted by Clark and others also indicates that students who have met with some educational success and who judge their experiences in school to be fair are more likely to believe in the American ideal of meritocracy. That is, they are more likely to think that opportunities are available to everyone and that those who work hard will be rewarded. Students who have had more negative educational experiences which they judge to be in some way unfair are more likely to reject the meritocracy ideal.[17] These studies show, too, the internal contradictions that poor, low-income, and minority youth often contend with as they try to make sense of their circumstances. Those who have experienced school failure and other negative outcomes often have strong critiques of the opportunity structure and its tendency to reproduce itself. Yet, these same youth also tend to blame themselves for their failures and for what they did or did not do that undermined their chances for success. Jay MacLeod's work offers classic examples. The mostly white, low-income boys he refers to as the "Hallway Hangers" challenge the achievement ideology and argue that they do not have the same opportunities as others do ("Hey, you can't get no education around here unless if you're fucking rich, y'know?"; "We don't get a fair shake and shit"). At the same time, though, these young men fault their personal shortcomings and lament their actions and prior choices ("I just screwed up"; "I guess I just don't have what it takes").[18]

In my own research, I have found far greater buy-in of the achievement ideology among working-class and low-income black youth who experienced school success, but this was coupled with an awareness of how hard it could be for people like them to get ahead. These youth, whose hopes of social mobility rested primarily on education, persisted in school, holding on to what they believed was their best chance for achieving a better life. The older adolescents, especially, were not oblivious to racial inequality and discrimination. In fact, numerous students reported incidents of perceived discrimination at school. For example, Curtis, a cocky, high-achieving, rising senior at Everton High School, recounted an incident in which he felt a teacher had treated him unfairly because of his race.[19] According to Curtis, he and a few other students had not received a packet (handed out by the homeroom teacher) for their pre-calculus class. When Curtis went to the head of the math department to request a packet, she implied that he was lying about not having received one.

> *Curtis*: ...Other people didn't get theirs either, and they went after theirs and she just handed it right to them, but when I went to her and asked, you know, to explain what had happened, and told her I didn't get one, she pretty much insinuated that I was lying. I was like, "You're not going to, you're not just going to call me a liar when I know what happened and I see how, you know, hassle-free, you're giving these other packets. You're going to give me one like that too."
> *Interviewer*: You said that to her?
> *Curtis*: Yeah. Oh, I mean I was like, "I'm not going to be discriminated against just because you think that I'm lying. That's not the case." And she's like, "Well, okay," and she gave me the packet...
> *Interviewer*: Why do you think she accused you of lying and just gave everybody else—?

Curtis: I don't know, and that's why I said I felt discriminated against because it was like, "Wait a minute, these other people just were in here and just got theirs, what's the problem here?" And I hate to say it was because I was black, because I was the only black person in that class, but you know I don't know what it was all about.

With a 4.5 (weighted) GPA, Curtis was one of the highest achievers among the sixty-five participants in the study of high-achieving black students my colleagues and I conducted. The fact that he was aware of ongoing racism and discrimination, however, did not diminish his ambitions or his desire for academic success.[20]

Other high-achieving black students expressed confusion and disappointment when they experienced situations like the one Curtis described. Still, few seemed to think that discrimination and racism were insurmountable. Most had faith in their ability to achieve despite the odds. They continued to strive despite any obstacles they encountered because they "want[ed] to be successful in life," as Lynden, a senior at City High School explained. "I want to do better than my mom, and nobody [in my family] has ever went to college. My mom and dad didn't go to college and I want to do better. I want to go to college. And make something of myself."

Lynden effected what he called a "g'ed up" or "gangsta" style; he dressed from head to toe in the latest urban gear, complete with oversized clothing, doo-rag, and lots of "bling."[21] Nevertheless, he was engaged in school and striving for success. His academic successes and subsequent rewards (e.g., he made the honor roll and he had his name listed in the local newspaper for his achievements) confirmed his belief that he would be recognized as an intellectually capable person with the potential to "make something" of himself. By rewarding his efforts, the school gave Lynden a formal and "expert" evaluation of his potential. From his perspective, this institutional recognition confirmed that he would be judged based on his performance in the classroom, not on his race, family background, or preferred style of dress.

Lynden had few examples in his own family of people who had achieved much upward mobility, but that did not prevent him from thinking that his life might be different. Black students who see their parents and other relatives struggle to make ends meet do not necessarily reject schooling and adopt identities oppositional to mainstream norms. Many of the students I interviewed believed that their relatives' struggles were a consequence of the poor quality of their education or the fact that they had had too little education or had made bad personal decisions. Such beliefs were often fostered by the relatives themselves. For example, when we asked Clearview High School senior James what, if anything, his parents said to him about school, he responded: "They say, 'Well James, the worst thing that happened to me in my life was I didn't go to college. I didn't seek my final degree. We don't want you to do that. We want you to go and be the best you can be.'"[22] Indeed, although students and their parents sometimes voiced complaints about schools and teachers, few blamed schools, racism, or discrimination when they discussed their failures. Most blamed themselves.

This was especially true of the parents at Linwood Elementary School, many of whom lived in the low-income housing projects surrounding the school.[23] As they discussed their educational hopes and expectations for their children, the parents expressed regret about the choices they had made in their own educational careers.[24] Interestingly, at no time did they suggest that the schools might have failed them. Now in the most precarious of economic situations, either unemployed or working low-wage, unskilled jobs, the parents stressed the importance of education for their children.

> I hope [Kyle] goes to college. I'm gonna try to make him go to college. 'Cause that's something I wanted to do, but I never pursued it because when I was—, I quit school in the eleventh grade. I really, and then went back. Two months from graduation got pregnant. Didn't never go back, just didn't. Just didn't go....'Cause you can't go get a job, say, at City Hall, without a high school diploma. You can't go get a job at McDonald's, not without a high school diploma. They want a GED. You've got to have some kind of education background to get a job, and a proper job. I mean you want to get a good job, now. You've got to have college, you know, degrees and stuff. You know, the right college, you've got to have a degree. You've got to have a diploma. You've got to have a diploma to drive a trash can! If you don't have it, you can't get it. So, you've got to have an education. It's very important in life and learning in life.
>
> *(Ms. Parker, Linwood parent)*

> Actually I dropped out when I was fifteen. Then I moved to PA—Pennsylvania with my mother, and I went up there and I finished up to the eleventh grade. So that's what I'm going to school for now— to get my GED, my high school diploma....From Tuesday through Thursday. So, um, I just wasn't doing nothing. Now I wish I could go back and do it, but I just—at that time I wasn't doing nothing. I didn't see myself doing no work. I didn't want to be there. [*Prompt: What did you see yourself doing at that time?*] I, mm-mm. [*She laughs.*]

I don't know. I honestly do not know. And I pray to God that my kids don't be like that. And I can, take my son—he probably would like— no, my daughter [is] probably like that. 'Cause that girl don't want to do nothing. She don't want to do—I believe if somebody tell her she old enough to drop out of high school, she'd drop out. 'Cause that girl just don't want to do nothing. [*Prompt: What do you tell her?*] She—if she know like I know, she better stay in. 'Cause it's getting harder by the year. It's getting harder by the day. Everybody asking for high school diploma. 'Cause I told my kids if I could turn that around, I would be done finished school—way long time ago like I supposed to have. And I tell 'em, "Y'all better finish." But she got a good head on her shoulder, all of 'em do. 'Cause she says she wants to go to college...they better get it [education] while they can. I'm serious. They—they better get it while they can because now that I'm going back to school—I'm learning more, which I could've learnt then, you know, and got it all over with. Now I'm twenty-nine years old, back at school again, I ain't got no business being in school without no trade. [*She laughs lightly.*] You know? So, I told 'em, I said, "Y'all better get it while you can, because I mean, leave these streets alone, leave these babies alone, leave these little boys alone." I tell 'em, I said, "'Cause if you don't want to be set back, like,"—okay, like for example, I tell 'em, I said, "Look at me. I haven't finished school, your daddy haven't finish school. Your daddy repeated ninth grade for four years straight. You don't want to be like him."

(*Ms. Moss, Linwood parent*)

Despite their own limited education, Ms. Moss and Ms. Parker, like many other parents in my research, expressed little ambivalence about education as a means for achieving upward mobility, either for themselves or for their children. They believed they would have been better off if they had completed more education. Lacking access to other resources (e.g., steady income, powerful social networks) that might help their children get ahead, these parents stressed the importance of education and hoped that their children would not make the mistakes that they had made. There was little in the parents' or the students' narratives to support John Ogbu's claim that, "Many [blacks] see little evidence among their own people for believing that success in adult life or upward mobility is due to education."[25]

While Ms. Moss's and Ms. Parker's pro-education views are not exceptional among *Linwood* parents, my point is not to argue that they are representative of all low-income black parents. Instead, I present their comments to balance sweeping assertions of the sort that Ogbu and others make that poor and low-income blacks see little value in education.[26] These mothers are like other poor and low-income Americans (and like the boys Jay MacLeod studied and the "hard living" students Julie Bettie describes). All face the same painful contradiction of being poor in the "land of opportunity." One way they are able to make sense of their position is to see it as an outcome of their own failure to take school seriously and get the kind of education that is a prerequisite for good jobs.

Most students I encountered, even those at schools like Linwood, where poor and low-income families predominate, repeated the common refrain that if they work hard in school they will do well in the future. Contrary to frequent reports of a pervasive sense of hopelessness and pessimism among contemporary black youth, these students made statements signifying their belief in the utility of education. They readily made connections between their own school performance and their chances of going to college, getting a good job, and making a decent living. The higher their own achievement, the higher their aspirations and the greater their optimism about their individual prospects for the future. This pattern was most evident among high school students. The relationship between achievement and occupational aspirations was less clear among elementary school students, because, as a group, their aspirations were less well developed (e.g., "[I'm] gonna be either a teacher, a doctor, or a dancer."). They also restricted themselves to a narrower range of future careers than did their older counterparts. Most young students aspired to be police officers, doctors, lawyers, teachers, or professional athletes. Nevertheless, most students, regardless of age or achievement level, expressed some faith in the promise of the American dream. They seemed to *want* to believe in their own efficacy, that they had some control over their lives, and that their effort and skills, above all else, would determine their success.

To be clear, faith in the promise of the American dream did not prevent the students from critically assessing society's treatment of blacks and other people of color; nor did it preclude feelings of uncertainty about their own chances of making it. This combination—continuing to strive even while believing that African Americans are not always treated fairly—is not as surprising as it might first seem. The students' behavior is no different from the behavior of scholars and other professionals of color who critique the U.S. opportunity structure but continue to work to achieve personal success within that very structure, and routinely encourage children to "stay in school."[27] African Americans, as W. E. B. Du Bois's work reminds us, have always faced these kinds of internal tensions.[28]

Such tensions are also evident among the "rags to riches" young men that Alford Young studied, and among the high-achieving, low-income students of color described in Prudence Carter's and Carla O'Connor's research.[29] Again, like many adults who strive to achieve despite knowledge of, and even personal experience with, racism and discrimination, disadvantaged youth who are aware and critical of larger structures of inequality do not necessarily hold fatalistic attitudes or behave in self-defeating ways. The dilemma is not, however, simply one of being both black and American. There is also a tension borne of the task of nurturing an individual self within a society in which persons with black skin, like your own, are viewed and judged as a single, undifferentiated group. In post-desegregation America, that means living one's individual life with hopes and dreams similar to those of other Americans, until something happens to remind you of your difference.

Since desegregation, African American youth have been socialized to believe in the ideal of meritocracy. Like other Americans, most believe that with hard work, anyone can achieve success. African Americans are generally willing to risk believing in this achievement ideology because they understand that their chances for success and economic well-being will be greatly reduced if they do not work hard. If they have doubts about the degree to which the achievement ideology applies to them, these misgivings are partially assuaged by personal experiences of success in school, and in the labor and housing markets.

For those whom the school defines as successful—students like Lynden, Jasmine, Yvette, Curtis, and Marguerite—their experiences of success encourage a sense of hope that barriers are continually being broken down and that any existing obstacles can be overcome. After all, these students' academic success offers them evidence that people of color can be and sometimes are rewarded for their efforts. Despite their own modest family backgrounds and the fact that neither their parents nor their siblings had a college degree, Curtis's and Lynden's achievements gave them high hopes for their future: both planned to attend college. Curtis had aspirations of becoming a pathologist and Lynden hoped to pursue a career in computer programming.

Lower-achieving, low-income and minority students have a very different perspective. Their faith in the American ideals of fairness and meritocracy is less strong: they see that many individuals in their racial/ethnic and socioeconomic categories encounter much more difficult circumstances than people in other categories and/or classes. In schools in which differences in the educational experiences of the "haves" and the "have nots" are unmistakable, lower-income and minority students quickly learn their place in the school's achievement hierarchy and many come to expect and accept that opportunities for people like them will be limited. To be sure, students' experiences outside of school as well as those of their parents also inform their perceptions of the opportunity structure. The evidence suggests, however, that their own schooling experiences are of far greater consequence in shaping their views. Students from disadvantaged backgrounds who are academically successful are less likely to express the type of resignation and pessimism that their lower-achieving peers sometimes do. There is a deep irony in the fact that the institution that is supposed to level social differences and to render background characteristics unimportant, instead more often openly reinforces and exacerbates those differences. An African American student in Annegret Staiger's study captured this incongruity nicely. Remarking on the marked racial disparities in curriculum placement at his school, he said, "It's weird how in school and in life we are taught not to discriminate or to segregate, but yet we are going through this every day at school."[30] As I explain below, to make sense of the misalignment between what they are told and what they experience, students draw on various alternative sources.

Cultures in Action among Students

How people assess their experiences depends, in part, on their own social position and on the cultural tools available to them. Minority and low-income students are more likely to experience negative educational outcomes (e.g., lower grades and less rigorous academic placements, higher retention rates, and more disciplinary actions). It should not come as a surprise, then, that these students also are more likely to reject some aspects of the dominant meritocracy ideology. After all, that ideology often does not accurately represent their experiences, as studies like Julie Bettie's, Jay MacLeod's, and Katherine Newman's so vividly illustrate.[31]

When people's experiences are contrary to the ideology of the dominant culture, they can turn to other sources to make sense of their seemingly abnormal experiences. They may use explanations available in existing micro cultures or subcultures or create new subcultures. Studies of low-achieving, working-class students provide examples of this process. To preserve their self-worth, these students draw on gender and class-based discourses that allow them to construct narratives that accomplish two goals simultaneously: The narratives accentuate differences between them and their higher-achieving peers and they devalue the goals and pursuits to which their higher-achieving peers attach great importance. For instance, in his study of a group of working-class boys in England, Paul Willis describes how the boys, whom he called "the lads," regularly ridiculed their middle-class, higher-achieving peers for their conformist behavior. Drinking, fighting, sexual activity, and the ability to make themselves and others laugh, gave "the lads" a sense of superiority over their "submissive" counterparts, who they believed were not having any fun. In a discussion of the ways in which their lives were more exciting than their "childish" peers' lives, one "lad" explained to Willis,

> I mean, what will they remember of their school life? What will they have to look back on? Sitting in a classroom, sweating their bollocks off, you know, while we've been...I mean look at the things we can look back on, fighting on the Pakis, fighting on the JAs [i.e., Jamaicans]. Some of the things we've done on teachers, it'll be a laff when we look back on it.[32]

William Corsaro's concept of "public negotiations" provides another useful way to think about how these youth are using available symbols (in this case from working-class culture) to make sense of their experience and, in the process, creating new meanings. He explains that:

> [Culture] is produced and reproduced through public negotiations. In these negotiations, social actors link shared knowledge of various symbolic models with specific situations to generate meanings while simultaneously using the same shared knowledge as a resource for making novel contributions to the culture and for pursuing a range of individual goals.[33]

In the United States and elsewhere, lower-achieving, working-class males routinely draw on discourses of masculinity to dismiss their higher-achieving peers' success.[34] For example, in an ethnographic study of a predominantly black Washington, D. C., high school, Fordham and Ogbu found that "persistent rumors" circulated around the school that male students who took a "large number of Advanced Placement courses" were homosexuals.[35] Lower-achieving students of color also routinely draw on discourses of race.[36] Julie Bettie describes lower-achieving Mexican American students' use of the acting white slur to hurt their higher-achieving peers' feelings as a "defensive strategy for coping with race-class injury."[37] Thus, as Ellen Brantlinger asserts, "The directionality of exclusiveness is not just from high to low," although, of course, the consequences are not the same.[38] Still, low-achieving minority and low-income students are quite adept at devising ways to stigmatize and exclude their higher-achieving and higher-status peers.

The argument I make in this book is that students' attitudes toward formal education, including attitudes that are oppositional toward schooling and achievement, develop largely from their experiences in school. This argument offers a different perspective on the attitude-achievement link than the view most widely accepted today, which implies that attitudes predict achievement. The approach I advocate is not new, however. In earlier research, scholars argued that working-class students who were not able to realize the goal of academic success constructed subcultures that rejected, at least publicly, the school's values and assessments.[39] These studies were conducted in the early years of school desegregation, when many public schools were still largely segregated. The researchers concluded that the oppositional attitudes and behavior of white students were a consequence of these students' failure to achieve academic success and gain the esteem of their peers and teachers.

Arthur Stinchcombe, for instance, in his 1964 study of high school students' rebellion, argued that students who are not academically successful "find other elements of the culture to use as symbols of identity."[40] Stinchcombe found that it was not that failing working-class students did not desire academic or occupational success (most had internalized the dominant achievement ideology). Rather, their failure in school created what he called a "psychological strain." The students then had to reconcile their achievement goals with the harsh realization that these aims might be unattainable. Put in this position, the students chose to reorient their goals and redefine success on their own terms, ones that did not hinge upon the validation or esteem granted by the school.[41] By detaching themselves from the source of negative evaluations, the students were able to reconstruct and maintain a positive sense of self in spite of the evaluations and judgments of the institution.[42]

In the post-desegregation period, some black students exhibit oppositional attitudes and behavior similar to the kind Stinchcombe described among white students. Interestingly, despite these similarities, the old explanations (like Stinchcombe's) have disappeared. In their place we now find explanations that question the cultural orientation and values of African Americans. What is needed, I believe, is a return to the lessons learned from earlier research, in which students' school experiences were central to understanding attitudes and behaviors that appeared inconsistent with school norms.

EXPERIENCES AND STUDENTS' ATTITUDES AND OUTCOMES

Many things influence the kinds of experiences we have. The most important of these are the social structure of the society in which we live, the institutions with which we come in contact, and our location within both this broad structure and particular institutions. A ten-year-old Muslim girl from a wealthy family growing up in Iran and attending a private school will have much different experiences than a ten-year-old Muslim girl from a working-class family growing up in Detroit and attending a public school. To make sense of our experiences and decide how to act in particular situations—as part of the ongoing process of trying to influence what will happen to us in the next moment—we rely on the knowledge made available to us in the cultures in which we have been socialized.[43] These cultures include both macro ones (e.g., those related to our national identity) and micro ones (e.g., those related to our membership in specific racial, religious, and social class groups).

Each culture provides a particular vantage point from which to view and interpret the world, and these interpretations may either complement or contradict one another. When they are contradictory, we tend to favor the vantage point that provides a view that presents us, in our own estimation, in an acceptable light.[44] Research in psychology and social psychology has consistently demonstrated that people's behavior is often motivated by the need to feel a sense of competence, worth, and esteem. As the data provided in the forthcoming chapters will demonstrate, much of what we observe among youth in school today reflects their attempts to negotiate experiences in ways that allow them to achieve these same self-affirming goals. By claiming that they did not work hard enough, low-performing students not only blame themselves, they also protect themselves from the perception that they are not intellectually capable.

Here I am drawing on Ann Swidler's conceptualization of culture as a tool kit, in which she views culture as a set of "symbols, stories, rituals, and world-views" through which meaning is experienced and expressed.[45] Sociologist Orlando Patterson has dismissed this view as being "too open-ended and voluntaristic" in its "conception of culture as a tool kit from which people selectively draw their strategies of action as it suits their purposes."[46] Yet I find these qualities precisely what make Swidler's theory of culture most compelling and useful. All Americans participate simultaneously in various cultures, in addition to the overarching national or dominant culture. Our specific religious, social class, racial, ethnic, and regional backgrounds offer us a range of possibilities for interpretation and subsequent "strategies of action." As Troy Duster remarked in his 2005 presidential address to the American Sociological Association, people interpret what they see differently because they "bring very different personal and social histories, perspectives, sexual orientations, [and] religious or secular views," to bear in any given situation. Moreover, an individual's multiple social locations and affiliations may offer divergent perspectives. Consequently, in making sense of their experiences, individuals often have to select among competing interpretations.

When the role of culture is understood this way, the widely accepted argument that black youth cast achievement as acting white because they do not value education seems misguided. Not only does it present a static view of culture, it also suggests that culture supplies the values that drive our actions. However, Swidler contends that culture shapes values and action because people come to value those things for which they have the cultural tools to be competent. Useful examples of this approach to understanding the connection between culture and values are found in school- and youth-focused studies such as Paul Willis's, Jay MacLeod's, and Arthur Stinchcombe's. In each case, the author describes how, failing to meet the school's standards and expectations, the group of poor or working-class boys became increasingly alienated from the institution. Consequently, the boys created their own subculture in which the knowledge and skills they possessed, including toughness, masculinity, street smarts, and physical strength, were among the most highly valued attributes. Consistent with Swidler's argument regarding the influence of culture on action, we can see how the boys' "actions and values [were] organized to take advantage of [their own] cultural competence."[47] The boys' subculture also provided them with an alternative view of their school failure. Rather than accept the school's negative evaluation of their academic capabilities, they can argue, as the working-class "lads" in Paul Willis's study did, that they did not want what the school had to offer.

The tool kit argument, then, seems to point us in the right direction. It draws our attention to the existence of the range of possible interpretive tools available to individuals. And, it prompts us to ask, "Under what conditions do individuals in a given society draw on cultural tools other than the macro or national culture to understand a particular experience?" But that question in turn points to the need to modify the tool kit conceptualization somewhat. As Marguerite's, Yvette's, and Jasmine's remarks (presented earlier in the chapter) made clear, the school's judgments and evaluations strongly affect students' self-assessments and aspirations. Yet, in the tool kit argument, institutions appear passive. Thus, I reformulate Swidler's view that people "come to value ends for which their cultural equipment is well-suited," in order to accommodate the powerful role institutions and their agents may play in judging and determining our competences.[48]

Various studies have shown that schools play an active role in contributing to student outcomes.[49] These studies shed light on the ways in which school practices and policies, whether intentionally or not, privilege white middle-class culture and consequently undermine the achievement of minority and low-income students. Annette Lareau's research, for instance, makes clear that the middle-class approach to parental involvement in schooling is not "better" than the working-class approach. Rather, middle-class students accrue advantages because their parents' approach is more consistent with what schools currently expect and reward.[50] Shirley Brice Heath's work reveals the influential role of teachers' typically unacknowledged cultural expectations. She documents ways that cultural miscues and miscommunications around language may place students of color at a disadvantage in schools.[51] In one example, Heath describes how black children who are accustomed to receiving direct orders (e.g., "Sit down") sometimes find themselves in trouble in classrooms with teachers who express themselves in indirect terms (e.g., "What should you be doing now?"). My point here is that the practices and policies of schools have real effects, and these effects are neither neutral nor class- or colorblind.

Ironically, earlier studies of educational outcomes were faulted for attributing too much power to institutions and too little to individuals. Herbert Bowles and Samuel Gintis, for instance, were harshly criticized for developing explanations of educational outcomes that portrayed social structures as all-determining and made no provisions for the possibility that students might act of their own volition.[52] Other scholars, such as Paul Willis, Jean Anyon, and Jay MacLeod, used ethnographic methods to redress this imbalance by showing the ways in which students do resist and/or cooperate with structural forces in the production of outcomes.[53] Their work opened up interesting new possibilities for how we think about the interaction between social structure and human agency with respect to schooling outcomes and social mobility. Yet, more recently, it seems that we have taken a step backward—at least with respect to black students and acting white. In this area, attention to the effects of local structures and individual experience has waned. We seem to have forgotten Richard Sennett and Jonathan Cobb's earlier call for more attention to "the child's own experience in school."[54] To explain complex interactional situations, we must pay attention both to the actors and the institutions involved, and to the responses of each to the other.

Conclusion

I have argued in this chapter that black students' pessimism or optimism about the future, their ideas about academic success and making it, are best understood through an examination of their personal school experiences and meaning-making, rather than through an assessment of the African American community's history or culture. Culture is not irrelevant here, but it does not drive values and action. Instead, culture is a resource that individuals draw on to make sense of the world around them. For students in post–desegregation America, that world, unfortunately, includes racialized tracking.

Regardless of how students interpret racialized tracking patterns, however, it is the school structure that sustains the patterns and makes them a reality with which students must contend. As I describe in chapter 2, many black students are presented on a daily basis with a visual image of achievement that is racialized. This image keeps the myth of black inferiority intact. I argue that this experience explains how and why youth associate academic achievement with whiteness. The institutional context has direct bearing on students' judgments about the degree to which their skills are well or poorly suited to the demands of schooling. Thus, we must not overlook or downplay "the institutional authority in which the school is embedded."[55] Indeed, Annette Lareau and Elliot Weininger's call for greater attention to "the micro-interactional processes through which individuals comply (or fail to comply) with the evaluative standards of dominant institutions such as schools," is exactly right.[56] As I explain in the next chapter, constructing school success as acting white is how some black adolescents choose to read and respond to the cultural spectacle of racialized tracking while simultaneously discounting the inferiority explanation.

Throughout this book, I argue that local school structures and students' experiences within those structures are central to understanding the stories students construct about themselves and others, about achievement and educational opportunity, and about succeeding in the larger society, as well as students' responses to and choices under particular conditions. In the next chapter, I closely examine the schooling experiences of a group of sixty-five high-achieving black students in nineteen high schools in North Carolina in order to document when and where students' casting achievement as acting white emerges. The evidence shows that by paying particular attention to the local school context and individual experience, and by understanding culture as a tool for making and expressing meaning, we gain a clearer picture of how and why some black students associate whiteness with academic success.

On Becoming A Cultural Object

Academic Achievement and Acting White among Black Students

And, the guy—the black guy—made a comment: "She thinks she's white. She thinks she's something, something, something. She's too—she acts too white." I'm like, "How do I act white? Just because I don't act ignorant like you, doesn't mean I'm any less black. And I have common sense, I know how to act and because I want something better in my life, obviously than what you want because you just act like you don't care."

Yvette, black female, Massey High School (79% white; 13% black)

IT IS RARE TO PICK up a book or an article about black students today and not find some reference to acting white. Although its meaning is often contested, as Yvette's comments (above) suggest, black youth often use the term to convey that a black person's behavior, style, or tastes signal white rather than black cultural patterns and traditions. In effect, to accuse someone of acting white is to call her racial authenticity into question. For many black Americans, this is insulting and hurtful.

Some scholars insist that there is nothing "authentic" or "natural" about being black.[1] But racialized name-calling, including challenges to racial authenticity, have a long history among black Americans. For instance, African Americans' use of the term "Oreo" (to signify a person who is black on the outside but white on the inside) probably has been in circulation since 1912, when the cookie that inspired the slur made its debut. Moreover, according to J. Martin Favor, author of *Authentic Blackness*, "The perceived necessity to delineate ideologically and aesthetically that which is most 'real' about African American experiences has been a driving force behind social and artistic movements," including the Harlem Renaissance.[2] Indeed, the roots of practices attempting to establish the boundaries of "real" blackness extend deep into the past.[3] However, these practices appear to be more pronounced today, according to historian Nell Painter.[4]

What is new about attempts to establish the boundaries of "real" blackness is the addition of academic achievement and other achievement-related activities to the list of out-of-bound behaviors and preferences.[5] Up through the 1970s the acting white slur was used primarily as a way of ridiculing how certain blacks spoke or how they aligned themselves politically or socially. Even more commonly, the term was used as a broader and vaguer commentary on others' general way of being (e.g., "lacking soul"). What changed? Why has academic achievement become a cultural object? That is, why do some black youth now consider academic success, and such behaviors as taking advanced classes, a symbol of whiteness?

Many people view students' current use of the acting white slur in an academic context as simply part of the "oppositional" nature of black youth culture.[6] In holding this view, they implicitly accept two claims: first, that this contemporary usage is part of a collective or social identity in opposition to whites; and second, that it represents a cultural frame of reference that black Americans have developed in order to maintain boundaries between blacks and whites.[7] Yet few have questioned when and how academic achievement became part of this boundary-making.

In this chapter, I draw on the experiences and narratives of academically successful black students in different school contexts to show how the new usage of the acting white slur is connected to the school organizational practice of tracking. I also explore what tracking means, more generally, for these students' social life at school. I focus primarily on high-achieving black adolescents because these youth are most often the targets of racialized ridicule.[8] Their experiences provide a critical vantage point from which to learn about the conditions under which students cast achievement as acting white. The high achievers' narratives also help us understand why some high-achieving students are the targets of their black peers' scorn while others are not.

Logically, a discussion of when, where, and why students cast achievement as acting white must begin with the youngest students. How do children in elementary school view high academic achievement and high achievers?[29] Do young black students also use the acting white slur to refer to their high-achieving peers? And if so, under what conditions do they do so? Looking at young students' experiences can provide important clues to understanding the process by which students come to view academic achievement as a form of acting white.

In my research involving elementary school students, I have found no evidence that preadolescents use the acting white slur in any context, even when racialized placement or achievement patterns are a part of their schooling experience. However, we cannot conclude from this that children are not familiar with or that they never use the term, because a few of the high-achieving adolescents recalled being teased about acting white in elementary school. But the absence of a more consistent pattern of younger students using the term suggests that black children are no more likely than others to begin school predisposed to think about achievement in racial terms. As the following examples illustrate, the young students interviewed had not yet begun to grapple openly with or make sense of the racial differences on display in various forms at their school.

Achievement and the Salience of Race among Preadolescents

In 2001, Georgetown Elementary School was 87 percent black and 11 percent white (see *Minority Underrepresentation* study). Located in a rapidly growing urban area of North Carolina, Georgetown is a magnet school that draws many of its black students from a nearby public housing complex and its white students from wealthier surrounding neighborhoods. At the time of the study, the small population of white students accounted for nearly 60 percent of the school's gifted population.[10] More than one hundred miles away in a rural part of the state, white students at another predominantly (71%) black elementary school, Holt, accounted for that school's entire gifted population.[11]

Students in these schools were exposed to daily images of "whiteness as giftedness."[12] Especially in classrooms in which "gifted" children were "pulled out" for special instruction, students regularly witnessed a starkly racialized image of ability each time the gifted students stood and left the room. According to a Georgetown teacher we interviewed, in one fifth-grade classroom, every white student in the class had been identified as academically and intellectually gifted (referred to as AIG or AG), but not one of the black or Latino students, who made up the majority of the mostly black classroom, had been so designated. In this classroom, as at Holt in general, the recurring image of the white children leaving the room to receive instruction for the "academically intelligent," as some children put it, signals to all present that only white children are intelligent.

The effect of the repeated public coupling of whiteness and giftedness is similar to another type of cultural spectacle, that of public punishment in schools. Ann Ferguson has shown how the treatment of young black boys in public school constitutes a "powerful learning experience about social location and worthiness."[13] As she makes clear, in the school context, cultural spectacles like these single out, name, and display what constitutes "bad" and "smart." In doing so, they affirm the "institutional power" of schools to make such judgments.[14] Images of "whiteness as giftedness" similar to those at Holt and Georgetown, are repeated in various forms in classrooms across the country.[15]

The immediate impact of these images on elementary-age students' attitudes toward achievement is not clear, however. The young informants at Holt and Georgetown did not refer to these racial patterns. In fact, they rarely mentioned race at all. Furthermore, none of the black students mentioned acting white in any context; nor was there any evidence that they shunned or ridiculed the "intelligent people" simply because of their perceived intelligence or achievement. Instead, black students expressed a desire to participate in their school's gifted program.

Remarks made by Kris, the sole black participant in Holt's gifted program (added after we initiated the study), are especially informative. Kris reported feeling "good" about his placement in the gifted program because he was able "to be with people [on his] level and compete with people" on the same level. He described his parents' reaction to the news of his placement as being as if he had "just won a million dollars or something." Kris elaborated, explaining that his parents were happy for him because "they knew [he] had wanted to be in AG for a long time." Kris expressed no ambivalence about his placement in the gifted program, and there was no indication in his account that he endured any social problems with his classmates as a result.[16]

The comments of other black students at Holt seem to support what Kris told us. While another black male sixth grader, Jake, did not directly express an interest in the gifted program, he casually mentioned that two of his best friends were in it. On the other hand, for the four black girls interviewed at Holt, being left out of the gifted program was either disappointing or confusing. Each reported that she had consistently been on either the A/B or A honor roll. The girls were not certain of all the specific requirements for placement in AG, but they believed that academic performance was an important component. Thus, fourth-grader Mae believed she was "smart enough" to be in the gifted program; and Morgan (Kris's sister), another fourth-grade student, explained that she would like to be in the program because she is "a pretty smart girl." Similarly, Candy, a sixth grader, claimed that "most of my classmates think I should be in AG." The students' remarks reflect positive attitudes toward the gifted program in particular and academic achievement in general.

The absence of blacks in Holt's gifted program seemed to have had little effect on how the black students interviewed there viewed either the program or high-achieving students more broadly. It was a little surprising that none of the children at Holt ever mentioned race. However, this finding is consistent with the general lack of race talk found either across the 100 interviews conducted with elementary school students in the six schools, or during the seven or more months of fieldwork I conducted at three of those schools. Although students at Madison Elementary (see *In Their Own Words* study), the all-black public school, sometimes used race or color to describe others, those were rare occasions. One of those occasions came during a field trip toward the end of the school year. Some of the students were explaining to me why their previous teacher had not allowed them to go on their end-of-the-year trip the year before. According to one student, that teacher did not like black kids. She was "vanilla colored," added another. Very few of the young informants at any of the other schools mentioned race at all, with the exception of a white fifth-grade student at Georgetown who reported that "the African American kids" ask her why she is "trying to act black" when she uses slang.[17]

Even when prodded to describe others, elementary school students seemed to shy away from referring to race. For example, asked to describe his teacher, Kevin, a white fourth grader at Holt, responded: "She's pretty tall, black hair, nice, fair, very strict, and funny sometimes." Henry, a white fifth-grade student at Georgetown, described his AIG classmates by nearly every physical characteristic but race.

> *Interviewer*: If I looked at the group of students in your AIG class, describe them to me. Describe what they look like.
> *Henry*: Well, there's [Teddy]. He's a little bit taller than I am. Basically he has the same build as I do. But, and then there's [Shia]. She's pretty big for her age. And then there's [Jaylyn]. She skipped a grade and so she's smaller than most other people in there. And there's [Monica] who, she has long hair and she's, like, just—a girl.

It is very likely that each student Henry described is white, especially if his was the fifth-grade classroom of all-white gifted students the teacher described.[18] Thus, as scholars such as Richard Dyer and others who study white privilege have argued, Henry may simply have taken his AIG classmates' white skin for granted.[19] That does not explain, however, why so few young informants of any race mentioned the race of others.

It may also be that white students were reluctant to mention race because the interviewers were black. However, even black students rarely mentioned race. It is important to note that, except for obtaining demographic information, I did not raise the issue of race with preadolescents (and I instructed research assistants to take the same approach). Race is a sensitive topic that makes even adults uncomfortable, so it seemed inappropriate to inject the topic into discussions with young children. Therefore, we discussed race with preadolescents only if they raised the issue.

The preadolescent informants' lack of race talk suggests, as some social scientists have theorized, that race is not an especially important marker of difference for young children.[20] However, given my conversation with the Madison students, the experience of the white student who reported that black students questioned her about trying to "act black," and the older students' recollections of their classmates' use of the acting white slur (below), it may be that preadolescents are more likely to publicly acknowledge race within their own peer groups, but not within earshot of adults. Indeed, the children's general silence on race in the context of the interview may also reflect some level of awareness that, as Paul Sniderman and Thomas Piazza found, it is considered not "appropriate to speak of the issue of race."[21]

There are some studies that have found evidence of race talk among preadolescents, however. In most cases, though, the children were in contexts in which discussing race was encouraged by adults.[22] For example, Amanda Lewis conducted an ethnographic study exploring the construction of race in different elementary school contexts.[23] At a Spanish-language immersion school, teachers readily initiated discussions and engaged with students on issues dealing with race and ethnicity, power, status, equality, and justice. As a result, the students at that school were more aware of their own and others' racial, cultural, and ethnic identities. They also were more comfortable using racial terms and discussing race and inequality compared to students at schools in Lewis's study in which the issue of race was not openly discussed. These findings indicate that in settings in which adults openly and explicitly engage the topic, race may take on more meaning for preadolescents and they may be more comfortable openly discussing it. In general, though, it is obvious that race is not as salient a category for preadolescents as it is for older youth, and the former are not as comfortable with the topic as the latter.

As the next section shows, the adolescent informants often introduced the topic of race. They readily recalled the racial composition of their elementary schools and classrooms, and the race of their former peers and teachers. This suggests that although preadolescents may not openly acknowledge race, neither are they color-blind. When racialized patterns of achievement such as those described at Georgetown and Holt exist, they likely do make an impression on children, even if they are reluctant or unable to articulate that impression at the time.

Achievement and the Salience of Race among Adolescents

By the time they reach high school, students seem to have shed their preadolescent reserve regarding race talk. For all of the sixty-five high-achieving black adolescents we got to know during their junior and/or senior year (see *Effective Students* study), race was a salient category, regardless of the schools they attended. (See table 2.1 for demographic information about these students.) Whether it was during informal conversations we had as we walked with them to and from class, or during the formal one-on-one interviews, students spontaneously mentioned race, with little or no interviewer probing. For example, unlike the preadolescents, when asked to describe particular groups of students or classrooms (e.g., "If I looked in your AP English classroom, what would I see?"), for example, adolescent informants often included racial descriptors. Although there were differences among adolescents in the degree to which they believed race matters in everyday life, they all were racially aware, and no one was reluctant to discuss race when we raised it to follow up, clarify, and/or obtain more details (e.g., "Is the person you are talking about black?").[24]

Adolescent participants acknowledged that race began to take on more importance for them and their peers during middle and high school. For Vanessa, a junior at Everton High School (75% white; 21% black), the attention to race began in high school. As she explained, this was when the "faction comes in." Vanessa linked increased racial awareness to students' expanding knowledge base. Learning more about historical events such as slavery and the Civil War had repercussions.

> I don't think as a child you ever really notice it [race], and then you start reading books like Frederick Douglass' and you start reading about all these people more in depth, and that's when, like I mean, in elementary school they don't tell you about all the bad things that

TABLE 2.1 Selected Characteristics of Sixty-Five *Effective Students*

	N	%
Female	44	68
Male	21	32
Foreign Born[1]	7	11
Family Income[2]		
$5,001–$20,000	2	4
$20,001–$25,000	5	10
$25,001–$30,000	3	6
$30,001–$39,000	6	13
$39,001–$50,000	6	13
$50,001–$70,000	11	23
$70,001 - $90,000	6	13
More than $90,000	6	19
Parent Education[3]		
Less than high school	1	2
High school diploma or GED	7	14
Some college	9	18
Vocational or AA degree	10	20
BA degree	13	26
More than BA	10	20
Family Structure		
Lives with mother and father	38	59
Lives with mother only	20	31
Lives with other relative or guardian	7	11

[1] *All foreign-born participants are female.*

[2] *We obtained annual household income in a survey of parents (50) of participating students. Forty-eight parents reported income information.*

[3] *Information listed refers to parent completing the survey. The majority (78%) were mothers.*

happen in elementary. You read all this in high school, you get all these books about and you see movies about how it happened and what happened, and that's when your eyes are opened...I see like [white] girls like that I grew up with, and I never, they always talked to me, they were always friendly with me, now I see them with Confederate flags and everything, and they're just like out there like 'white is supreme.'...but I just see a whole different side than I seen when we were in elementary school because they've been introduced to, like we've been introduced to our black history, they've been introduced to their white history...

Other participants did not articulate as clear an understanding as Vanessa's of how the black-white racial divide began, but their accounts of when racial issues surfaced, particularly with respect to achievement, were quite consistent. In all but two cases, they cited middle or high school as the starting point.

Race-related tensions and misunderstandings among adolescents often revolved around friendship choices and the peers with whom students socialized inside and outside of class. Such problems were most pronounced among students who attended schools in which stark racial differences in placement and achievement were the norm. In this context, achievement became another cultural marker of difference along which youth could and sometimes did draw boundaries. Darren, another participant from Everton High, discovered this in middle school when he joined the Beta Club, an organization that among other things is intended to reward achievement. Darren was teased by his black peers, especially the males: "They would say, like, you know, 'Why you're the only black boy in the Beta Club? There's nobody else in there.... There ain't none of your brothers in there. Why do you want to be with all the white people?' Stuff like that." When asked how he handled the "heat" he was getting from his black peers about his membership in the club, Darren replied, "Just took it. I just took it. I knew I was doing alright."

Acting White and the Cultural Spectacle of Achievement in Racially Diverse and Predominantly White Schools

Among the sixty-five high-achieving students who participated in the study, thirteen reported being accused of acting white for particular achievement-related behaviors. Experiences with the kind of racial isolation in advanced classes and programs that Darren described were prominent in each of these thirteen students' accounts. Sabrina, a student at Anderson High School (59% white; 33% black), explained how "this whole 'you want to be white' thing" first started for her in middle school. It was a consequence of the racial composition of the advanced classes to which she had been assigned.

I think the fact that, like—'cuz usually, um . . . like I said, most of my friends come from classes I've been [in], and we just end up in a tight bond, and since like, you're like, a black person in honors class, there's not many black people around you, so, like you bond with the white students with you and stuff like that, but. . . . I'm just mainly—I go with people who I have things in common with, and like, I guess education would be a big staple in that also, so, I just happen to like, bond with people, and like, just 'cuz the most of them are white, or there're some that are black, it's just . . . they just kind of seem like, "Oh, you just wanna be white," or whatever.

Sabrina's segregation from the majority of black students continued in high school. As shown in figure 2.1, in the six different classes in which we observed her during her junior and senior years, black students were underrepresented in all but one, public speaking/debate, an elective. In that class, blacks accounted for 39 percent of the students. In each of the other classes (all AP), black representation ranged from a low of 9 percent in AP calculus, where Sabrina was one of two black students in a class of twenty-two, to a high of 24 percent in twelfth grade AP English, where she was one of four black students in a class of seventeen.[25]

In this book's introduction Sandra was in a similar position at Earnshaw School of Excellence (49% white; 44% black). Being "the only black person" in her advanced classes had left her isolated from other black students in the middle school grades. She had had little choice other than "to make friends with a lot of white students." Sandra explained how being seen with only white students led to problems so serious with a group of black girls that she

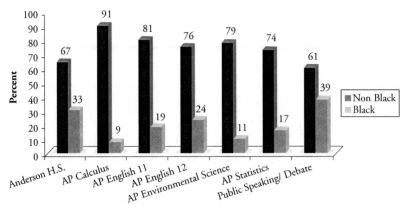

FIGURE 2.1. Racial Composition of Anderson High School and Sabrina's Observed Classes, 2002–2003.

contemplated transferring to a private school.[26] She described how the girls tormented her because they believed that she did not "want to be with other black people," and that she thought she "was better than them" and "trying to act white." Sandra went on to explain how the girls' teasing moved from "making fun of me because they thought that I was snobbish," to "everything else. It went into how I dressed, how I talked, everything else. I couldn't walk down the hall without someone saying something to me." The whole experience left Sandra feeling "pretty devastated" and "depressed."

Sandra remained at Earnshaw through her senior year, and although life for her improved in the higher grades (the girls who had tormented her left the school), her advanced classes were still considerably segregated. During her senior year, in both Integrated Math and AP English, she was one of three black students in classes of twenty-one (14%). In her standard Spanish class, however, she was one of seven blacks in a class of eighteen students (39%).

Lynden's experiences at City High (69% white; 16% black), though not as difficult as Sandra's, had similar elements. He recalled that when he was a freshman, other black students began referring to him as "White Pretty Boy" because he had been socializing mainly with white students whom he had met in his advanced classes.

> 'Cause the majority of my classes was with white people so I was friends with them and they were like kind of, and they were smart, and I was smart with them or whatever. . . . Like ninth grade year, ninth grade, the whole ninth grade year, I didn't chill, I didn't do nothing. Basically, my dad had me on lockdown and stuff like that, but I really didn't do anything. So it was like [the black students were saying about me], "He don't—he don't—he ain't all that." So I was like, "Okay." So I started chillin' more with black people and stuff.

By not "chillin'" with fellow blacks, Lynden became socially vulnerable. His behavior was interpreted as a sign that he was conceited ("he ain't all that") and therefore he deserved to be teased by the group.

When we met him, Lynden was in his senior year. He was still taking advanced classes, but he was also firmly embedded in the black crowd at City High. He explained that after ninth grade, he started "chillin' more with black people" at school and was able to change his peers' initial perception of him as conceited. He reported that he still cared about his grades and that he made good grades. Now, though, his academic standing was not an issue for his peers. "They don't care," he said. "It don't matter. I mean, I'm chillin' with them; it don't matter."

When we observed him at school, Lynden, with his doo-rag, baggy clothing, and bling, rarely seemed to go unnoticed as he walked through the halls between classes. Usually he greeted other black males with a nod, "What's up," or the customary fist bump; and he suavely tapped, winked at, or hugged at least one girl (not always black) along the way. Occasionally, he would stop to talk to fellow blacks as they congregated in the second-floor hallway, leaning against the railing overlooking the school lobby, a spot the group favored. The only way Lynden appeared to stand out from the black majority at City High was in the classes he took. By all other typical measures—in dress, gestures, and speech—he appeared to be just like any other black student at his school.

For Yvette, whose remarks about acting white opened this chapter, problems with racialized teasing related to achievement began in elementary school. A student at Massey High School (79% white; 13% black), Yvette recalled being accused of acting white in both her predominantly white elementary school and at Massey. "Isn't that sad?" she commented during our first interview. "Elementary school, you're getting told by people that you're not black enough because you're so smart." She could recall no problem, however, being a high-achieving student in her predominantly black middle school.

> *Interviewer*: They said stuff to you about acting white [at Emerson Middle School] too?
> *Yvette*: No, it wasn't that bad there because there were a lot of black people in aca- in advanced classes, like, I have to say, like, in my English class there had to be like ten black people in there. That's a lot. That was a lot.
> *Interviewer*: So you didn't really get that at that school? Then you came to [Massey High School]. What happened there?
> *Yvette*: More white people than black people. The black people that are doing good are trying to "act white." [*Tone is sarcastic.*]

The difference in Yvette's experiences across the three schools is telling. The only time she did not hear students' casting achievement as acting white was when she attended a predominantly black middle school where many black students were enrolled in advanced classes.

Other students who reported racialized teasing related to achievement seem to have been less fazed by it than were Yvette and Sandra. Juliana said that her black peers at predominantly white Everton were critical in their remarks about the racial composition of the classes in which she enrolled, but she seemed to find their comments humorous.[27] Laughing when we asked whether they ever teased her for doing well in school, she replied:

Yes. It's kind of funny, too. They be like, "Oh, Juliana done turned white on us."... They be like, "She done turned white on us. Be up in the white people class. Act like she don't know nobody." I'm like, "Come on! I'm still the same person, ain't nothing different." They'll be like, "Yeah, we'll see. Whatever. You come with nine letter words to us and we'll see what you're talking about."

Robin, who completed her junior year at Shoreline (72% white; 15% black) before transferring to a private school, recalled being called a "nerd," when we asked if she had ever been teased "about being good in school." She explained that, "Some people used to tease me about what math I was in and stuff. How I'm always in the white classes." In fact, Robin reported that it was not until her junior year that she "actually had another black person" in her honors English class.

The perception among students that advanced courses are "white people" classes is not limited to schools in North Carolina, or even the South. Anthropologist Annegret Staiger makes this clear in her study of a large multiracial high school in California. She notes that black and Latino students often referred to the school's gifted program as "a program for White students only."[28] This perception presents a dilemma even when it does not lead to being taunted for acting white. As adolescents, most high school students are grappling with internal doubts and questions about their identity and where they belong. For black students, the experience of racial isolation as well as the messages conveyed through racialized tracking (e.g., advanced classes are "white people" classes) create additional social and emotional challenges.

MAKING SENSE OF RACIAL DIFFERENCES IN COURSE ENROLLMENT

A troubling consequence of racialized tracking is evident in the foregoing examples. As adolescents try to make sense of the racial patterns they observe, they inevitably construct meanings that reflect racial stereotypes. At Rolling Hills High School (77% white; 18% black), racialized tracking left Phillip with the perception that black people "don't take honors and AP classes." Phillip, a senior, began this discussion with Valerie, one of the research assistants, one morning after leaving his honors physics class. As they walked to his third-period class, Phillip mentioned to Valerie that Tanya, a classmate in physics and another participant in the study, also was in his math class. "There are only one or two black people in all of my classes," he continued.

When Valerie asked Phillip if it had always been that way, he replied, "Pretty much, because black people just don't take honors and AP classes. If you go to a regular class, there are more."

This situation is difficult for many adolescents (and adults) to make sense of. As a black honors student in Beverly Daniel Tatum's study of the development of racial identity said about his experience with racialized tracking, "It was really a very paradoxical existence. Here I am in a school that's 35 percent Black, you know, and I'm the only Black in my classes.... That always struck me as odd. I guess I felt that I was different from the other Blacks because of that."[29] Left to make sense of this "odd" situation for themselves, it is not that surprising that some adolescents turn to the acting white slur. How else are they to understand why only one or two black students are enrolled in the most rigorous courses and programs—unless of course they are to believe the stereotypes about racial differences in intelligence, work ethic, or the value of education?

High-achieving black students might challenge as "really stupid" the idea that "you're acting, like, white or something if you're trying to be smart," as Reeva, a student at Mullins High School (51% white; 41% black) did. Nevertheless, these students did not seem any better able than their lower-achieving peers to make sense of the absence of blacks in advanced classes. Jordan, a rising senior at Latham High School (81% white; 8% black), thought that he had "been the only black student" in his honors courses on "many, many occasions," because the other black students at his school were bused in from poorer areas of the county.

> You're not going to walk into an AP course or an honors course and see many of them [black students]. Go into an academic course you'll see almost all of them. And I'm not really sure why that is. It may have been because where they pulled some of these black students from, a lot of them come from [a neighboring town] and that's more of a lower-middle-class area. And I guess that's why, just where they pulled them from.

Reeva's explanation for the low number of black students in advanced classes at Mullins showed a similar degree of confusion. Even as she said that she would "like to see more minorities" in her honors classes, she seemed to believe that the only thing preventing that from happening was the students' own racialized attitudes about achievement.

Other students in schools with racialized tracking held similar beliefs, which, accurate or not, contributed to the sense of difference and the widening social gulf between blacks and whites and among blacks. Under such conditions, adolescents seemed to feel more pressure to adhere to the perceived norms of their respective groups. Lynden and Tanya, for example, reported that as ninth graders, they felt they had to "have the attitude like [I'm not] all about school" or "like the attitude, 'We don't care about grades,'" in order to fit in with their black peer group at school. Tanya explained how this kind of thinking emerged for her at Rolling Hills High School:

> I don't know—because it's always been, it seems like it's always been—the smart people are the white people, and me being a black person, I wanted to fit in with the black people too. So I figured if I went in there acting like all the brainiacs, they'd say, "She's another goody-two-shoes," not paying me any attention.

Although Tanya portrays this pattern of "the smart people" being white as having "always been," she, like Yvette, reported having had a different experience in middle school. There, her school's pre-college program to prepare minority students for college resulted in "classes [that] were more equally proportioned; they were white and black. There'd probably be maybe ten black people in the advanced class." In high school, however, this pattern changed, and Tanya was at a loss to explain the transformation.

> *Tanya*: There were so many smart minorities, and then it was like when you get in high school, it's like you get in those higher classes, there are two or three [students of color].
> *Interviewer*: Well, what happened? They were all in middle school, where'd they go?
> *Tanya*: I don't know.
> *Interviewer*: Are they in high school? Are they in your high school, or did they go to—?
> *Tanya*: They're in my high school. I don't know if they're not taking the harder classes or because it's so many classes to offer, they just kind of split up, and the number gets smaller. I don't know—but every class, I guarantee you, there's only, in my pre-calculus class there were two black people. In my honors history there were two...

Figures 2.2 and 2.3 depict this pattern, which we observed while shadowing study participants at Rolling Hills. As Phillip mentioned, he and Tanya were the only two black students of twenty-two (9%) in the honors physics class during the spring of their senior year, although the school's student body was 18 percent black (see figure 2.2). In Tanya's honors English class in the fall of her junior year, she was also one of two blacks, but this time in a much larger class of thirty-seven (5%). By contrast, in the standard Spanish class in which

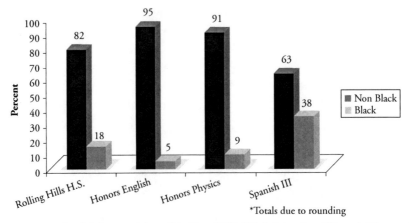

FIGURE 2.2. Racial Composition of Rolling Hills High School and Tanya's Observed Classes, 2002–2003.

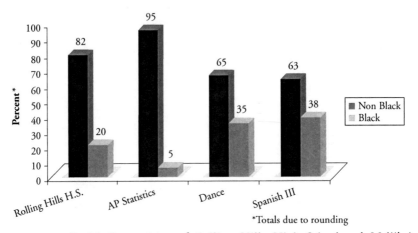

FIGURE 2.3. Racial Composition of Rolling Hills High School and Maliika's Observed Classes, 2002–2003.

she was enrolled during that same semester, Tanya was one of six black students in a class of sixteen (38%). We observed a similar pattern of black underrepresentation in advanced classes and overrepresentation in lower-level and elective classes in visits to Maliika's classes at Rolling Hills (see figure 2.3). For example, Maliika was the only black student in her AP statistics class of twenty (5%), but was one of nine blacks in her dance class of twenty-six (35%), and one of six blacks in her standard Spanish class (the same class in which Tanya was enrolled).

Unable to explain the dwindling presence of black students in advanced classes, Tanya interpreted the situation as an indication that black students were freely choosing not to take advanced classes, presumably because of their low regard for the kind of people ("brainiacs") who generally take such classes. In her first year of high school, Tanya was afraid to be associated with that group, especially, too, because those students did not look like her.

RACIALIZED TRACKING AND ANIMOSITY AMONG BLACK STUDENTS

As Tanya's comments and those of other students indicate, racialized tracking fosters a growing sense of difference between black and white students and among blacks. To make matters worse, the difference also implies status. Thus, in addition to prompting students to reinforce racial stereotypes as they try to make sense of the racial disparities in placement and achievement, racialized tracking reinforces a pecking order that leads to animosity and resentment between the students at the top and those at the bottom. This is not surprising. As Jerome Karabel and A. H. Halsey have pointed out, "The structure of the educational system upholds those meritocratic values that justify differential rewards, and the separation of the 'successful' from the 'failures' provides daily object lessons in inequality."[30]

No one seemed to understand this dilemma better than Shelly. In discussing the classes she and another high-achieving informant at Anderson High (59% white; 33% black) were taking, Shelly described the emergence of the academic hierarchy and its social consequences:

> When I was in elementary school, I don't know, those [years] were so great, maybe because you're so young. I don't know if it had to do with being separated from people, but I remember being in classes with people that were all at different levels, and it was all like, it didn't matter because you're all, you know what I'm saying, you got to interact with all different people. And then in middle school, they separate you out and then they tell you, like, you know, who's in the slow class, and you know, who's in the honors class. And then they expect the kids that are in the lower-level classes not to have some kind of animosity towards you. I would call it animosity. That's the term for it. Kind of [*pauses*] distaste for you, you know. It's like they give you a target on your chest and then they give people arrows to shoot at you.

When this process of separating out appears to students to reflect existing social status divisions, the animosity intensifies. Janet Schofield and Andrew Sagar describe precisely this phenomenon in their explanation of how the unequal achievement of black and white students in a newly desegregated middle school in the late 1970s created "resentment and hostility" between the two groups. According to Schofield and Sagar, "The black students often perceive the highest-achieving white students' performance as an arrogant display, a deliberate flaunting of knowledge that downgrades other class members."[31]

Not surprisingly, then, when a token number of students from less privileged backgrounds are given opportunities that place them among the higher status group of "others," separated from peers of similar background, they risk high social penalties for displaying any hint of haughtiness or arrogance. As other studies have shown, white students are similarly open to scorn. White students in lower-level classes often accuse their peers enrolled in advanced classes of being "stuck up," "snooty," and "high and mighty."[32] Regardless of race, the higher achiever who is perceived as arrogant provokes resentment and anger among those left behind academically. In part, this is because high school students who lack strong academic credentials are increasingly aware that this will limit their prospects for social and academic advancement. Thus, a reward that was widely coveted when students were younger, as we found among the elementary school students, can now, it seems, only be envied—and its recipients resented.

This resentment is what many academically capable American high school students fear and attempt to ward off by "just laying low," as Keisha, a student at Garden Grove High School (54% white; 32% black), put it. She described being disliked by all of her classmates for being "the smart one" as early as elementary school.

> So I was kind of an outcast. The only people I had were my teachers. So I'd go to school, I was the brain. I knew how to read and do algebra, and I was just so smart and I didn't have any friends....No one liked me. You know how it is. There's always that one person in your class, no matter if they're doing it on purpose or not, they're "the smart one."

Keisha's recollection that her elementary school classmates resented her for being smart is inconsistent with younger students' reports of their experiences (though consistent with Yvette's). But, as she explained, her experience was complicated by her "foreign" status. Aside from being a "brain," she had difficulty fitting in with her classmates because she was an immigrant.[33]

> I got picked on a lot because I was African. I had an accent. I wasn't like everyone else. I wasn't black and I wasn't white. And I wasn't anything that a child could define. I was just foreign. And I tried to

socialize but I guess the accent got in the way. And that's all they saw. And little kids I guess they were just ignorant or something. I just couldn't make friends, no matter how hard I tried because I was not cool, I guess, because I was foreign. And to top it off, I was smart. No one wants a brain.

By the time Keisha started middle school, however, she "knew better" about how to manage her performance in order to make friends and not alienate anyone. She noted that she still made "those straight A's," and everyone knew she was smart, but that she was not as open about it, or, as she said, not as "straight up with it."

Avoiding Becoming a Target of "Distaste"

As we have seen in many of the preceding examples, the intense underrepresentation of black students in high-track classes in racially diverse and predominantly white schools leaves the high-achieving black students who take those classes isolated from fellow blacks. This, in turn, puts them at risk of being perceived as haughty or conceited, especially when they appear to be distancing themselves from the group. Recall how Lynden's, Sandra's, Sabrina's, and Juliana's black peers reacted to their enrollment in "white people" classes or to their socializing with only white students. Insulted by what they perceived as an intentional act on the high-achieving student's part to put them down, some students responded with a put-down of their own: the acting white slur. It is well known among African Americans that the term acting white has the power to condemn. Thus, the term can be counted on to swiftly undercut the visual display of white supremacy as well as dismiss as irrelevant the school's norms and evaluations. As such it allows lower-achieving students to gain a degree of symbolic power in the face of an otherwise embarrassing experience.

Two points are worth noting here. First, not all of the study participants encountered hostility from fellow blacks for socializing primarily with white students. Consider Adonis. His response when asked about the various cliques at his school and why he socialized mostly with white classmates rather than the "rich black people" (of which he considered himself a part), suggested that he felt constrained in his friendship choices: "Because all of our, my classes they, it's hard to get like a black person in the class. I mean, I only had one black person in my class over the last year, and that was out of six classes. Actually no, it was like four. I had two in one class and one in another."[34] Yet in his account of life at Latham High (81% white; 8% black), Adonis reported no problems with black peers.[35]

Second, students like Adonis, Lynden, Sandra, and Shelly strongly denied that their choice of friends or achievement behaviors were intentional acts to distance themselves from fellow blacks. These students felt a connection to their black peers and they wanted to fit in and be a part of the group. As Shelly expressed it, "I am them; they are me; that's my culture." Thus, many informants were disheartened by their peers' rejection and teasing. To avoid this situation, those who were isolated from fellow blacks in advanced classes often reported that they made an effort to fit in. Some did this by paying attention to the way they dressed and by adorning themselves with jewelry and other markers of black fashion tastes.[36] Shelly revealed that she dressed "like a normal black girl," so as not to put herself "out there" to be "ridiculed."[37] Sandra also reported that she altered the way she dressed; and she said that she watched BET (Black Entertainment Television) and listened to urban radio stations to be more in sync with her black peers. A number of the boys sported one or two diamond stud earrings. Lynden and his brother Glen confided that they changed their style of dress once out of their father's sight.[38] They shed the casual shoes and "collared shirts" tucked into non-baggy pants that he required them to wear in favor of hip-hop styles more common among their black peers (Starr, a participant who attended Garden Grove High School, referred to the style one day in class as "the Black People's Uniform," of baggy jeans, a tee shirt, and sneakers or Timberland boots). Both boys insisted, however, that this look was their preferred style of dress.

Many participants attempted to fit in simply by, as Lynden said, "chillin' more with black people." Selina, a student at Massey High School, zeroed in on the issue of being a part of the group when asked how other students at her school felt about high achievers.[39] Note that her perception of the treatment of black high-achieving students, as well as her own experience, is different from that of her schoolmate Yvette, quoted previously.

> I don't—I don't think—I don't really think it's a big deal. I really don't, because see, a lot of the high-achieving black students, there's mostly girls rather than boys. And, they—they're—they're mingling with the other black kids just as much, so I don't think about it—it's really not an issue. I think if they were all secluded, then, yes, then it would be like, "Gosh, look at that group of, you know, dorks" or whatever, so.

Selina's comments indicate that "mingling" with other students helps high-achieving students avoid being perceived negatively or shunned or ridiculed by their peers.

Amaria, too, endorsed mingling ("hang[ing] out") as a good way to avoid negative reactions from peers. Although she moved to the United States with her family from Africa when she was a young child, Amaria did not experience any hostility from her peers during her first years in American public schools (unlike Keisha), and in high school she believed that her peers looked up to high-achieving students. Nevertheless, Amaria found that being a part of the group was key to avoiding the "hate" that is common among teenagers.

> *Amaria*: You have people who hate on you! [*She laughs.*] Well, it—
> Yeah people will be like, um, um, "She thinks she's smart," and this
> and that. "She thinks she's—," but you're always going to have people
> like that. I don't have too many people like that, I guess 'cause I hang
> out with everybody and like, they know me. So but, if you—if—a lot
> of people, if they don't know you, and you don't hang out with them
> then they'll start hating on you, but I don't have any people like that.
> I just see people doing that to other people.
> *Interviewer*: Why do they do that to other people? One of the things
> you just said was if you don't know them, then they do that. So—
> *Amaria*: Yeah. If you don't, if they don't know you, then they'll, they'll
> just hate on you. It's just typical teen stuff. And then like, um, I think
> for me, er, not—well—yeah for me too. But, if you're not, if you're
> just really smart and you don't, if you're not in like a lot of like activ-
> ities, you don't, you don't interact with a lot of people, then you just
> one of those.... It just seems like you're outcasting yourself. People
> tend to hate on you, but people are, teens are always going to hate on
> other people for some reason. [*She laughs.*] I'm serious! If you have nice
> clothes, they'll hate on you so, but it also depends—like if you hang
> out with other people then they have no, no reason to hate on you
> 'cause they're friends...

Amaria's remarks suggest that any indicator of status difference can spark resentment among adolescents if a teen is seen as antisocial.

"Chillin'" or "hang[ing] out" with fellow blacks outside of class was not simply a strategy the high-achieving participants employed in order to fit in with others or demonstrate their allegiance to the group. Friendship ties were a strong motivation for seeking out peers. As we have seen, high-achieving black students often had few black classmates in the advanced courses they took. In addition, in many schools, opportunities during the day to interact with friends outside of class were rare. So, when such opportunities occurred, students tried to make the most of them. An experience with Tanya and her friends at Rolling Hills is illustrative. During one of our visits to campus to shadow Tanya, the senior class had a mandatory assembly to select their class flower, color, quote, and song. After Valerie, the research assistant, had settled into a seat at the back of the auditorium with Tanya and her friends, all of whom were black, Tanya turned to her. Almost apologetically, Tanya explained to Valerie that the students were not usually as segregated, but that the only time she got to sit with her friends was during assemblies. Tanya's comments prompted Valerie to look around and take note of the degree of racial segregation. Ninety-nine percent of the black students were seated together in the back section of the auditorium.

To get a sense of why the opportunity to connect with black friends at the assembly was so important to Tanya and others in her position, consider Keisha's description of her experience at Garden Grove. She was no longer the outcast she had been in elementary school. Still, in responding to an interview question about the environment in her advanced courses, she described feeling alone because she was the only black student in her AP classes and had little in common with her white classmates.

Interviewer: Now talk about the environment in those classes. What's the environment like in those honors and AP courses that you've taken? Is it different than—

Keisha: Yes, there's no one to talk to. No friends. Just a really, really—when I was a freshman, I took Spanish III and I was the only freshman there. It was just me and this other black girl. And that was just it.

Interviewer: So why do you not have any friends or no one to talk to in these classes?

Keisha: 'Cause all my friends take different classes. They don't, I mean Starr, she was in my English class. But my friends aren't taking like the AP Calculuses and the AP Spanish.

Interviewer: OK. Well talk about, a little bit about those students who do take those classes that you take. Who tends to take those classes? You keep giving me this smirk and the smirk tells me there's something—

Keisha: [*She laughs.*] Oh, the nerds.

Interviewer: Who are the nerds?

Keisha: It's nothing. I'm just—I'm always this one black girl in a sea of just nerds. White people. And I know that sounds bad, but I don't have any other way of explaining it.

Interviewer: OK, well let's talk about that, because it's conceivable that the nerds could be all kinds of other people, but are all the white people nerds?

Keisha: Unh unh.

Interviewer: Are all the nerds white people?

Keisha: Unh unh. No, it doesn't go either way. But—my math class—that's what keeps coming to my mind. They only talk about *Star Wars* and *Star Trek* and—painful memories. I don't have anyone to talk to.

Keisha's account of her experience as the lone black student "in a sea" of "white people" highlights the isolation students in her position sometimes feel. It also helps us understand that the loneliness stems from feeling different and left out.

Adding Insult to Injury

Concerns about fitting in, especially for high-achieving students, are typical among adolescents, regardless of race. For many black youth, however, such worries may be heightened by an awareness of the importance African Americans attach to a sense of community and connectedness with others of their race.[40] But not all informants tried to fit in or cared to be associated with the normative black youth culture they observed at their school.[41] Curtis and Shawnie, for instance, openly sought to distance themselves from the black majority and the negative behaviors they believed to be the norm among this group. These behaviors involved what informants— attempting to distinguish between the different cliques at their school— usually described as "ghetto." Although generally acknowledging the existence of diversity (e.g., "And then within the black community, you got the different groups"), informants explained that the "ghetto" black students stood out because of the way they dressed, talked, and carried themselves: "and then you have the really ghetto black people who are always loud and always fighting"; "They're the worst. They're the loudest, they pick on everybody else, start all of the fights"; "they're loud and they wear saggy pants...people see their underwear hanging out and everything"; "they're always like loud and ghetto." It is important to understand that, unlike Curtis and Shawnie, most informants did not view the behaviors of the "ghetto" crowd as the norm among black students. Still, Shawnie and Curtis made no apologies for their desire to distance themselves from the behaviors of the black crowd, but in the process they also demeaned and offended their peers. Both students admitted that they could be "condescending" and "arrogant" at times, and as might be expected, they were not well liked by many of their peers, especially blacks. Both students faced ongoing racialized ridicule and ostracism.

Among the seven informants at Everton High School, Curtis and Juliana (quoted above) were the only ones to report racialized teasing. But whereas Juliana indicated that the students who teased her were her friends and only joking, Curtis could make no such claims. As we learned from Curtis's school-mate Vanessa, some black students were antagonistic toward him because of their belief that he "look[ed] down upon" them. She explained her perception of Curtis's predicament:

> I've seen this one guy Curtis, he's like, he's just like he knows every-thing. On his break time he reads the dictionary. He just, he wants to do it all, and they look at him like he's such a sell-out, and he's always [*Unaware that she is referring to another participant, I interrupt to ask*: Is he black?] Yeah, he's black, and he never wants to interact with people who are not like him or who don't achieve as much as he do...They look at him and he's like an outcast, so like the black students they don't really like him at all. And I'm looking at them like, "Why don't you like him?" And it's not because he's achieving more than them, it's because he separates himself from them. But he doesn't want to deal with them, that's why they don't like him. I don't think the black kids have a problem with higher-achieving black students if you talk to them, and if you act like a person towards them. It's the ones who choose not to conversate with them, act like, I can see that they act like, "No, I can't talk to you because you don't do what I do," and I can see that, and that's where they have the problem.

Vanessa went on to say that she could "actually picture Curtis bleeding and nobody would—, laying on this floor bleeding, just blood oozing everywhere, and I think they would just pick on the boy and not try to help him."

For his part, Curtis was aware of his peers' intense dislike of him and real-ized that some saw him as "the whitest black boy" they knew. In interviews with him, Curtis acknowledged that his behavior "comes off as being rude or snobby." His disdain for fellow blacks was obvious in many of his remarks. He was especially hard on black males, disparaging their leisure activities ("it wasn't like I had to wake up with a basketball in my hand"); familial patterns ("I don't have like eighteen cousins that all go to the same school"); style of dress ("I don't sag"); and speech ("I don't curse every other word"; "I'm not the 'What's up, man?' and that kind of thing").

Curtis's stereotypical and demeaning views of fellow blacks, and his self-confessed fear of being similarly perceived, undoubtedly affected how he interacted with his peers. Vanessa's analysis seems dead-on: Curtis "separate[d] himself" from other blacks; "he doesn't want to deal with them." This, in turn, as Vanessa pointed out, probably intensified his peers' negative perceptions and hostile treatment of him. Although Curtis is an extreme case, his social problems give substance to remarks other study participants made about the importance of high-achieving students interacting with fellow blacks and not treating them with disdain.

Shawnie, a student at Parker-Berger High School (55% white; 36% black), was by her own admission in a position similar to Curtis's. When she was asked how she was doing academically relative to fellow blacks, she quickly distanced herself from the group.

> *Shawnie*: Better than others. A lot of times I don't even associate with the black people at our school because, I don't know what it is, but we just don't have anything in common. Like, we don't, like, I'm thinking totally different than them. And so, like, I see them in the hallway, like, walking down the hallway, yelling out rap songs and … and being loud. It is just not my personality, it is just not me. So I don't even, like, try to get with that because I know what they're about kind of, you know. I kind of know, you know, they are not really as motivated. I don't know, it just seems, their classes are where I get—they're not as motivated and they're just trying to get by. And so I don't—they don't even know I'm better because as I see—as I've gotten older and in classes, the number of black people in my classes is less and less and less and less. And it's like I remember people there and I talked to them, and they're like there are less and less black people. And I'm, you know, like proud of myself. Like I think Bonita is like number two, and she's like the only other person I know beside Wanema; me, Wanema, and Bonita are the only black people that were junior marshals. And so like them, and then like [between] everybody else is such a big gap, or to me it is. I guess it's just my personality, too, because Wanema and Bonita can really associate with them, but I just can't. [*She laughs.*]
>
> *Interviewer*: Does that ever cause any conflict between you [and the other black students], or is it …
>
> *Shawnie*: Yeah, I kind of already have a reputation as—they think I'm like snooty or think I'm too good for them, or whatever, and I've dealt with that since I was like in elementary. They assume that I know— that I'm trying to be white, or whatever.[42]

Students such as Curtis and Shawnie were less concerned about fitting in or meeting their peers' expectations and more concerned with how their teachers and other authority figures perceived them. Similar to the group of high-achieving black students Signithia Fordham studied at Capital High, these students made a conscious effort to distance themselves from the average black student.[43] It is important to note, though, that Curtis and Shawnie did not necessarily adopt what Fordham described as a "raceless persona" in order to be high achievers.[44] These students distanced themselves from what they viewed as negative aspects of black peer culture while maintaining a personal commitment to blacks in general. For example, Curtis took issue with his black peers' use of the "n" word, pointing out that he found it ironic "seeing how black people are the ones who should be fighting for civil rights and stuff." He also reported expressing concern and disappointment when he realized during his junior year that he was the only black male in the junior class to earn a GPA of 3.5 or higher. "I hadn't paid attention to it until I looked around at the list, and there was nobody on there," he said. "I couldn't believe it. It was just like, where is everybody at?...and it kind of shocked me, it's like, you know, that's a shame."

The self-centered and superior attitudes displayed by Curtis and Shawnie in the comments quoted above were typical of these two students. Thus, it is not hard to understand why other students might resent them. But Shawnie and Curtis are unique cases. The other eleven students who experienced taunts of acting white and other racialized teasing did not strike us, either as we shadowed them during the school day or as we talked with them during interviews, as arrogant or condescending in the way that Curtis and Shawnie did. Furthermore, unlike these two, most of those accused of acting white expressed surprise and disappointment at how their peers perceived them.

To summarize, as the informants' experiences illustrate, the intense under-representation of black students in advanced classes presents a social predicament, in addition to limiting opportunities to learn for the majority of black students. If black students who have the opportunity to take advanced classes are not sufficiently attentive to how they present themselves in daily life at school, they run the risk of further alienating their black peers, who may perceive them as arrogant or haughty. Indeed, almost all reported instances of allegations of acting white for achievement-related behaviors (or reports of fears of such accusations), included remarks about being perceived as thinking that one is "better than" others (all thirteen informants), is "stuck up" (six informants), or is "arrogant" (four informants).

THE PATTERN OF RACIALIZED TRACKING IN RACIALLY DIVERSE AND PREDOMINANTLY WHITE HIGH SCHOOLS

We observed more than three hundred classrooms across nineteen high schools between January 2002 and May 2003 as we accompanied informants to their AP, honors, and general education courses. (Table 2.2 lists the high

TABLE 2.2 Percent White and Black of *Effective Students'* Schools, 2001–2002 (Listed Alphabetically)

High School	Size	Percent White	Percent Black
Anderson	2011	59	33
Banaker	1093	6	89
Bloomfield	2021	76	17
City High	1393	69	16
Earnshaw	1306	49	44
Everton	1610	75	21
Flamingo	1416	25	60
Garden Grove	2044	54	32
Latham	1947	81	8
Lucas Valley	1934	65	24
Massey	1993	79	13
Mullins	1560	51	41
Parker-Berger	1821	55	36
Pearce	2413	50	37
Rolling Hills	1288	77	18
Shoreline	1747	72	15
Vanderbilt	1866	47	37
Wade	1690	71	14
West End	1089	78	18

schools and the percent black and white composition.) Not surprisingly, we saw the most significant underrepresentation of black students in AP courses, especially AP calculus and AP biology, and in advanced math and science courses more generally. Black students seemed to be somewhat more equitably represented in advanced English and history classes.

The observations conducted while shadowing students at school confirmed the general pattern of underrepresentation of black students in advanced classes reported by informants who were attending predominantly white and racially diverse high schools. The pattern was more pronounced in some schools than in others, however. For example, at Anderson and Garden Grove, both racially diverse schools, the pattern of black underrepresentation in advanced classes and more proportional representation in lower-level or elective classes was clear. At Garden Grove, Amanda was one of eight black students in her Spanish class of twenty-one (38%), but she was one of three blacks in both her AP English class of thirty-one (10%) and her AP physics class of twenty-five (12%) (see figure 2.4). In Keisha's classes at Garden Grove, we observed that black students comprised fifty percent or more in her allied health sciences classes during her junior and senior years, but their representation fell at or below 10 percent in her AP English and AP chemistry classes (see figure 2.5).

At predominantly white high schools such as Massey, Wade, and Shoreline, however, the pattern was less well defined. At Shoreline (72% white; 15% black) and Wade (71% white; 14% black), black students were underrepresented in the majority of classes we observed. In many standard math, science, language, and English classes, their numbers neared or exceeded parity

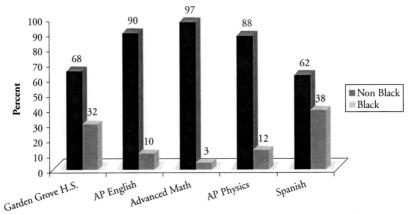

FIGURE 2.4. Racial Composition of Garden Grove High School and Amanda's Observed Classes, 2002–2003.

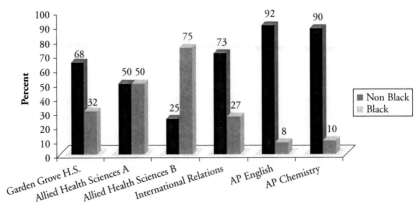

FIGURE 2.5. Racial Composition of Garden Grove High School and Keisha's Observed Classes, 2002–2003.

relative to their representation in the school population. However, in physics, chemistry, and honors English classes, they represented less than 10 percent of the students. In the three AP classes we observed at Wade High School, one informant was the sole black student in each class. At Massey High School, black students were just 13 percent of the student body, and their presence in most of the twenty-one different classes we observed was small. However, they were proportionally or overrepresented in five of the classes, one of which was an advanced class (honors English). In other classes, their representation ranged from 3 percent (psychology) to 13 percent (AP European history).[45]

The pattern showing greater underrepresentation of black students in advanced classes at more racially diverse schools is consistent with the findings of previous studies using national survey data.[46] However, some of the differences in underrepresentation we found may be accounted for by the variation across schools in the number of AP courses in which informants were enrolled. This matters because black students were most significantly underrepresented in AP classes. At Anderson and Garden Grove high schools, 11 of the 27 and 13 of the 33 different classes observed, respectively, were AP classes, compared to just 1 of 24 at Shoreline, 3 of 34 at Wade, and 2 of 21 at Massey. This difference in the course-taking patterns of students across schools was not simply an artifact of the classes we were able to observe. Interview and survey data from the informants confirm the difference. For example, as a group, the six informants at Shoreline reported taking just three AP courses, compared to nineteen AP courses for the group of four informants at Anderson. It may be that at the predominantly white schools, black students are more likely to be crowded out of advanced classes.

At any one school, we were able to cover only a small sample of classrooms over the year and a half period of study. Thus, the observations in individual classrooms provide only a glimpse of the racial organization of schools. However, the observational findings are consistent with other data.[47] For instance, data collected by North Carolina's Department of Public Instruction show that in the aggregate, minority students were underrepresented quite significantly in the advanced curriculum in almost every school in which black students were not the majority (see table 2.3).

Table 2.3 shows the level of disparity (a score of 1 indicates proportional minority representation and 0 indicates no minority representation) in minority representation by high school in AP courses that most schools are likely to offer (English, calculus, biology, and history). At Everton High School, for example, where minority students comprised 21 percent of the population, in 1999–2000 there were no minorities in AP calculus or any of

TABLE 2.3 Minority[1] Representation in AP Courses, Grades 9–12, 1999–2000

School Name[2]	English			AP Calculus			Biology			History			% Minority in School Population
	% Minority in Course	Disparity Index	Total Students in Course	% Minority in Course	Disparity Index	Total Students in Course	% Minority in Course	Disparity Index	Total Students in Course	% Minority in Course	Disparity Index	Total Students in Course	
Anderson	23	0.67	396	7	0.21	28	0	**0.00**	19	12	0.36	90	34
Banaker	79	0.87	184	68	0.75	62	73	0.80	22	86	0.95	281	91
Bloomfield	7	0.39	597	0	**0.00**	57	0	**0.00**	16	8	0.41	263	19
City High	4	0.27	225	3	0.17	135	8	0.45	210	10	0.55	113	18
Earnshaw	21	0.42	273	10	0.20	20	15	0.31	78	20	0.40	263	50
Everton	9	0.40	354	0	**0.00**	34	0	**0.00**	8	9	0.38	199	22
Flamingo	44	0.66	71	27	0.40	15	NA	—	—	46	0.69	120	67
Garden Grove	17	0.52	444	2	**0.07**	41	4	**0.13**	24	18	0.54	220	33
Lucas Valley	12	0.40	518	3	**0.11**	63	7	0.24	28	3	**0.10**	169	30
Massey	5	0.31	791	0	**0.00**	28	7	0.46	30	2	**0.14**	293	15
Mullins	19	0.44	393	15	0.34	136	8	**0.18**	52	14	0.33	379	43

Parker-Berger	15	0.38	279	7	0.19	28	6	0.16	16	15	0.39	113	38
Pearce	16	0.43	688	7	0.20	452	10	0.28	39	11	0.30	598	37
Shoreline	6	0.26	757	4	0.15	54	3	0.11	150	11	0.45	232	25
Vanderbilt	12	0.27	446	8	0.18	172	13	0.28	64	19	0.43	735	44
Wade	7	0.37	478	4	0.22	50	6	0.33	51	6	0.35	252	18
West End	13	0.60	410	7	0.32	14	14	0.64	14	7	0.30	59	22

1. African American, American Indian, and Hispanic.

2. Data for 1990–2000 were not available for Latham and Rolling Hills High Schools. Both were relatively new schools at the time of the study.

the advanced biology courses. The same was true for Bloomfield High School, where minorities comprised 19 percent of the student population. Shoreline, Massey, Garden Grove, and Lucas Valley high schools each had two curriculum areas, generally math and science, in which the disparity index was close to zero (0.15 or lower) in 1999–2000.

The two exceptions in the table to the general pattern of black underrepresentation in advanced classes at racially diverse or predominantly white schools are City High (69% white; 16% black) and West End (78% white; 18% black). In both biology and English AP courses at West End, the representation of minority students is just over half the rate of the students' presence in the student body. West End and City High were also among the smallest schools in their respective districts, with student populations of less than 1,500.[48] Furthermore, City High has actively undertaken efforts to reduce the achievement gap between black and white students, including adopting a program designed to prepare minority and low-income students for success in advanced classes.[49] In light of these efforts, it is not clear why minority students remain significantly underrepresented in most of the AP subject areas.

Combined, my observations at City High look somewhat consistent with the general pattern displayed in table 2.3. Black students were significantly underrepresented in most of the advanced classes I observed, but they were overrepresented in a few others. For example, I shadowed Glen, Lynden's brother, on a day that he had pre-calculus, an advanced math class, followed by an honors African American history class. Of twenty-seven students in the math classroom, Glen was the only black student (4%). In the history class, however (and not surprisingly), Glen was one of fifteen black students in a class of twenty-two (68%). Additionally, black students were overrepresented in the honors English class in which Courtney and Lynden were enrolled; on the days I visited, there were between five and seven black students in classes of eighteen to twenty-one. Although as Courtney acknowledged, there were "a lot of black students" in his honors English class, he also pointed out, "But, the rest of my honors classes and AP, I'm the only black."

My observations at West End High School (78% white; 18% black), on the other hand, were not, even in the aggregate, consistent with the pattern shown in table 2.3. In the observed classes, black students were underrepresented in advanced classes such as AP biology (6%) and AP European history (5%), but overrepresented in standard and elective classes such as business (30%), leadership (29%), and English (30%). Accompanying Amaria in the fall of 2002, for instance, I observed 21 students in her first period Spanish III class, of whom 4 were black (19%); 26 in her algebra III class, of whom 3 were black (12%); and 32 in her advanced earth science class, of whom 4 were black (13%).

Acting White and Achievement at Predominantly Black High Schools

By contrast to the intense underrepresentation at the seventeen racially diverse and predominantly white schools shown in table 2.3, at the majority-black schools, Banaker (6% white; 89% black) and Flamingo (25% white; 60% black), the disparity index was .60 or higher in all but one curriculum area (AP calculus). Observations at the two predominantly black high schools match the evidence provided in the table. The advanced classes in those schools were usually majority black (although, as in the other seventeen schools, black students often were underrepresented in those classes relative to their overall enrollment in the school), and blacks also were more likely to be among the highest-achieving students in the school. Under these conditions, high-achieving black students experienced a much different social environment.

Unlike their high-achieving black counterparts at racially diverse and predominantly white schools, students in these schools did not report any problems with students casting achievement as acting white or other racialized ridicule and ostracism. Discussions about acting white with informants at these two schools were, therefore, much less in-depth than were those with informants at other schools. Banaker and Flamingo informants generally had few or no stories to tell about allegations of acting white for achievement-related behaviors. Banaker students Lavern and Sonya, like their schoolmates who participated in one of our previous studies,[50] reported that accusations of acting white for achievement were not a problem at their school. According to both girls, their classes were "mostly black." Lavern reported that no one at Banaker had ever accused her or anyone she knew of acting white. When asked whether she had ever heard the term, she acknowledged that she had. She then described her older sister's experience of being accused of acting white in middle school, although not for achievement-related behaviors.

Sonya said she had heard other students at Banaker being accused of acting white, but, again, never for achievement-related behaviors.

> *Interviewer*: Since you've been here have you ever heard anybody talk about or accuse someone else of acting white?
> *Sonya*: Uh, yeah.

Interviewer: Who, what?

Sonya: The way they talk, the way they act. Yeah. My good friend, she always gets accused of acting white 'cuz she talks, she talks very proper and I guess black people don't talk proper. Yeah, right [*sarcastic tone*]. Yeah. She gets that a lot.

Interviewer: Do they ever say that about people who do well in school? Like, is it ever just about them?

Sonya: No, I haven't seen that. When they say you're acting white, they just do if you talk a different way, like talk proper.

Neither Sonya nor Lavern reported being teased for doing well in school. And neither had felt the need to downplay their achievement, although both were careful to point out that they were not boastful. Lavern believed that her peers were more likely to "look out for each other" academically than to tease each other. And Sonya reported that she "never felt that being smart was bad, or doing well in school was bad," nor did she feel that that type of environment existed at Banaker. "I've never seen that," Sonya explained. "Like, I don't know if it's me, but I just, I just didn't see that at all."

Sonya was so unfamiliar with students at Banaker belittling "smart people" that she questioned whether that type of environment existed anywhere in the real world.[51] When asked why she questioned this, Sonya explained:

> Because they don't single you out, or talk bad about you. I just don't see that. I mean, I see things like that on TV, but when I look at TV, sometimes I'm like, "that just doesn't happen at my school." Like the whole clique thing, like, I look at it in the cafeteria, and I just don't see that. You know how you see on TV, there's just different people in the cafeteria in their own little sections. And I look around, I'm like, why isn't this school like TV?

Like many other predominantly black urban high schools, Banaker had its problems, including low test scores and a citywide reputation as a "bad" school, in terms of both the academic and social climate. The Banaker students we interviewed, however, disagreed. They perceived the socio-academic environment for achievement as encouraging.

The same can be said for Flamingo, where there were no accounts of allegations of acting white for achievement. Informants there did report some teasing for achievement, but they were also careful to explain that the teasing was not antagonistic toward high achievers or achievement per se. For example, when asked how she thought other students at Flamingo felt about high-achieving students like herself, Kathy admitted that peers had called her a "bookworm" when she was younger. They still teased her for being a "nerd," she said, but she explained that it was not the same as seen on television.

> They're alright, they really don't, you know how like a lot of times on television they say, "Well, the nerds are in this class," and stuff. It's nothing like that around high school, and that's what I was telling my mom the other day, she was like, "Do they really act like this stuff?" I was like, "No, in high school we don't classify people as either you're a nerd and nobody can talk to you, or something like that."

Another informant, Sylvester, described the type of teasing he experienced at Flamingo as "playful" rather than hostile:

> People will be like, "Man, [Sylvester] know the answer." A lot of people, as far as being like teasing me, it's just like, "Hey, he's the person you want to ask." If they ask a question, the teacher goes, "Answer this question," and they don't know, they're like, "Ask [Sylvester]," you know what I'm saying. So they try to get it off of them and then just put it on somebody else. They don't always get peeved at this person always knowing the answer. "He's always raising his hand, thinks he knows everything." It's not like that.

These students' accounts are strikingly different from those of participants at racially diverse and predominantly white schools. At the predominantly black schools, students did not seem to feel that they had to walk a fine line between being a high achiever and being perceived as arrogant.

Neither Michelle nor Kwame, the other informants at Flamingo, reported being aware of any teasing for achievement in their high school. But Michelle, who at the time of the study was poised to be either valedictorian or salutatorian of the senior class, reported that her peers recently admitted to her that in middle school, they used to make fun of her behind her back. They told her they recalled calling her a nerd "when they used to call [her] name up for all the awards."

Like their counterparts at Banaker, participants at Flamingo also did not have to endure racial isolation in their advanced classes, because, as they described, those classes were majority black. When we asked Kwame whether the racial composition of the advanced classes was similar to that in standard classes, for example, he was quick to point out how Flamingo was unique in that respect.

> *Kwame:* [*He sighs lightly.*] I would say there's more, well, at Flamingo, it's like, different. There's more, I would say the racial breakdown is

not, in the honors classes, not what you would think it would be. Or you'd think there would be more whites versus minorities and stuff like that. And it's not typical. Because I think, in our class, our English class is more minorities than there are of the whites and stuff like that. So—and it, that's how it's always been, you know, like the top, like, I'd say like the top ten, or even fifteen, is majority black. And stuff like that. So—it's, it's pretty good.

Interviewer: And is it the same within the AP courses, too?

Kwame: Mm-hm [Yes].

Kathy made similar comments regarding the highest-achieving students at Flamingo and the racial composition of advanced classes: "I think the number one person in our class is black, and, like I told you, a lot of the honors classes are mostly black, or the classes that I've been in were mostly black, anyway." The observations while shadowing students at Flamingo and Banaker support the students' claims about the racial composition of their advanced classes. All classrooms observed at Banaker were close to or majority black, ranging from 50 percent in one class (AP/IB calculus) to 100 percent in several others (e.g., AP environmental science, honors English, student leadership). At Flamingo, all but three of the nineteen classrooms observed were majority black: AP chemistry (45% black), standard chemistry (47% black), and technical theater (30% black). In all other classrooms, including AP calculus, AP English, honors physics, culinary arts, and psychology, black students comprised between 52 and 79 percent of those in attendance.

Casting Achievement as Acting White: A Reinterpretation

The observations and narratives of high-achieving black adolescents at nineteen high schools reveal two key facts. There is a pattern of underrepresentation of black students in advanced classes in predominantly white and racially diverse schools; and this pattern creates the necessary condition under which black students interpret academic achievement as a "white thing." However, though necessary, this condition is not sufficient to lead to accusations of acting white with respect to achievement for individual students. If it were, we would find evidence of this phenomenon in any school with a pattern of significant underrepresentation of black students in advanced classes. We also would find that the acting white slur affects every black student who is on the other side of the racial achievement divide.

Instead, consistent with previous research, the evidence shows that not all high-achieving black students endured racialized teasing or ostracism from fellow blacks because of their achievement.[52] The majority did not. In fact, students within the same school often had very different experiences. For example, when I asked Lynden's schoolmate and friend, Courtney, about being teased for high achievement, he dismissed it. "That sounds like something out of an eighties movie," he said, faintly echoing the comments of informants at the predominantly black schools.

Similarly, the experiences of high-achieving black students at schools such as Garden Grove, Shoreline, Massey, and Earnshaw differed. At Earnshaw, for instance, the other participants did not face the treatment Sandra endured. Neither Zorayda nor Sharon reported any harassment or accusations of acting white for achievement-related behaviors from fellow blacks during any of their seven years at Earnshaw. Sharon admitted that peers had teased her, but "it was never about academics. It was never about school."

Zorayda, on the other hand, said she had been called a "nerd" for doing well in the middle school grades by both black and white friends, with whom, incidentally, she continued to socialize in high school. She claimed that the advanced classes at Earnshaw were not racially segregated. From her perspective, it was just that "people tend to stereotype that the white kids take the honors and AP classes and the black kids take the standard classes." Noting that she has "black kids in [her] AP classes," Zorayda argued that the stereotype was "not true." Despite this, she added, "of course, I have a lot more white kids [in my AP classes]." Zorayda attributed this fact, however, to the racial composition of the school, explaining, "but there's a lot more white students here." And during this discussion, she revealed that she wanted to attend a historically black college, explaining, "because I'd feel normal and like, Wow! I'm not the only black person here."

Ironically, the underrepresentation of black students in some of Zorayda's advanced classes may have skewed her perception of Earnshaw's racial composition, which was more than 40 percent black for most of the time she was in high school. For example, in the fall of her senior year, Zorayda was one of three black students among the twenty-one (14%) students in her honors physics class. However, in some respects, Zorayda's perception of the presence of black students in her advanced classes was accurate. More than once while shadowing her, I registered surprise at the sheer number of black students in the room. In Zorayda's honors English class that same year, she was one of twelve black students in a class of nineteen (68%).

Nonetheless, relative to their proportion in the wider school population, black students were usually underrepresented, and sometimes significantly so, in Zorayda's advanced classes. Her inaccurate but positive perception of racial balance in those classes is important, however. If that perception is widely shared among the sixth- through twelfth-grade black students at Earnshaw, then Sandra's experience of racial isolation in advanced classes and of ostracism and ridicule for appearing to distance herself from fellow blacks because she was the only black student in advanced classes, is not likely to be repeated.

Conclusion

As every other generation has done, contemporary black youth have taken their cues about what is and what is not authentically black from patterns they repeatedly see and hear in their daily lives. What these youth are doing is not unique. They are receiving information from the environment, making sense of it within the repertoire of symbols and knowledge at their disposal, and responding based on their perceptions of the current situation. For many black adolescents, particularly those attending racially mixed and predominantly white schools, school life is dominated by a tracking system that is unmistakably racialized. These students observe advanced classes that are composed almost entirely of white students and lower-level classes that are more diverse (even overrepresenting black students at times). In addition, they are presented with honor rolls, gifted programs, Beta Clubs, and National Honor Society rosters that are predominantly white. These patterns, some of which emerge as early as elementary school, create and sustain an image that signals a racial hierarchy in academic ability and achievement and makes a cultural spectacle of achievement. I have argued that this image is key to understanding why and how some contemporary black adolescents construct academic achievement as a "white thing."

Some black youth draw on discourses of race from the cultural tool kit of the wider African American community when faced with schooling experiences that do not appear consistent with previously held mainstream understandings of how things work. In other words, culture provides a perspective to make sense of an experience that is inconsistent with the American ideals of fairness and meritocracy. The American achievement ideology offers no explanation for the visually apparent racial disparity in tracking found in many public schools, other than to suggest that black students as a group do not work as hard as others do, or that they are not as intelligent as others are. Faced with these stereotypes, black youth seek alternative explanations to account for the observed racial disparity.

It is difficult to determine precisely when the acting white concept originated, but it seems fair to say that it has been in existence for nearly a century. Thus, it is a readily available "tool" within black Americans' system of symbols and meanings. In interpreting their experiences in desegregated schools, contemporary black youth may use this tool to give themselves, if only symbolically, a sense of power and control. By claiming that taking advanced classes is acting white, the students are also suggesting that they are freely choosing not to take those classes. In that context, the current use of the acting white slur with respect to achievement makes sense. It allows those who experience racialized achievement hierarchies at school to actively construct meanings that indicate preferences, tastes, and wants. Especially for youth at the bottom of these hierarchies, asserting control in this manner is preferable to passively accepting the insulting message implicit in racialized track placement, namely that black students are academically inferior and/or lazy.

What it means to act white will continue to change over time and across place (region, neighborhood, school) as each generation of black youth adapts the concept to incorporate differences they observe in the life chances and outcomes, styles of dress and speech, tastes, and so forth, of blacks and whites. Both inside and outside of school, black American youth are engaged in producing and re-creating meaning in ways aimed at disrupting existing social arrangements and understandings. Their current use of variants of the word "nigger" (e.g., niggaz, nigga) is one striking example. Ridiculing high-achieving peers may be another. The acting white slur simultaneously affirms the existence of the institutionalized link between whiteness and achievement and rejects the validity of that link. In that sense, the taunt is a small act of rebellion that symbolically, at least, reclaims power.

In the post-desegregation era in which tracking is the new form of segregation in many schools, some lower-achieving black students may reject the institution that has determined that their skills are not well suited to the demands of schooling. Additionally, when these youth perceive that their more successful peers are behaving in an arrogant or obnoxious manner, they may counter that behavior by leveling what they know will be a most effective insult: the accusation of acting white.[53] Julie Bettie encountered a similar response to racial disparities in achievement among Mexican American students in the California high school she studied. In explaining why, lacking "a political and cultural discourse on class," working-class Mexican American students accused their more academically successful middle-class peers at Waretown High School of "acting white," she writes, "It was a way of saying, 'I don't understand your success and my failure, so I'll minimize your achievement by accusing you of acting white.'"[54]

Desegregation created a new social world, one that abruptly declared blacks and whites equal. Prior to desegregation, especially in the South, blacks and whites tended to occupy separate worlds, each with its own institutions and array of distinct cultural traditions and practices. Integration threatened to disrupt those cultural distinctions by creating a world in which blacks and whites lived and worked side by side. Many African Americans, although favoring integration for various political, economic, and social reasons, also strive to hold on to their own cultural practices and styles.[55] Yet even as they have tried to preserve old traditions and meanings, African Americans also have had to create new meanings by which to understand and deal with the new environments in which they live, work, and socialize.[56]

The history of race relations in America has been characterized by relentless attempts to monitor and control racial and other differences (e.g., gender, sexual orientation), especially through the imposition and maintenance of discriminatory policies and practices.[57] This history shapes how contemporary black youth interpret the patterns of racialized achievement they observe in their schools. Their "blackness" and their connection to the larger experience of being black in America is the one thing that most see themselves as having in common. Black Americans cannot always articulate clearly and do not always agree upon what it means to be authentically black.[58] Nevertheless, many believe that there is a community-wide expectation that they embody and express "blackness" in their everyday interactions, especially with other blacks, but also in the presence of whites. Failure to meet this expectation leaves one open to accusations of being "uppity" or "selling out." Knowing the peculiar history of blacks in America and being aware that ongoing discrimination and racism exist, African Americans generally understand the importance of this expectation, even if they cannot clearly articulate a rationale for it, and even if they do not always live up to it. Some scholars refer to this understanding as a sense of linked fate.[59] Thus, as Prudence Carter has argued, some youth use the acting white slur "as a form of social control."[60]

For some, the commonality among blacks matters a great deal (in both positive and negative ways), and for others it means little.[61] This is an important point, because as I show in the next chapter, adolescents' vulnerability in the face of peer pressure is connected to the degree to which they feel the need to fit in. The strength of this need affects how much time, effort, and energy they expend to meet it. However, it is not necessarily the case that the more black youth feel a sense of community with and connection to other African Americans, the more likely they are to be concerned with fitting in with their black peers. Some students, as we learned in this chapter, distinguish between acceptable and unacceptable black teen practices and choose to identify only with what they consider acceptable. Moreover, as Erin Horvat and Kristine Lewis and other researchers have shown, black students do not always feel they must sacrifice their racial identity in order to do well in school.[62]

SCHOLARLY MISINTERPRETATIONS OF STUDENTS' CASTING ACHIEVEMENT AS ACTING WHITE

The argument I make that the expression of school achievement–related behaviors as acting white is found only in the post-desegregation era directly contradicts the assertions of numerous commentators and scholars, including Jawanza Kunjufu and Signithia Fordham. Yet both Kunjufu and Fordham label as resistance to acting white comments and experiences of black students that do not appear to be racialized.[63] The accounts both researchers refer to reflect black students' concern with being characterized as or called a "nerd," "brainiac," or "sucker"; or they refer to the students' reluctance or refusal to enroll in advanced classes. The following is an example of Fordham's interpretation of such data, presented in *Blacked Out,* her more in-depth analysis of the students at Capital High:

> Instead of confronting school officials or constructing an open rebellion or multiple rebellions, they resist the construction of Otherness by avoiding certain courses—World History, for instance, as well as specific school-related activities like the chess club and the math club. This response is most visibly manifested in their concentration in the academic track labeled "regular" and in their wholesale shunning of the advanced placement program, the segment of the school's curriculum that is most likely to lead to academic success at Capital and admission to the nation's elite colleges and universities.[64]

I can find no evidence in Fordham's work to support her interpretation of the Capital students' avoidance of particular courses as racialized behavior. When compared to the comments and behaviors of students of other racial and ethnic backgrounds at other schools, the Capital students' concerns look generic, indistinguishable from those of the average American adolescent.

American students of all racial and ethnic backgrounds commonly shun school activities popularly defined as "dorky." These often include the most rigorous academic courses as well as certain extracurricular activities, such as chess clubs and debate teams. Consider the following comment from a debate team member that Gary Alan Fine quotes in his study of debate teams at two predominantly white, upper-class high schools: "In Randall's Park there's still a negative feeling among students because they think that debate is one of those really academic activities, and academics is still kind of downplayed and shunned.... I think it's a negative thing only because, wow, that's just too smart a kind of thing."[65] This kind of "negative feeling," showing disdain for certain scholastic activities and achievement-related behaviors, is prevalent in many American secondary schools.[66] It is part of what some researchers refer to as an "oppositional peer culture."

One study of more than 20,000 high school students in Wisconsin and California in the 1990s found that "one out of every six students deliberately hides his or her intelligence or interest in doing well in class because they are 'worried what their friends might think.' One in five students say their friends make fun of people who try to do well in school."[67] Moreover, many students expend considerable energy attempting to avoid the stigma attached to "the geeky crowd."[68] Most qualitative accounts of life inside the contemporary American junior or senior high school, including Fine's ethnographic study of "talk" among debate team members and Patricia and Peter Adler's study of preadolescent culture and identity, find some evidence of the existence of this oppositional peer culture.[69] As the Adlers wrote about the students in their study (most of whom were white), "Some boys who were scholastically adept tried to hide their academic efforts or to manage good performance in school with other status-enhancing factors so as to avoid becoming stigmatized."[70]

That the kind of anti-intellectualism prevalent in many American high schools is a common feature of American culture was made quite clear during the 2008 presidential election season. Examples were abundant—as were print and online media commentaries on specific instances of anti-intellectualism. For example, after many people publicly praised the first debate performance of Republican vice presidential nominee Sarah Palin, one online blogger, Mitchell Bard (2008), wrote:

> Rather than reward knowledge and intellect in this country, we reject it, saying that it makes the candidate "arrogant" or "boring" or "elitist" (or, as two Southern Republicans referred to Barack Obama, "uppity," but that is a whole other discussion). No, the U.S. has become an anti-intellectual society that scorns intelligence and ability and wants leaders that are "just like them."[71]

In light of the anti-intellectualism and general "oppositional" nature of American youth culture, it is not clear what, if anything, race has to do with the Capital students' choice of courses and activities. Nor is it clear that we can understand the students' "concentration" in the "regular" track by looking only at their attitudes.[72]

In both scholarly and popular accounts, students' casting achievement as acting white is often characterized or defined in ways that leave the phenomenon disconnected from the context in which black youth are schooled. Indeed, a major difficulty with this area of research is that there is little consensus on the root of the problem: where, when, and why does this application of the acting white slur to achievement emerge. Attempts to test the effect of the taunt by measuring differences between black and white students on particular characteristics (e.g., attitudes toward school, popularity) often start from the same flawed assumptions about the underlying processes.[73]

For example, when economists Roland Fryer and Paul Torelli designed a national study of the effect of "acting white" on student achievement, they operationalized the phenomenon as "any statistically significant racial difference in the relationship between popularity and grades."[74] This is a troubling misspecification, and it leads to problems of interpretation. As we learned in this chapter, high-achieving black students' unpopularity is not simply a consequence of their grades and achievements. Fryer and Torelli's study showed that popularity peaked at a 3.5 grade point average for black students (although not in the more segregated schools). White students, however, continued to gain popularity as their grades increased. The researchers interpreted these findings as evidence supporting the notion that black students avoid doing well in school because they view it as acting white.

The analysis presented in this chapter suggests problems with Fryer and Torelli's conclusions about the diminishing popularity of the highest-achieving black students in racially diverse schools. Their findings more likely reflect these students' extended isolation from fellow blacks due to their enrollment in predominantly white advanced classes and their inability to penetrate white friendship networks beyond a superficial level. The findings in this chapter show that, in predominantly white and racially diverse schools, the highest-achieving black students spend most of the school day in the company of whites, away from the vast majority of other black students. With few opportunities to interact with other black students at school, it is not surprising to find that the highest-achieving black students do not receive as many friendship nominations as their lower-achieving black peers.

Fryer and Torelli's research underscores the need for clearing up the conceptual confusion that surrounds adolescents' use of the acting white slur in reference to academic achievement. We cannot construct valid measures unless we begin with an accurate definition of the problem we seek to investigate. Recall the examples of Curtis and Shawnie. Their cases were atypical, but they offer a strong reminder of the importance of attending carefully to the narrative accounts of students and systematically analyzing the details of their school experiences. A more superficial investigation or a more abstract level of analysis invites misinterpretation of high-achieving black students' unpopularity as a reflection of their peers' contempt for their academic accomplishments. After all, as this chapter has shown, even the students themselves sometimes make this mistake. The lesson here is that studies investigating whether black students hold particularly negative racialized attitudes toward achievement and how those attitudes affect their academic achievement would be strengthened by the use of better measures for capturing the effects of the acting white slur and by greater attention to the impact of school and classroom racial composition. Refining our questions and the measures we use to answer them may reveal a tipping point in racial composition above which black students, no longer able to tolerate inequality, call upon the acting white slur.

Finally, a word about gender. I set aside this issue in the foregoing analysis in order to outline the general process by which school organizational practices affect the particular meanings students construct about achievement and race. As I have shown, these practices affect both males and females, but the importance of gender should not be discounted. Prudence Carter and others have clearly identified gender as an important factor in minority youth's school performance, behavior, and attitudes. In her book *Keepin' It Real*, for example, Carter described how parents may send different messages to their male and female children about what is expected of them, and how students' performances of masculinity and femininity may collaborate with social conditions to influence achievement outcomes. Thus, future research should consider the impact of gender on how students respond to the school structures this chapter identified as significant. Possible gender effects on how students respond to their peers' casting achievement as a form of acting white should also be investigated.

As this chapter revealed, many informants felt concerned, at some point in their school career, about how other students perceived them. This aspect of school life is an important one that has not received the kind of careful scholarly attention from sociologists that it deserves. In the next chapter, I examine adolescent vulnerability to negative peer influence, exploring why some students are more likely than others to conform to the norms of peer environments in ways that may put them at risk for academic underachievement or failure.

| THREE | Susceptibility To Oppositional Peer Cultures |

If a teacher would ask a question, "Does anybody know how many days are in a year?" Uhm, before I knew better I'd raise my hand and say the answer. But I just kept it cool. If she asked me, I'd say I'm not sure, you know? Try not to know everything. Try to make people like you.

Keisha, *black, Garden Grove High School (54% white; 32% black)*

'Cause I didn't care what they thought. I don't really care what other people think about me. I'm going to try to do good. If you don't want to do good, that's on you. If you don't like me, that's on you. You think I want to be white, fine. Think that.

Yvette, *black, Massey High School (79% white; 13% black)*

A PEER CULTURE THAT DISPARAGES "REALLY academic activities" and students who appear to strive too hard for academic success exists in many American secondary schools.[1] Of particular concern to educators, parents, and researchers are the consequences of this "oppositional" peer culture for academically successful students, because, regardless of their race, achievement can make them prime targets for their peers' ridicule and ostracism. For high-achieving black students, as I showed in the previous chapter, there is an increased potential for ridicule when school life is dominated by achievement and tracking structures that are unmistakably racialized. How vulnerable are these students to pressure to conform to the norms of an oppositional peer culture? Why are some high-achieving black adolescents more vulnerable than others? Are black students more vulnerable to racialized oppositionality (e.g., taunts about acting white) than to the more general type of oppositionality (e.g, taunts about being a nerd) that many high-achieving American adolescents face? What are the consequences of conformity for students' academic performance? Members of the group of sixty-five high-achieving black students provide some interesting, and sometimes surprising answers.

Many of these students were relatively unaffected by the norms of an oppositional peer culture during their secondary school career. Forty-three percent (of which 64% were female) reported that they neither had been nor feared they would be ridiculed for achievement-related behavior. These students also said they never downplayed their achievements or ability. However, more than half of the sixty-five students said that they were affected in some way. Either they had been teased about their achievement-related behaviors or, anticipating teasing, they had adjusted their behavior in advance to avoid it. What is intriguing about this group of thirty-six students, however, is the differences among them in their ability to withstand the pressure to conform to the norms of their local peer environment.

Yvette and Keisha (quoted above) were among those affected by achievement-related teasing or ridicule, and as their remarks indicate, they responded very differently. Keisha represents students at one end of the spectrum. This group is disturbed by their peers' taunting and worries about being a target, particularly of racialized and intra-racial ridicule. These students attempt to ward off the ridicule by adopting the styles (dress, speech, or hair) of the local black peer culture, or by concealing their ability and achievement from others. At the other end of the spectrum are students like Yvette. They adamantly dismiss peers' ridicule of their achievement-related behaviors and claim to make no attempt to adjust their behavior or personal style. Differences in the reported severity of the taunting do not account for the differences in students' reactions. In fact, some students who did not face direct ridicule nevertheless feared it enough to adjust their behavior to avoid the possibility of such an experience. What explains these differences? What makes some students more vulnerable to these pressures, while others are more secure?

In this chapter, I examine in depth the factors that enable high-achieving black adolescents to resist, reject, or ignore pressures to conform to the dictates of their local peer environment and the factors that leave them most vulnerable. I profile six adolescents to show how the *strength* of their sense of *identity* (i.e., who they are *and* are not), their *goals and aspirations*, and their *beliefs* all significantly affect how they respond to negative achievement-related peer pressure at school. Interestingly, the factors that are generally cited as the best predictors of adolescent susceptibility to peer influence (e.g., type or amount of parental input, type or quality of peer and friendship networks) do not emerge as especially useful. Instead, students' personal characteristics and the context in which they encounter peer pressure provide more insight into why some high-achieving black adolescents were more likely than others to succumb to pressure to conform to oppositional aspects of the peer environment at their school.

Adolescence and Peer Influence

Adolescence is considered a particularly vulnerable period in the American life course. Youth must deal with rapidly occurring physiological changes, with changing social roles, and with forging an identity independent of their parents. Concerns about appearance, identity, fitting in with peers, and belonging become increasingly important and may leave teenagers especially vulnerable to peer influence.[2] John Hewitt contends that by the time they reach junior high school age, American youth are strongly under the influence of a peer culture whose priorities "may be sharply at odds with parental values."[3] Adolescents typically do not want to be perceived by their peers as too different from the norm or, worse yet, as weird, as this can lead to teasing, ridicule, or ostracism. Hence, to fit in with peers, teenagers sometimes act against their parents' wishes and even their own better judgment.

The finding that peers have significant effects on adolescents' school behaviors, attitudes, aspirations, expectations, and other education outcomes has been fairly consistent over time.[4] That this influence can be both positive and negative is also well established.[5] For instance, membership in an academically oriented friendship network has positive consequences for an adolescent's academic performance while membership in a delinquent friendship network is associated with a greater number of problem behaviors over time.[6]

Adolescents are also influenced by people with whom they have very little interaction. Peggy Giordano's study of peer messages in high school yearbooks shows that less intimate peers can be much harsher critics than close friends.[7] Moreover, urban neighborhood studies such as Elijah Anderson's *Code of the Streets* (Philadelphia) and Mary Pattillo-McCoy's *Black Picket Fences* (Chicago) also indicate that youth are influenced by a wide range of people, including those they do not know and with whom they have no relationship or contact, such as television actors and movie stars.[8] Indeed, close friends, acquaintances, random schoolmates, neighbors, and strangers may all serve as part of an adolescent's reference group, shaping norms and providing models for things such as how one should dress, wear one's hair, speak, spend one's leisure time, and behave in school. Thus, identification with distant others and respect and/or admiration of others, in addition to intimacy and closeness, also may contribute to social influence among adolescents.

Just how much influence one adolescent has on another, however, varies depending on the particular behavior, context, and individuals involved.[9] Nina Mounts and Laurence Steinberg's research on peer influence on grades and drug use bears this out. They found that some teens are more susceptible to peer influence on positive behaviors than they are on negative behaviors.[10] Similarly, how much influence parents have on teens varies according to the behaviors involved and the relationship between parent and child. For example, Mounts and Steinberg found that students who described their parents' style of parenting as authoritative were more likely to benefit from having high-achieving friends than adolescents with parents who were less authoritative.[11] Bruce Biddle, Barbara Bank, and Marjorie Marlin's study of parental and peer influences on adolescents' drinking behavior and academic achievement found that parents are more likely to exert influence through norms while peers are more likely to exert influence through modeling.[12] In sum, research on adolescent behavior shows that peer influence is important, but that its significance varies; likewise, in varying degrees, parental influence continues to be a force in teenagers' lives.

Developing greater knowledge of the factors that help adolescents deflect potentially harmful peer influence is important, and may be especially so for black adolescents. Studies report that youth of color, especially males, are influenced to a greater degree by their peers on matters related to school achievement.[13] Among the academically successful adolescents we interviewed and observed, reactions to peer pressure varied widely. These students' narratives show that to understand peer influence, we must have some information about individuals' sense of identity, goals and aspirations, and beliefs. Adolescents who had a firm sense of who they are (and are not), clear goals and aspirations, and a set of strongly held beliefs about right and wrong, adamantly refused to succumb to peer influence that might interfere with their success. I call this group *secure* adolescents, because they seemed most immune to negative peer influence.[14] On the other hand, adolescents who were less grounded in their beliefs, or who were still trying to figure out parts of their identity or what they wanted to do in the future, tended to be more concerned with fitting in, either with a particular group or with the wider student population. I call youth in this group *vulnerable* adolescents, because their lack of clarity in all or some of these areas left them most at risk for negative peer influence.

For the analysis in this chapter, I draw on the experiences of the thirty-six adolescents who reported having been affected by the norms of an oppositional peer culture.[15] I use a case study approach, focusing on six students, in order to better illustrate the dominant characteristics of archetypical *vulnerable* and *secure* adolescents. To provide additional examples of patterns across the cases, where appropriate, I also include experiences reported by other participants. It is important to emphasize that the two analytical categories I use here represent points along a continuum. During adolescence, the process of coming into one's own with respect to various ideas, issues, goals, and so forth, is a fluid one.[16] The case studies provide snapshots of this ongoing process. They show how at particular moments in time, the combination of their sense of identity, goals and aspirations, and beliefs affect how the students respond to the norms of an oppositional peer culture.

The data suggest that most of those I label *vulnerable* eventually became more secure in the face of oppositionality. Similarly, those I label *secure* were at one time more vulnerable to this type of peer influence. The data also show that some adolescents who lacked clarity in some areas (e.g., identity), had greater clarity in other areas (e.g., goals). Importantly, however, lacking clarity in even one of these key areas made adolescents susceptible to peer pressure.

Peer Pressure and the High-Achieving Black Adolescent

Among the thirty-six adolescents who reported experience with teasing or ridicule related to achievement, or who perceived that an oppositional environment existed in their secondary school, twenty-five generally ignored, resisted, or rejected the characterizations (e.g., acting white). The remaining eleven admitted that they made adjustments to try to conform to their peers' norms and expectations. Here, I profile two students who resisted pressures and four students who tried to conform.

Tommy and Sandra had direct experience with ridicule and they both adjusted their behavior to prevent further harassment. Tanya and Carl did not experience ridicule directly, but they were nevertheless affected by the perception that an oppositional peer culture existed at their schools. Both adjusted their behavior in advance, hoping to avoid being teased (or worse).

These four students are archetypical *vulnerable* adolescents. They stood out among others as being especially concerned, at some point in middle or high school, about their peers' perceptions of them and about the possibility of being ridiculed for their achievement-related behaviors. Gwen and Curtis, on the other hand, seemed the most impervious among our informants to the experience of or potential for ridicule related to their achievement behaviors. They represent the archetypical *secure* adolescent, largely unconcerned and unyielding in the face of ridicule.

Table 3.1 provides summary background information for Tommy and Sandra, Tanya and Carl, and Gwen and Curtis. As the second-to-last column in the table indicates, the type of oppositionality these students encountered or perceived to be present at their school differs. Among the larger group of thirty-six high-achieving adolescents, across all three school types (predominantly white, racially diverse, and predominantly black), most experienced "general" oppositionality.[17] That is, they were mocked and teased in nonracial terms, called names such as "bookworm," "nerd," "goody-goody," "the rolling book bag," "teacher's pet," and "smarty-pants," by black and other peers. I distinguish this kind of taunt from the type of specifically racialized name calling (e.g., acting white, "Oreo") described in the previous chapter. Only participants at predominantly white and racially diverse schools experienced this type of ridicule related to their achievement.

High-achieving adolescents were also scorned and ridiculed in ways that highlighted other types of status-based resentment. These insults included alleging that the high-achieving student was "a wannabe," "stuck up," or "uppity"; behaved as though she thought she was "better than" others; or acted "high and mighty." Insults like these are used both within and across racial, ethnic, and class groups. Most often, however, they are directed toward in-group peers and signify that others feel put down in some way by the targeted student's behavior. This type of oppositionality is categorized as either class-based or intra-racial, depending on whether the insults are intended to call attention to the targeted students' crossing of class boundaries (usually lower- or working-class ones) or racial/ethnic boundaries.[18]

The aim of this chapter is to investigate why some high-achieving adolescents conform to the norms of a peer culture that is oppositional to the goals and values of schools in order to avoid ridicule, while others do not. To that end, I focus on students whose experiences cover all types of oppositionality. However, these students do not represent all three school types. They all attended predominantly white or racially diverse schools. It is in those schools that participants' reports of ridicule were the most striking and, in some cases, painful. It may be that, in those schools, the experience of any type of

TABLE 3.1 Archetypical *Vulnerable* and *Secure* Adolescents' Family Characteristics and Responses to Oppositional Peer Cultures

Student	Mother Education	Mother Occupation	Father Education	Father Occupation	Family Income	Oppositionality Reported	Response to Oppositionality
Curtis	A.A.	Administrative coordinator	NA[1]	NA	$25,001–$30,000	Racialized, general, intra-racial	Rejected
Gwen	H.S.	Teacher's aide	NA	NA	NA	General	Rejected
Tommy	H.S.	NA	H.S.	Correctional officer	NA	General	Conformed
Sandra	M.A.	School counselor	B.A.	Clerical worker	$70,001–$90,000	Racialized, intra-racial	Conformed
Tanya	H.S.	Customer service	H.S.	Tractor operator	$70,001–$90,000	Anticipated intra-racial	Conformed
Carl	A.A.	Lab technician	NA	NA	$30,001–$39,000	Anticipated racialized, intra-racial	Conformed

[1]. *Not available. Father's education and occupation are not available in cases where the father is not living in the home; some parents did not provide information on family income.*

oppositionality is made worse for high-achieving black students by the presence of a visible racial hierarchy in achievement and tracking.

Secure Adolescents: "I Don't Care"

I don't care what anybody else thinks! I only care about my work. I don't care. . . . I really don't care, because it's just me.

Karen, black Massey High School (79% white; 13% white)

Karen's comments are representative of the remarks made by *secure* adolescents. These students insisted that they did not conform to their peers' expectations and actively resisted norms that might derail their achievement. The possibility of significant consequences, such as being disliked or losing friends, does not deter them. "I don't care," is part of the answer most give when asked about their reactions to their peers' opinions of them, or to teasing and ridicule. Gwen and Curtis exemplify the *secure* adolescent.

CURTIS

Well, some of {the black students} are like, you know, "Well, why are you high and mighty?" You know, "why are you," kind of, sort of, like, "why are you so uppity?" But, I mean I never let it get to me because their opinion doesn't really matter when it comes down to it. I mean at the time it probably upsets me a little bit, but I get over it real quick, {He laughs.} I mean real quick, because it comes down to what it is I want to do and how I'm going to live my life.

Curtis was the youngest of three children, the only boy, and the only one still living at home in the trailer park with his divorced mother. Neither of his siblings had attended college. Curtis, who was ranked 4th in his graduating class of 370 at Everton High School (75% white; 21% black), was determined to do so. With a 4.5 (weighted) GPA and SAT scores above 1400 (both self-reported), he was among the most motivated and achievement-oriented of the high-achieving study participants. In fact, in class with Curtis on Senior Superlatives Day, we heard some of his white female classmates in AP calculus announce that they had nominated him "Most Likely to Go Buck Wild in College," because he was so calm and focused in high school.

Almost all of Curtis's decisions seemed directed toward achieving his goal of earning a medical degree and becoming a pathologist, a desire he said he had had since he was a child. The clarity and longevity of his focus is evident in the following exchange:

> *Interviewer*: Now the first thing you said was that a lot of [African American males] don't think it's cool [to do work and be smart]. Has that come up?
>
> *Curtis*: Yeah, it has, it's like [they say], "[Curtis], man, why are you always studying and why are you—," always almost, [I'm] like, "I have to; otherwise I don't do good." It's like, "Whatever, man," I mean that's their attitude that they don't—I guess because I have known what I want to do since I was really young, and I've done research on what it takes to get there, I've had some kind of, like, direction…

Curtis encountered general, racialized, and intra-racial oppositionality at school. Yet he seemed determined not to let anything get in the way of achieving his goals. Ridicule from peers, whether black or white—even the perception among some blacks that he was a "sell-out"—he dismissed as unimportant. For instance, when asked to describe the kinds of things his peers "pick at" him about, he responded:

> Like I had, you know, "You're the whitest black boy I know," that kind of thing. Some people could take offense at that. I don't personally because, you know, in some respects it's probably true. [*He laughs.*] Yeah, people say that kind of thing, and in some respects it's probably true, and if that's the way they feel, then you can think that. But that doesn't change me, who I am, and I'm not going to feel insecure because you have an opinion.

His peers' low estimation of his black identity performance may not have troubled Curtis because he preferred to distinguish himself from the "typical" black male student.

> And I think that's kind of funny, seeing as how black people are the ones who should be fighting for civil rights and stuff still, but yet they slack off when it comes to—, like to me "nigger" is a derogatory term. I wouldn't let my friend refer to me that way, but yet that's thrown across the school like it's like an everyday hello. And I think, to me that's kind of like taking for granted what was done in the sixties and the seventies, because it's like, here I am using a term that was once used to degrade me.

The degree to which Curtis is able to disregard his peers' perceptions and comments is unusual, especially among adolescents. As discussed in chapter 2 and explored in this chapter, black adolescents (and even adults) often are highly offended by comments that question their racial identity.[19] In Curtis's case, dismissing the comments that challenged his blackness and his life choices had the positive effect of making him less vulnerable to peer pressure. His resolve was bolstered by his belief that he was "doing the right thing," whereas other black students were not. Moreover, he took pride in "doing [his] best," a commitment he said he learned from his mother's side of the family: "I really just believe, you know, we believe in doing your best."

Curtis appeared to be neither discouraged nor disturbed by other people's opinions of him. As noted in the previous chapter, being taunted for acting white did not prompt him to adapt his dress, speech, or other behaviors to conform with those of his black male peers. He knew who he was not (e.g., "stereotypically black") as well as who he was. He said that he did not dress like the "typical African American male," meaning that he did not wear "Fubu or the hat backwards or the bandana or the doo-rag." "I mean, that's just not me," he emphasized again. Curtis also knew what he did not want to become. He believed black males were hindering their own success: The way they dressed prevented teachers from seeing them as serious students; and the way they spoke made them sound "ignorant." This lack of respect or admiration for his black peers protected Curtis from losing focus: His disregard effectively neutralized any negative influence peers might have had on him.

That his attitude was off-putting was not lost on Curtis; he acknowledged that to others, his self-confidence "comes off as rude or snobby" and "arrogant." His "egotistical" personality, of which he also was aware, certainly did not win him friends, especially among the black students. This did not trouble Curtis because, as he explained, from tenth grade forward, he usually chose doing his schoolwork over spending time with his friends, most of whom, by then, were white. He drew comfort from his conviction that the choices he made would pay off for him in the future.

> Well, I mean there was, in you there was always that, that feeling that maybe I shouldn't be doing what I'm doing. But then I always came back to, "What are my *goals*, you know, where am I going to be, how much is this night out with my friends going to mean to me, you know, five or ten years from now?"...I'm glad I didn't go because I don't think that I would have been where I am now...If I had stayed

with that group of people, I would be where they are now…which is in the D – C range, and that's not where I want to be.

Just how many real friends Curtis still had by his junior and senior years is unclear. As noted in chapter 2, Vanessa, another high-achieving student at Everton, spontaneously mentioned Curtis during an interview. She remarked that white students did not like him any better than the black students did. She said that she had "heard white students who he claims are like his best buddies talk about him behind his back."

Curtis's AP classmates seemed not so much to like as to tolerate him, mainly because of his academic ability. As he walked into the room and took his seat in AP calculus one April morning, the only other black student in the class told Curtis that his group mates, three white females, had been talking about him in his absence but that she "took up" for him. "I don't care," Curtis replied as the girls denied the accusation. Valerie, the research assistant, noted that Curtis did not seem to be on friendly terms with his group mates. Unlike the other clusters of students, who chatted pleasantly about topics other than schoolwork as they worked, Curtis's group was all business. Moreover, whereas the students in the other groups all sat facing one another, only two of the girls in Curtis's group faced each other. All three girls talked among themselves throughout the morning, but none of them talked to Curtis unless he initiated by asking a question or commenting on a math problem.

Initially, Curtis spoke only to the group mate seated in front of him, although the other two girls were listening. When he made a suggestion, no one responded to him, but they all appeared to take his advice, turning the page when he suggested they skip a problem or writing when he gave an answer. After working on his own for a while following a few brief exchanges with the girls, Curtis said, "Well, I got an approximation, so—," but the girls ignored him and continued their own discussion. Curtis did not offer his answer but instead asked, "Did y'all do part b?" The girls replied, "We got an answer." He asked, "Is it right?" The girls did not respond, and for the rest of the period Curtis worked alone.

Curtis was an outcast among much of the student body, and he was not especially well liked by teachers, either. Several incidents made this clear. One morning, while Valerie was waiting in the main office for Curtis to arrive, she observed a disagreement between a teacher and Curtis and his mother. Sounding irritated, the teacher complained to the principal that Curtis's mother had let him out of the car in an area not designated for drop-offs. Although the teacher had asked them to move on, Curtis had "insisted on getting out anyway." As the group disappeared into the principal's office,

Curtis defended his actions, explaining that he had been in a car accident the day before. Later that day, Curtis recounted the incident to Valerie, explaining that as he had gotten out of his mother's car, "The teacher approached me and started berating me. I told her, 'Look lady, why are you hassling me about this? You better get out of my face. I was in a car accident yesterday. You better be glad I'm here today!'"

That same day, during his second-period class, the classroom teacher approached Curtis at his desk and spoke to him in a whisper about his "mouthing off" in the parking lot earlier. At the end of the period, as Valerie was leaving the room with Curtis, the teacher asked her, "Where in your notes did you write: 'Curtis works on AP calculus in [his Economic, Legal, and Political Systems class] because he's so smart and already knows all this stuff'?" Recall, also, Curtis's run-in with the math teacher whom he perceived as having accused him of lying as well as discriminating against him when he told her he had not received a math packet (see chapter 1).

Whereas the experience of being disliked, or worse, being a social outcast, was uncomfortable or even unbearable for some participants, Curtis was unfazed—unless, as the math packet story demonstrates, he perceived the situation as having direct implications for his achievement. He dismissed his peers' opinions of him with the frank statement that from his perspective, the only opinion worthy of his attention was "how they think I do in school, like do they think I'm doing well and I'm going to be successful in college." So firmly was Curtis committed to his own academic achievement and future goals, and to his sense of who he was and was not, that he appeared immune to the pressure to conform to any other set of norms or expectations.

Curtis's behavior and attitudes protected him from negative peer influence, but they also made him appear socially inept. He seemed to have very little sense of perspective. He was unable, or unwilling, to recognize when his behavior crossed the line from being self-protective to being rude and obnoxious. Adolescents with personalities like Curtis's no doubt exist in every school and, like Curtis, they probably are not well liked. In Curtis's case, however, the situation is made worse by the presence of a racial hierarchy in achievement and his placement as one of the few black students at the top of that hierarchy. In this context, his behavior is all the more intolerable and insulting to his black peers.

There is no equivalent of Curtis among study participants at either of the predominantly black schools. Therefore, it is not possible to compare his experience of racial isolation at the top of the achievement hierarchy to a similar black student in a different schooling context. However, a different comparative lens may be useful. The year that our participants were graduating from high school (2003), the top graduating senior at Banaker (89% black) was an Asian student (Rebecca), one of the few in the school. If the cheers she received from schoolmates during the school's Awards Day program were any indication, Rebecca was well liked. Students in the packed auditorium cheered wildly each time her name was called as the recipient of another award (she received several). And during my interview with Sonya about two months before the awards program, she used Rebecca as an example to explain her belief that students at her school do not tease others for doing well academically.

> *Sonya*: No because [Rebecca], you know, she's number one, and she dances and she's down to earth and—
> *Interviewer*: [Earlier] you said she doesn't do anything but study.
> *Sonya*: Oh, she does study, but she, but she has to do community service for IB, stuff that's not just focused on school, but she dances and she loves dance. But she studies a lot, but she gets things done and she does, she just has that tolerance for things like that. I mean I think she deserves every bit of it.
> *Interviewer*: And the rest of the school doesn't see her in a negative—
> *Sonya*: No, they really don't. They're like "Oh [Rebecca]," they'll usually say "the Asian girl." I was like, "Yeah, she's—", they're like, "Yeah, she's cool." Nobody doesn't like her because she's smart or anything. It's just, I don't see it.

Rebecca was one of only a handful of Asian students at Banaker, but her achievements and placement at the top of her class of mostly black students did not result in resentment or ridicule. She was considered "cool" among her peers because of her participation in a popular extracurricular activity and because of her "down to earth" personality.

Generally, adolescents in Curtis's position at the top of the achievement hierarchy, as we learned in chapter 2, are very conscious of how they act around their peers. In fact, his is the position that high-achieving adolescents, regardless of race, seem to fear most: being perceived as haughty and unidimensional, and being despised and outcast as a result. Adolescents in David Kinney's research on high-achieving students' transition from middle school to high school discussed why this situation "really would be terrible." One white male explained that, in order to avoid being an outcast because of his intelligence, it is important to him that he "strikes a balance between intelligence and being a normal human being."[20] Indeed, Curtis's situation is the kind of negative example adolescents likely envision when they consider the costs of being "too studious."

GWEN

Gwen, a student at West End High School, shared Curtis's orientation toward achievement and a commitment to her own goals, but there the resemblance ended. Gwen, who described herself as "always participat[ing] in something," was well liked by her peers, both black and white. Surprisingly, she thought that a lot of students did not like her—an impression I could find very little evidence to support. On the contrary, she seemed to be popular. For example, in her senior year, students at her majority-white high school nominated her for senior class representative; she won the homecoming queen contest (a surprise to her); and she was nominated for "Best Personality," "Most Likely to Succeed," and "Outstanding Senior." As she walked through the school's halls and stairwells between classes, other students frequently acknowledged Gwen, saying "hi," or "what's up," and she responded in kind. Sometimes she stopped to talk to friends, even when she was running a little late. Not many of the high-achieving students enjoyed this level of general popularity.[21]

Gwen was also well liked by school counselors and teachers. On my first visit to her AP European history class, in which she was the only black student, her teacher, a white female, raved about Gwen, telling me what a good student she was. "One of my best students!" she exclaimed, "probably the best in [the] class." She noted that Gwen was "always a very active participant" during class discussions. The teacher also mentioned that Gwen had been in her class in tenth grade and that she had been "great then, too." Another white female teacher described Gwen to me as an "overachiever." A young black female teacher was, according to Gwen, a mentor who told her about various academic opportunities. This teacher also stepped in when Gwen did not have the resources to participate in or take advantage of particular opportunities. For example, if she lacked a dress to wear to the prom or to an awards banquet, her mentor would provide them.

Gwen's accomplishments, including her overall popularity, were especially notable, given that she lacked some of the standard material status symbols so important to high school students. She was one of the few study participants who did not have access to a car in her senior year; she did not care about how she dressed; and by most standards, her family background was modest. She lived with her mother, a teacher's aide, and her grandmother in a small, prefabricated house bordering an old, black public housing community. Yet, unlike many similarly situated black adolescents (such as those described in Pattillo-McCoy's study), Gwen stayed the course of high academic achievement. Like Curtis, she saw and was motivated by examples of what she did not want to become and where she did not want to "end up." Unlike him, she did not speak scornfully of any particular racial group.

> *Gwen*: But, um, I look at other students and it makes me want to do better, so that I won't end up the way they are. And I get it [motivation] from there.
>
> *Interviewer*: When you say "end up the way they are," describe those students that you look at and say, "I don't wanna be there."
>
> *Gwen*: Right, they're—they just—they just settle for less, you know, they either drop down or they leave, or they just don't care. You know, and they just get through, you know, just cheating or something. That's how they get through school.

Gwen also had positive motivating forces in her life. Her older brother was a sophomore in college and a role model with whom she regularly competed to see who could get the highest grades and GPA. Since neither of Gwen's parents had attended college, her brother provided her with information about which courses to take in high school and how to prepare for college. He stressed the importance of staying focused. He told Gwen, for instance, that she needed "to get an A or a B for college." She took her brother's advice seriously, as she was intent on following in his footsteps.

Gwen's father, who lived nearby, was also a motivating force. He provided the inspiration and encouragement for her aspiration to become an astronaut ("he wanted to be an astronaut when he was younger, but he never got the opportunity, so, it's like, me, I'm his second chance in being an astronaut"). He gave Gwen her first telescope when she was eight.

Gwen described herself in interviews as much more focused and academically oriented now than she had been a few years earlier. With senior year and graduation approaching, the days when she "dressed to impress" and "was more concerned about what's the latest styles" were well behind her. She also had reduced the number of distractions in her life. During her first two years of high school, she had had a boyfriend and "lots of friends." As a junior preparing for college, Gwen no longer had a boyfriend at school; and by choice, she socialized with just "a few friends" who were similarly focused on achieving their goals. By senior year, she again had a boyfriend, but he attended a different high school.

In the classes I observed during her junior and senior years, Gwen was all business. She typically worked independently, but every so often, she exchanged questions and comments with classmates seated nearby. When she had friends in class, she interacted more. For instance, she and her good friend Keishaun, a black female, were in the same advanced English class. There, Gwen seemed more relaxed, especially as the two girls playfully competed over grades. "I'm beating you," Keishaun said to Gwen one day in class as she compared their respective grades. "Wait a minute, this can't be right," Keishaun remarked in disbelief, "Your interim [grade] must be wrong." "Oh no, you not [beating me]!" Gwen responded. "I got a eighty-three," Keishaun replied after double-checking the numbers. Shortly afterward, when the teacher returned the students' exams, Keishaun leaned over to see Gwen's grades and gasped as she looked at her paper, "Gwen," she said joking, "I'm so disappointed in you." To which Gwen replied, "What? It's only an A minus." Both girls laughed.

Gwen maintained that her primary focus was her academic performance and future. Thus, she was especially proud when she was inducted into the National Achievers Society, an organization, sponsored in part by the National Urban League, that recognizes the achievements of black students.[22] Asked why she wanted to be involved in this society, Gwen explained, "I just like to take advantage of all opportunities." Gwen saw the opportunities as a way "to get out of here, move beyond this area." She recognized the competitiveness of the college selection process and wanted to be "in a good position" when it was her turn to apply. Toward that end, she also was involved in a weekend academic program at a nearby university. The program aimed to help minority students from area high schools prepare for college. On her own time, Gwen investigated college Web sites, hunting for information about school tours and admission criteria.

Gwen also took AP and honors courses, including German, throughout high school, and was generally known for being a "hard worker." She described herself as "never slack[ing] off. I finish one thing, I gotta start another. It's like there's no time to waste, *at all*." Although even in early adolescence she had always earned good grades and done her "own thing," these actions became more important to Gwen as she looked ahead to where she wanted to go in life. She was so focused on her goals of graduating from college and "going where the money is" that whether other people liked her and what they thought of her were not important.

I know that I'm not liked by some people, so . . . Because, I'm just—I just—I'm just not like them. I'm just doin' my own thing, you know. I don't always like to talk about what they talk about and if they are like constantly getting in trouble or doing this and, you know, and, that's just not me.

Having a clear sense of who she was and was not seemed to help Gwen, as it did other *secure* adolescents, resist pressure to behave in ways that were inconsistent with those ideas. Gwen's self-image included being a "hard worker." Although this was a trait she was proud of, she acknowledged that it prompted other students to tease her sometimes. Even Amaria, another study participant and Gwen's "really good friend" at West End, teased her about her focus. "I used to pick on her and tell her she has no social life," Amaria recalled. Gwen described the "hard worker" crowd and her reaction to the teasing she experienced as follows:

> *Gwen*: The ones that—when you see them, they're constantly doing work. They're—they won't settle for less, you know, they—if they have a C, they won't settle for a C. They'll push for a B or an A or, um, the ones who—who really just don't slack off at any point. They're— they're always working on something. You know, and it's like they don't wait 'til the last minute or, you know, they're—they're just really—they're really worried about being on top, you know, being the best, you know, being recognized because of how hard they work....
>
> *Interviewer*: There's no stigma attached to that? People don't make fun of those—those hardworking students—or anything?
>
> *Gwen*: Well, sometimes, they may have a joke every once in a while. But, for the most part, most people that I see just don't really pay attention. But, like, um, with me, it's like, everyone kind of knows me in some way, so I get a few jokes once in a while.
>
> *Interviewer*: Like what?
>
> *Gwen*: Like, well most people say, oh, I'm a nerd, or "You're always doing this and you're always doing that," or "You need a life." You know, things like that, but I don't let it bother me 'cause it's just for fun.

My observations confirmed Gwen's behavior to be just as she described: She was highly focused at school and she did not hide her ambition to excel. There was hardly a time when she was observed that she was not doing schoolwork. No matter what was going on around her, Gwen was "constantly doing work." For example, at an assembly during which U.S. Army recruiters were making presentations to various classes, Gwen was busy working while other students chatted, dozed, or stared blankly at the presenter. Once in a while, she would lift her head up from her notebook and stop writing to pay attention to the presenter, but it was never long before she resumed her work. On another occasion, during an exam in her German class, Gwen was the only student who worked nonstop. Other students wandered around the room, talked to one another, and otherwise annoyed the teacher. Gwen rarely lifted her head from its position bowed over the paper on her desk. She seemed oblivious to the discussions going on around her.

In class after class, while other students whispered and fooled around, Gwen worked. She was never idle. When she finished an exam or an assignment in less than the allotted time, she turned her attention to other work. She sometimes joined other students in brief conversations, but she was rarely the initiator. Moreover, Gwen was never unprepared for class; in fact, she was usually over-prepared. Once, when her AP biology teacher asked students to take note of something in their textbooks and commented that she knew they did not have the book with them but should take a look at it when they got home, Gwen pulled out her textbook. She was the only student to do so. Later in the period, when the teacher asked who had read the chapter, Gwen was one of only three of the seventeen students in the room to raise her hand.

After English class one November morning, Gwen and I sat talking in the classroom during her lunch period (since she did not have lunch money, Gwen chose not to go out for lunch). Usually, she told me, she went to the library or stayed in the classroom and did her homework during lunch. On this day, however, she was free to talk because she needed a computer in order to do her assignments. She had decided to wait until she got home to begin the assignment. Gwen reported that she got all A's and one B on her last report card. Then she described how the other students in her English class had gotten "mad at" her because, "as usual," she had the highest grade in the class, the only A. At 97, her average was almost ten points higher than the next highest average. I asked how her classmates knew her grades. Gwen explained that they would ask the teacher what the highest grade was and who got it. The name supplied was always hers. In response, some of her classmates (both black and white) would say, "You're such a nerd," and she would reply, "You gotta be a nerd taking AP classes, because there's too much work to be fooling around." "It feels good to have the highest grade, to be at the top," Gwen admitted. I asked if it felt good even when others got mad at her. "Yeah," she replied, "it still feels good. It makes me feel smart." She explained that even in her AP biology class, where she was "like fourth from the top, it feels good, because that's not too bad."

Unlike the hostility Curtis encountered, Gwen faced only general oppositionality, which she portrayed as minor teasing. Although some adolescents were offended by any teasing, Gwen considered being called a nerd "a compliment." It fit with her "hard worker" image and showed that she was "trying to get somewhere." Moreover, for Gwen, being smart was not incompatible with being cool. She had never felt the need to suppress or camouflage her ability or accomplishments, even in front of her lower-achieving friends. This sets her apart from other high achievers (particularly males) in this and other studies:[23] "I felt like, you know, you—you can be smart, and you can be cool, and you can be pretty, and you can have your own style, you know? And still maintain everything. You don't have to be dumb to be cool or whatever." Gwen's accomplishments in high school demonstrate her ability to "maintain everything." Asked whether it was hard to achieve and sustain academic excellence in an environment where many students were less strongly academically oriented and focused, she said no.

> Because what I feel like, you know, this is me, it's my life that I'm working on, you know. If they wanna do that, that's their life. I might give them advice, or my opinion, but, you know, it's up to them to decide if they wanna take that advice or something, but for me, I mean, I look at it as, this is my future I'm working on, so, nothing else really matters.

For all her diligence, though, Gwen's academic record was not nearly as impressive as those compiled by many of the other high-achieving students. She was ranked in the top 25 percent of her graduating class and her SAT scores were less than 900 (both self-reported). However, being a hard worker and academically successful, taking advanced classes and striving for high grades, and achieving a (self-reported) 3.6 GPA, all were important aspects of Gwen's identity. Like other *secure* adolescents, she also had decided that her future success was more important than her peers' perceptions of her. She repeatedly stressed her future plans, and she voiced a certainty about some of the things she valued and about elements of her identity.

REJECTING NEGATIVE PEER NORMS

Curtis and Gwen were self-motivated, highly achievement-oriented adolescents who encountered aspects of an oppositional peer culture in high school. But throughout most of their high school years, both staunchly refused to be swayed by negative peer influence. They, like other *secure* adolescents, offered similar descriptions of the type of people they perceived themselves to be and had similar clearly defined goals for the future. They also used nearly the same language to signal their refusal to be influenced by other people's perceptions of them.

Secure adolescents consistently referred to knowing who they were, not just as individuals in the "me" sense, but as black people in the "we" sense as well.[24] Curtis, for example, spoke earnestly of his concerns about the absence of other black students among the group of Junior Marshals at his school. He was also dismayed by how some of his black peers took the struggles of the civil rights era "for granted" by using the "derogatory" term "nigger" "like an everyday hello." Curtis, Gwen, and other *secure* adolescents were comfortable with the identity they had crafted for themselves. They were also unambiguous and unwavering in the positions they took. They expressed clear ideas about where they were headed in life and what they wanted their future to look like. Overall, they were more future-oriented than their peers. During interviews they were more likely to make unprompted references to goals for college, career, income, or employment than were students who conformed to peer norms. *Secure* adolescents also conveyed a steely resolve not to let other people's opinions of them, particularly those that might threaten their goals or their self-image as successful students, penetrate their thinking. Like Gwen, however, many were able to do so in a way that did not alienate or offend others. While they were highly focused, these students were also personable and got along well with their peers.

Other studies of high-achieving black students' responses to peer pressure describe attitudes of indifference and determination similar to those of the *secure* adolescents portrayed here. For instance, in Roslyn Mickelson and Anne Velasco's study, an adolescent questioned about how he copes with criticism about acting white responded: "And that's just when I distance myself from people, 'cause I don't care. I mean, you can, you can say whatever you want to. I know what I'm doing, I know what I'm...I know I'm trying to get my grades right, and I know I'm trying to get off to a good school."[25] Many high-achieving black adolescents express a similarly strong sense of self-determination. This attitude may be one reason why racialized and other forms of oppositionality do not necessarily disrupt the achievement trajectory of high-achieving black students.

Curtis and Gwen provide especially vivid examples of traits observed among many of the high-achieving study participants. To the extent that adolescents had clear and strongly held ideas about who they were and where they were headed, they were less likely to conform to negative peer influence, even in school environments characterized by racialized tracking. Neither Curtis nor Gwen, nor other *secure* adolescents like Karen and Yvette, were particularly distressed or swayed by peer influence when they were younger, either. According to their accounts, these students seem to have come into their own earlier than others. They also seem to have had little concern about fitting in with their classmates or being liked. This sets them apart from their more vulnerable peers.

Vulnerable Adolescents: "I Kind of Like to Be Liked"

Well, I mean it'll bother me if I become an outcast to anybody, I mean white kids or the black kids. I mean that's just, I don't want to be an outcast to anybody.... I don't know, I kind of like to be liked, and I don't want to be hated at all, so...

Adonis, *black, Latham High School (81% white, 8% black)*

Unlike academically successful *secure* adolescents, those who conformed when faced with oppositionality were more likely to mention a desire to "fit in" and be liked, or at least to want to avoid being disliked or ostracized. Adonis's remarks highlight the intensity of *vulnerable* adolescents' concerns.[26] Their struggles to fit in among fellow blacks at predominantly white and racially diverse schools in particular, glimpses of which emerged in the previous chapter, are especially poignant. For many, peer problems surfaced during early adolescence, and in middle school specifically. For some, though, issues either continued in high school or first surfaced there.

These students' narratives show that during the time of their encounters with oppositionality, they were still in the early stages of forming their identities, formulating personal goals and aspirations, or internalizing beliefs. Sandra, the Earnshaw student who described herself as sometimes "devastated" by the comments of her peers, is an archetypically *vulnerable* adolescent. So, too, is Tommy, a student at Wade High School. Sandra's and Tommy's accounts reveal, sometimes touchingly, how *vulnerable* adolescents' lack of clarity concerning their identity, personal beliefs, or future goals can create a sense of general confusion that makes them especially sensitive to others' opinions and susceptible to peer pressure. In school environments where the racial divide in achievement between blacks and whites was stark, these students seemed to struggle most with the task of crafting a unified racial and high-achieving student identity. For them, racialized tracking appears to create a situation in which the concept of a "high-achieving black student" seems like a contradiction in terms.

TOMMY

A rising senior and a percussionist in the Wade High School (71% white, 14% black) band at the time of his first interview, Tommy had come a long way from the "bad boy" image he had tried to project in middle school.

Recalling his experiences trying to fit in during those years, he acknowledged an overall sense of confusion.

> I knew subconsciously, and on occasion the subconscious mind would come to conscious mind, but it was more, I didn't know what I was, and I kind of feel bad about that now cause it almost makes me feel as if "Where am I? Where am I going? And when?" kind of deal, thinking back, but I'm not going to let that get to me, I'm not.

Tommy is the younger of his parents' two sons. He said that his troubles began when his military family moved again and he started middle school as the "new kid." He had been moving around all of his life and never had the same friends for more than one grade. Tommy linked "moving around so much," to his early adolescent feeling that he "didn't know where [he] belonged."

> *Tommy*: Well, see, actually that story goes to the seventh, eighth grade years. Seventh grade year was my first year at [East Lexington] Middle School, and I was also trying to fit in. I was trying to fit in with the cool crowd, and the cool crowd was the African Americans, the black people who were like off in their own island and talking about rap...And I was trying to fit in with them because of the fact that they were cool, man, and I figured, "Hey, I'm black, and you know, I can fit in," but see—
> *Interviewer*: What made them cool?
> *Tommy*: I have no idea. [*He chuckles.*]
> *Interviewer*: Who decided that they were cool?
> *Tommy*: They seemed cool. I was a little twelve-year-old or whatever, however old I was, and yeah, so, see, I have a high vocabulary and I'm afraid to use it around certain people because they're like, "Hey, wait a minute, slow down, speak in English." And so I didn't fit in because of that, and I seemed like the nerd back in middle school, freshman and sophomore years, too.
> *Interviewer*: And you say you "seemed like," did they call you the nerd?
> *Tommy*: Some did, some called me geek, and some called me a nerd...

Tommy's desire to fit in led him to start his own gang (an extension of an existing clique), at the invitation of a group of black boys who seemed to be "running the school." In retrospect, Tommy acknowledged that going along with this plan was the "dumbest thing" he could have done. At the time, however, he was pleased: "Yes, as unbelievable as it may sound and as ridiculous as it is, it's still true. And so I was like, 'Finally I fit in,' and so I started swearing more and cussing more, and you name it...."

Tommy admitted that his "morals [were] in conflict with the gang," and so "it ended up failing" because he could not go through with the real business of a gang (e.g., fighting). Thus, besides picking a color and a name ("The Mack Gang Killers"), Tommy and his single fellow gang member at the predominantly white middle school did nothing more than strut around the school, displaying an attitude. However, in addition to adding "cussing" to his repertoire during this period, Tommy decided he "wasn't going to try as much." This, he hoped, would free him from being called a nerd.

> *Tommy*: ...and since everybody else was gittin' C's and D's, that's what I was going to get.
> *Interviewer*: Now prior to this, you had been doing okay in school?
> *Tommy*: I'd been making B's. B's and C's, instead of C's and D's.
> *Interviewer*: Now you're, are you consciously now trying to do this?
> *Tommy*: Yes.
> *Interviewer*: And how does one do that? What did you do?
> *Tommy*: You basically ignore the teacher in every possible way, and you don't do your homework, you just sit there and you're like, "Yeah, yeah, what's up?" And you just sit there in class and you pass notes, or maybe if somebody is needing some help on the test, you can kind of look over and you kind of give 'em the answers, if you know it.

Because Tommy's two-man gang was essentially inactive (neither boy even wore the chosen color), the few people who were aware of his "gang involvement" did not include either his teachers or parents. It was the change in Tommy's academic behaviors and performance that drew his parents' attention—and disapproval. Yet, neither their chastising, "whoopings," or other punishments, nor his mother's commitment to checking his homework every day, were enough to turn Tommy around. At the time, his primary concern was his peers' perceptions of him, not his parents'.

Doing poorly in school earned Tommy bragging rights that added to his tough, "bad boy" image. Letting his academic work slide was a way to achieve a goal he deemed valuable.

> It's bragging like to say that you got a "D" only because you go home, you tell your parents, well, [tell] all your friends that your parents are going to beat the snot out of you and you're going to be in so much trouble, and so then all your friends are like, "Ah, yeah, you da' man."...

Yet, Tommy explained that when his friends were not looking, he "would actually pay attention to the teacher and...be taking notes and...like, be writing down every single word that the teacher said and...giving the teacher hugs." It was not poor academic performance itself that Tommy believed improved his image in the eyes of his peers. Rather, it was the ability to endure the consequences of getting bad grades, namely, physical punishment.

Tommy's struggle to fit in with the "cool" black boys occurred during the early stage of his identity development, when he lacked firm convictions about his self, beliefs, aspirations, and goals. His sense of right and wrong was strong enough to prevent serious gang involvement, but without strong goals or a clear sense of identity, he found it difficult to decide whether it was more important to be cool or to be studious. Nor had he yet figured out, as Gwen explained, that the two could coexist. Recall that for Gwen, being smart *and* cool had never been complicated. For Tommy, that combination seemed impossible, and the choice between being a smart student and being one of the cool kids was a hard one. Throughout his freshman year and for most of his sophomore year, he continued to struggle to fit in, carrying with him the legacy of his relative lack of clarity in middle school and his lower achievement during those years.

Other participants also recalled experiences of losing their way and briefly going off course during similar times of confusion in middle school. This was the case for Lori, an Anderson High School (59% white; 33% black) senior who was also the mother of a toddler. Like Tommy, Lori recalled having gone through a "ghetto, thug stage" in middle school (although, unlike Tommy, she said she had maintained her academic standing and had even become student council president). During the period when she was hanging out with a group of "really bad kids" who "smoked and drank all the time," Lori tried smoking and drinking too. By high school, though, she had "[grown] out" of that "stage."

Jasmine, a senior at Lucas Valley High (65% white; 24% black), recalled a similar transition from middle to high school. She explained:

You know, when you're in middle school you care a lot of what your friends think. And school just like comes second to your social life. And when I got to high school I found that, you know, many people didn't care what, you know, what kind of clothes this girl was wearing or who was going to so and so's party or whatever. They were mainly focused on, you know, schoolwork and, you know, it made me think, you know, I should be this way too. And so I was like making goals for myself and I started caring less what other people thought of you.

Thus began Jasmine's transformation from an eighth grader with "horrible" grades into a high-achieving, organized high school student whose "main focus [was] getting into college."

Not so for Tommy. By the time he reached high school, his insecurities had intensified and his schoolwork continued to suffer. Now his concern was not just what fellow blacks thought of him, but what everyone, especially girls, thought of him. He began to worry about his looks and to doubt that he would be able to get a date. Consequently, he would blindly "follow some people. I would be, like, follow the leader." Reflecting on the insecurities that had continued to plague him through tenth grade, Tommy said:

> I look back at it and I'm like, "That was really dumb of me; of all of the things that I could have done in middle school, that had to have been the dumbest thing that I—," but as they say, "Hindsight is always twenty-twenty." And so freshman and sophomore years mean I'm so insecure with myself that I needed somebody to cling to, or some kind of clique and that's what it was about. And then I realized at the end of sophomore year, 'I'm my own person.' . . .

Tommy attributed this realization to his religious beliefs. In the midst of his struggles with insecurities, he was also "finding God." Thus, by the end of his sophomore year, he was more grounded in his beliefs and identity and had a better sense of the direction he wanted for his life.

> I realize that freshman and sophomore year I had totally messed up, because freshman and sophomore year I was about, you know, what my friends were thinking of me. I was about trying to fit in. And it wasn't until the end of sophomore year that I started to realize I'd messed up so much. . . . And so I finally figured it out on my own, it just happened. I can't take the credit, it was actually my Savior that showed me, you know, certain things that I shouldn't be insecure about, and it was Him that gave me the actual confidence that I have now. So let's give credit to where it actually deserves to be, in Jesus . . . I went to Christian camp and I rededicated myself to the Spirit of the Lord, and it's that Spirit that's within me that's actually guiding me now. It's not myself and, you know, my own will, but His will, as the Bible says, "Not my will, but Your will be done."

Tommy's recollections allow a glimpse into his development over time and indicate that religion was a major part of his self-growth. Only one other high-achieving participant invoked religion during interviews as frequently as

Tommy did. By the time we met him, in his junior year, Tommy's concerns about his peers' opinions had vanished. He maintained that he "could care less" and that "nowadays it's not about anybody else." Moreover, he was also "proud to be a nerd." In fact, he occasionally wore sports jackets and ties to school (this attire, along with his wire-rimmed glasses, gave him a slightly Steve Urkel–like appearance).[27] He also sometimes came to school wearing jeans on which he had written, "Jesus is real," "Jesus Fanatic," and "I love Jesus."

Religion provided Tommy with the means to develop a set of concrete beliefs, a clearer sense of self, and specific ideas about where he was heading in life. By his senior year, the distance from his former self was evident. For instance, he avoided taking the school bus because he had little tolerance for the antics of the ninth-grade riders who, he claimed, still had "that eighth-grade mentality that fighting is a measure of their self-worth." He was a bit "tired" of that mentality, he said. Finally comfortable with himself, he was able to act in a way that was consistent with his morals and values, a convergence that sociologist Steven Hitlin claims makes people feel more authentic.[28]

As a rising senior, Tommy described himself as "the kind of person that does everything by the rule book." For instance, although he believed that smoking "weed" was a problem at his school, he said it was not "a big problem" for him. If he witnessed students smoking weed, he would "just turn the other way and walk away." Furthermore, Tommy also had a "goal of [his] own," which he had not had a few years earlier. He aspired to attend UNC-Chapel Hill, be the first person in his immediate family to graduate from college, and the first in his extended family to graduate from a "major school." Tommy also hoped to "pull off a miracle" and "graduate with honors" from Wade High. Thinking of himself as a high-achieving student, or as he put it, "a genius," gave Tommy the confidence to believe in his own dreams and helped him sustain the hard work he put into achieving his goals.

Because he had spent the first two years of high school posturing rather than studying, Tommy's GPA was among the lowest of the high-achieving students (2.6 self-reported), and he was the only one who had never taken any advanced classes. His recent efforts to be a model student were paying off, however. One sign of this was that his counselor had included him in the pool of potential participants in our study of high-achieving students (based on his presence on the honor roll for at least two consecutive semesters). By the time we met him, he also seemed to have found his place socially. He was part of "the Band clique" (according to Tommy, there were only two cliques at Wade: Band and Junior ROTC) and he claimed to have many friends—"more than I can count." He was also well liked by teachers. For instance, during our visits to shadow him at school, his Spanish teacher referred to Tommy as "Señor Sociable." His twelfth-grade math teacher (who had also taught him as a freshman), called him one of her "favorite students" and chatted with him frequently during class.

Tommy was not popular outside of his own social circle, however, which may explain why he lost his bid for Student Council vice president. Furthermore, he seemed to have few black friends. Almost all the friends with whom he regularly socialized at lunch, playing cards, and chatting, were white, as was his former girlfriend. Similarly, nearly all the girls that Tommy frequently stopped to hug in the halls (this was his way of sharing some of the love that Jesus gave to him, he explained), passed notes to in class, and generally socialized with, were white. So, too, were the boys with whom we observed him socializing.

With religion, maturity, his parents' encouragement, and, strangely, an episode of the television show *The Fresh Prince of Bel Air*, Tommy eventually began to come into his own.[29] He developed a fuller sense of his racial identity, his direction in life, and his beliefs.

> Now there are black people like myself and some others that are willing to go somewhere in their life, be sixty years old and still doing something with their life. And those are the kind of people that I want to hang out with now, because you don't have to kill somebody, you don't have to beat up somebody to be black, you're black because you're born that way, and I just now realized that. So like the old saying goes, "Be black, be proud."

Tommy's struggle to understand what it means to be black is one shared by many adolescents of color, including some in this study.[30] Significantly, all of the participants who mentioned struggling to craft a black identity attended predominantly white or racially diverse schools where racialized tracking is prevalent. Although racial identity development is not as well defined a topic in the students' narratives as other aspects of identity (e.g., being a high-achieving student), it seems to have been more of an issue for middle-class black students and others, like Tommy, who did not grow up in predominantly black spaces or attend predominantly black schools. These students seemed to have a more difficult time figuring out how to be both black and a high-achieving student. (I return to this point later in the chapter.)

Perhaps the most important difference between students like Tommy and students like Gwen and Curtis, and even Sandra (described below), is that the latter had a clear focus on the future. Until his junior year, Tommy, who described himself as "a very sensitive type of guy," was not only still searching for a place to belong, he had not yet begun to consider where he was heading in life. As he gained greater clarity and confidence, he was less vulnerable to peer influence and thus able to assign less importance to his peers' perceptions of him.

SANDRA

Sandra was the youngest of three children, and the only one still living at home with her mother and stepfather. Of all the stories the high-achieving study participants shared about peer ridicule and ostracism, Sandra's was by far the most agonizing. She said her troubles began in "sixth and seventh grade," what she called her "shaky" years, at Earnshaw School of Excellence. Racially isolated in advanced classes as a sixth grader, she soon became a target of ridicule and was ostracized by some of her black female peers.

Extreme underrepresentation of black students in rigorous courses and programs in predominantly white and racially diverse schools is not unusual, but Sandra's experience reveals a consequence of that situation that has received very little serious attention from researchers or educators. For black adolescents who are still in the process of formulating their racial identity, racial disparities in tracking appear to further complicate the search for self, as Beverly Daniel Tatum has argued. Moreover, racial disparities in tracking may explain why, as Robert Crosnoe's research has revealed, integrated schools do not promote interracial friendships to the same extent achieved in integrated neighborhoods.[31] Since individual classrooms in desegregated schools often are not integrated, most black students in these schools have few opportunities to form friendships with white peers. Consequently, as evidenced in chapter 2, when interracial friendships do occur in such environments, they may be viewed as oddities and the participants may be ridiculed or even ostracized.

Zorayda and Sharon, the two other high-achieving study participants who attended Earnshaw, did not contend with the kind of racialized oppositionality that plagued Sandra. All three girls had started at the school in the sixth grade, all three took honors and AP courses, and as noted in chapter 2, Zorayda also reported having been teased about her achievement. But Zorayda laughed it off, while Sandra could not. For her, being the only black student in her gifted classes led to an ever-widening series of painful problems.

> *Interviewer*: At that time in middle school, you know, how did you feel about it? I mean, was it something that you pretty much just shrugged off, or?

Sandra: ...I couldn't walk down the hall without someone saying something to me. And so it got really bad, to a point where I was thinking about switching schools, because even though I love this school, you know, I didn't want to have to go through—and it wasn't everyone. And I did find, I did have friends that, you know, could shelter me [*She chuckles.*] from all that. But, you know, it was really rough. And I was really depressed for a while about it. Because I started trying to—in fact sometimes I started trying to distance myself from white people and tried to hang out with more black people, and tried to act differently. But it was all just really fake, and I didn't feel comfortable.

Sandra tried to fit in with the other black students by becoming more like them, but first she had to learn the role. She had grown up in a middle-class black family in a quiet suburban neighborhood, with a school-counselor mother and a household income in the range of $70,000 to $90,000. While these life circumstances are not particularly unusual for black Americans today, Sandra felt alienated from some of her black peers.[32] Thus, she tried to change her appearance and behavior. She "started trying to act like a slacker, like I-don't-care type of thing.... And [I] started trying to dress like them, wear my hair like them." At lunch, she also tried sitting at the "tables where it's all black people."

Unfortunately, these attempts at fitting in with the black students back-fired. Rather than being "welcomed with open arms," as Sandra had hoped and expected, the black girls got "mad" because they thought she was "mocking" them. The failure of these efforts prompted Sandra to go "to the other extreme." She reasoned, "Well, if I'm different, then I'm going to be different. And I was really different." She "wore crazy stuff that didn't match and black lipstick, and listened to crazy music that was—no one had ever heard of before. And ... I was reading books on Wicca."[33] That change, how-ever, left Sandra "totally alone." So over time, she gave up on that stylized self as well.

Sandra, who was ranked among the top 20 students in her graduating class of about 150 students, admitted, too, that she tried to downplay her achievement in front of other students. And although she continued to take advanced classes, she often thought about not doing so. In seventh grade, when she had had the choice to "either stay on with everyone else or go above" by taking algebra in the eighth grade, she "seriously thought about not going because [she] was afraid [she] was going to be ostracized even more." Later, in the upper grades, she also tried numerous times "to talk [herself] out of taking" AP courses for the same reason. She acknowledged that she wanted "people to see that [she was] successful," but

> At the same time, I don't want them to view me as arrogant about, that I think that I'm better than them, so I started that any time I make a good grade, I sometimes say that I didn't do as great, because I'm afraid that they might think that of me after a while.

With her black peers Sandra was especially careful.

> *Sandra*: . . . if it's with black people, other black people, like in my Spanish class, if I'm in a group with them, then I'll pretend I don't know how to do something, because I don't want them to think that I think I'm better than them. Or, if I say that, if I get a course test back, I hide it, especially if it's a really good grade, then I hide it because I don't want them to see that I made an A.
> *Interviewer*: Right, and you don't do that with your white friends?
> *Sandra*: I'm not as, like if I have to do it every time, and with black people I do it every time, but with them it's not all the time.

The difference between Sandra's response to the oppositionality she encountered and that of adolescents like Gwen and Curtis is striking. Gwen's encounters were of the general type and they clearly were not as severe as Sandra's, but Curtis's experiences were similar to, if not worse than Sandra's. Unlike Sandra, though, Curtis knew who he was and was not, and he seemed comfortable with his identity. Sandra was less self-assured and secure in her identity and was more susceptible to peer influence. Her lack of a clear sense of who she was, other than a high achiever, left an opening for other people's opinions to affect her developing identity. Sandra's case is among the more extreme in terms of the adjustments she attempted to make, but she was not alone in her attempts to downplay her achievements. Students like Keisha (discussed in chapter 2) and Adonis also attempted to hide or downplay their grades.

Adonis reported that in middle school he had had a run-in with black boys who called him "snowflake" and "whitey" because he wore his father's hand-me-down "Ocean Pacific" clothing rather than the "Tommy Hilfiger and Fubu" clothing popular among black kids and because they said he "talk[ed] all nice and stuff." After that, he tried to hide his grades from them. When asked why he did this, Adonis explained:

> It was just the way things were. . . . The first month of eighth grade. This is all just like in one year 'cause we got like, I mean sixth grade

there weren't that many black folks, and then we gained like one in seventh grade, which was [A. Z.], and then we gained another two, which was [Clarence] and [Stan], in eighth grade. They were new and they'd come from like different schools like [Everton] Middle School and stuff like that. So like "Yeah, man, you're smart, so you're smart," and so I like "Ah, I don't really make fun of those smarts, I got a B on that." And it says like 98 on the paper. [*So you'd lie?*] Yeah, and then like two months into it, it's not like it all like fell apart, it was just like it gradually like, "Yeah, you're smart, we know you're smart but you're cool anyway," so...

Adonis stopped lying because over time the boys accepted him and realized that he did not think he "was better" than they were. They also came to realize that although he "was better at school than they were; they were better at other things" than he was.

Although in this case Adonis's peers did not accuse him of acting white specifically because of his achievement, in his mind achievement was linked with race. Thus, he was certain that his "smarts" would be the next thing for which he would be perceived as acting white. Study participants jumped to this conclusion only when they attended predominantly white or racially diverse schools where racial patterns in achievement were obvious (see the discussion of Carl and Tanya below). Informants who attended predominantly black schools, where blacks were regularly among the highest-achieving students, did not make this leap, even though they, too, had heard peers use the acting white slur with respect to speech patterns and word choice. In Adonis's case, as is also evident in cases like Curtis's and Sandra's and others discussed in chapter 2, we see how institutional patterns can feed racial stereotypes about achievement and contribute to the peer problems some academically successful black adolescents face.

Sandra's experience was especially difficult for her to bear because it added to what she said was her already "low self-esteem." Judging herself against conventional standards of beauty, Sandra had concluded that she was unattractive. Moreover, she believed that her looks posed an additional life hurdle, requiring her "to be better than the average person in order to succeed."

Sandra: 'Cause of the way that I look. 'Cause I know that the world is pretty superficial and that I have to work ten times harder than some people in order for anyone to notice me. And mainly because of my appearance, that I'm afraid that when I go out into the world that I'm no longer in like a controlled climate like school, that I have to be better than the average person in order to succeed.

Interviewer: What do you mean by your "appearance"?

Sandra: Well, I am overweight and my face isn't very attractive. So, I try to be better at everything else to compensate for that.

What Sandra valued most about herself, the one thing that she believed gave her an edge, was her academic success and her drive to be the best. This made the peer ridicule and ostracism she faced especially threatening. Unlike Tommy, she could not try to fit in by slacking off, since doing so would undermine a core belief about herself and make it impossible for her to compensate for her looks by being "better at everything else."

Ironically, it was her idiosyncratic beliefs about the relationship between success and appearance, coupled with her concern about other people's perceptions of her, that helped Sandra stay the course academically. With *vulnerable* high-achieving adolescents, clear and firm educational goals and aspirations and a strong desire to succeed seem to provide protection from going off track academically. For instance, Adonis explained that his fear of failure and his desire to do even better than his parents overrode his need to be accepted by his peers. Similar concerns are clear in Sandra's explanation of why doing well in school is so important to her:

> Because I do care about how people perceive me. And I don't, I don't want people to see me as a failure, or as someone who's just average. 'Cause I want to make an A. [*She chuckles.*] I'd, well even though I know a B is above average, 'cause C is average, I don't like not getting a perfect score or not being the best. 'Cause my personality is that if I can't be the best at something, then I get really upset. There's just something in me that I want to be better. I want to do better in a class. I want to be at the top....I want to be someone that people remember as that overachieves, above average, stand out in a crowd...because I'm trying to get into a good college. I want to [*She laughs a little*], I want to have a good transcript. So I take challenging [courses]—and because I don't want to just go to school, and if I feel that I can do more than what's given to me, then I do more than what's given to me.

Sandra admitted that sometimes her drive to be the best was extreme. At times, even her mother told her that she "need[ed] to calm down."

> If I get an award, or I get a good grade, my mom is like, "Good job, I'm proud of you." At the same time, if I make a B or a C, my mom's like, "Well, that's still good, but it's not the end of the world, that's still a good grade."...She's like, "It's okay to push yourself, but you know, you're going to burn yourself out by the time you're finished."

In Sandra's case, as with many of the other high-achieving study participants, parents' opinions and expectations no longer seemed to play a primary role in shaping academic behavior. Although parents set particular norms and expectations for their children's achievement, the extent to which our informants held to those norms in the face of peer pressure varied.

The degree of concern with other people's perceptions the students expressed was a good index of their relative vulnerability to peer pressure. *Secure* adolescents cared only that other people perceived them as smart and hardworking and beyond that, they "could care less," as many remarked. Yet Sandra, a *vulnerable* adolescent, also wanted others to perceive her as smart, and she was just as, if not more, achievement-oriented than most other students. She differed from her more *secure* peers, however, in fearing that she would alienate her peers if they perceived her as arrogant because of her achievement. The more concern students expressed over how others perceived them and the more emphasis they placed on being liked and accepted, the more likely they were to try to conform to perceived peer norms.

Academically successful black students' concerns about other people's perceptions of them included the opinions of white students. Just as many did not want to alienate their black friends, some also were careful not to alienate their white peers. Sandra's concerns about how her white classmates perceived her led her to conceal certain parts of her developing identity from them. In the following passage, she describes her discomfort with classroom discussions involving the topic of race, and her worries over what her white classmates might think of her:

And I kind of feel uncomfortable in those kind of situations because I don't want to say anything, because [white students] would feel like all black people feel that way, and so I tend to edit my thoughts a whole lot more, because I don't want to be a, like to them as, "Oh, well, she's really militant." Or something like that. Or, we were having a discussion on Malcolm X, and Marcus Garvey and I didn't—I was afraid to say that, "Oh, well, I agree with some of the things that they say," because then you're labeled as militant and that, "Oh, well, you want to kill all white people." And I didn't want to be like that. And I didn't want them to think that all black people were like that either. And so I just didn't talk. Or some, I did say a couple of things in [Malcolm's and Marcus's] favor. And people were kind of like, you know, "Well, you're not supposed to be like that. That's not right to agree with them..." Yeah. I mean, or the Black Panthers. And they were shocked that I would know anything about them. And that I would know about what they were talking about, and what their viewpoints were, because I was only supposed to agree with Martin Luther King, Junior. I wasn't supposed to agree with [other black leaders].... Well, because I guess I hang around a lot of white people they would assume I would be, I wouldn't agree with anything that a more extreme black leader would know. Like that I wouldn't, I just wouldn't know about it. Because I wouldn't want to.... Yeah, I wouldn't want to have that influence. There's just a big misunderstanding as to who I am. So. They were just shocked that I would know anything about it.

That there was a "big misunderstanding" about Sandra's real identity underscores her own confusion and the mixed messages she sent as she tried to project a self that would fit the expectations of others.

Sandra's anxieties extended to even her friends' opinions of her. These, she said, were "pretty important" because "if they don't like something that you do, they're not going to hang out with you. And I don't want to be alone, so." Also telling were the descriptions of the people Sandra said she admired. First, she named another high-achieving student at her school, noting that this girl "got all A's," "was great at sports," "had a great personality," and "almost no one hated her."[34] She also said she admired her older sister, who had had similar experiences of racial isolation in advanced classes and "animosity from some black people":

She'll tell you flat out if she doesn't like something. And I wish that I could be like that and not care really what people, I mean she cares what people, what others think, but she's not afraid if she tells a person an opinion, she's not afraid that they're not going to like her anymore. And I wish I could be like that 'cause a lot of times what I think is not what I say, and I edit a whole lot what I think, because I don't want to step on anyone's toes.

Other study participants also reported that a sibling had had encounters with oppositionality similar to their own, but that they had responded differently. For instance, Ronnie, a *secure* adolescent at Wade High School, mentioned that her younger brother had gone off course academically in middle school trying to be "all cool and tough." These kinds of reports suggest, again, that family background factors, such as socioeconomic status, parents' expectations, and parenting style, are insufficient for understanding adolescents' vulnerability to peer influence.

Sandra's case is analytically significant because it illuminates an important association between clarity regarding identity, goals, aspirations, and beliefs, on the one hand, and the ability to resist peer pressure, on the other. Sandra tried repeatedly to adapt to the expectations of her peers, but she also set limits on the accommodating behaviors she was willing to undertake. Despite her almost obsessive desire to fit in, as a junior she would not conform to her peers' expectations by sacrificing either her identity as a high achiever or her goals of being at the top of her class and going to a good college. Her certainty and determination in these areas protected her from going off course academically, but they were little help in lessening the considerable stress she endured in the process. In all likelihood, Sandra would have been a *vulnerable* adolescent in any schooling context, but her difficulties were exacerbated by the racial isolation she experienced in the system of racialized tracking at Earnshaw.

ANTICIPATING OPPOSITIONALITY

In addition to those *vulnerable* adolescents who directly experienced some form of oppositionality, others reacted to the possibility of facing intra-racial or racialized ridicule from fellow blacks. These students adapted their behavior to fit with what they perceived as the norms among black youth *prior* to being the target of any harassment. Their cases further highlight how the presence of racialized achievement and tracking structures are confusing to black adolescents who are developing their sense of self. Indeed, this sub-group of *vulnerable* adolescents also demands close attention, because these students react to perceived oppositionality in ways very much like their peers who directly encountered ridicule. Some of the changes participants made in order to fit in with fellow blacks, such as wardrobe adjustments, may be relatively harmless in the long and short terms. Others, such as choosing to take fewer advanced classes, may have more important and longer lasting consequences for adolescents' academic achievement and general well-being. Conformity, in some cases, has high costs.

Shelly, a student at Anderson High, explained why she thought it was important for a high-achieving student like herself to "conform" to black adolescent norms. Pointing to the tee-shirt she was wearing with the word "naughty" across her chest, she said

> I dress—I don't really talk about this—I dress differently. Like if you look at me, you're not going to say, "Okay, she's smart and she's—" Once again, like with [some people having] pink hair, I'm trying to conform so that I don't stand out. So that's just for protection; at my school, that's the smart thing to do. [*She laughs.*] Conform. And then when you get out of high school, do whatever you want.... So, I dress like them. 'Cause I am them; they are me, and that's my culture, so I

do dress like a normal black girl. So I don't put it out there for myself to be ridiculed. Which they're not going to ridicule me, I don't think—but it's safe for me.

To explore this kind of preemptive behavior, I briefly describe the experiences of two other *vulnerable* adolescents, Carl and Tanya. Neither reported having encountered oppositionality directly, but both proactively conformed to perceived black adolescent norms. Carl's and Tanya's responses to the perceived norms of the peer culture in their middle and high school, respectively, and their descriptions of their motivations emphasize the roles social class and racial identity play in this aspect of school life. They also draw attention to the fact that adolescents may be especially vulnerable to peer influence during periods of transitions, when they are entering a new environment or facing a relatively new and unknown situation. Like many of the other high-achieving study participants, however, Carl and Tanya boldly rejected peer influence as they matured and developed greater self-knowledge, and in Carl's case, formulated clearer goals and future direction.

Tanya

Tanya (introduced in chapter 2) entered Rolling Hills High School as an academically successful student, and this was an important part of her identity. Still, as she explained, she worried that her academic abilities would prevent her from making friends. "When I first got into high school, I was just trying, I guess I was trying to fit in, but....Just trying to find friends, like not really knowing anybody, and I figured if I act like I'm all smart, they're going to be like, 'She's one of them goody-two-shoes.' " Tanya was not trying to find just any friends, however; her concern was with finding black friends.

As the incidence of racial segregation across classrooms and during assemblies (described in the previous chapter) indicates, the racial boundaries at Rolling Hills were well defined. According to Vanji, another participant from the school, aside from herself, Tanya, Philip and the handful of other black students who took advanced classes, black students at the school did not talk to white students. "It's really divided right down the middle," she explained of the black-white split—except when it came to sports rivalries with other schools. "Black people/white people are the same when it comes to sports....There's not the black [Rolling Hills] or the white, we're one school. But other than that, at lunch, you sit with your own kind. On the bus, when I used to ride the bus, black people sat in the back and white people sit in the front....Like a Rosa Parks thing." In this kind of environment, Tanya's anxiety about finding her place among the black students—

lest she should find herself in a situation like Sandra's—is understandable. Thus, to avoid becoming an outcast, she adjusted her behavior to fit what she perceived as the norm for black adolescents, including using "a lot of slang" and trying to project an "attitude like I wasn't all about school," just as Tommy and Sandra had tried to do. When asked why she thought that was necessary, Tanya said that what she had seen on television had increased her anxiety:

> *Interviewer*: Now, what made you think that you needed to do that in high school? What—did something happen that gave you the impression like, "I can't go in there being—"
> *Tanya*: No, you know how sometimes you just see it on TV, and people are just like, 'Hi, Steve [Urkel],'" and they'll always do something like throw him in the trash can, because he's smart. I didn't want to go to high school and everyone be like, "Okay, whatever."
> *Interviewer*: Okay, but did it happen at all in middle school? Did you ever feel you needed to do that in middle school?
> *Tanya*: No, middle school wasn't a big deal for me, but high school was just like, "Ah, high school," like a big step—
> *Interviewer*: So did you have this plan already in mind before you came to high school, that you were already going to—
> *Tanya*: I don't think so. I think it was going to class with all of the people, and I was like, "I've got to fit in, I've got to fit in."

In her first year of high school, concerns about fitting in may have contributed to Tanya's decision to "[run her] mouth" and get into a fight with a black girl who had been harassing her. The fight, which took place in the school lobby in front of the main office, led to Tanya's suspension from school for five days. She recalled:

> It was the dumbest thing I ever, it was right in front of the office, too [*she laughs*], the dumbest spot ever, for, I fought like five seconds and I got five days suspended for five seconds. I hated that, which messed up my year.... Well, when you're trying to do things, when you're suspended it's like always an "X" on your name, it's like, you know, she was suspended for this and for that.... Well, I wanted to do student council, and I was thinking about jumping right into the cheerleading the next year, and then I was like, "I'd better wait another year."

That fight was Tanya's first and last. During the remainder of her high school career, she repaired her institutional reputation and not only became the captain of the cheerleading team in her senior year, but went on to be inducted into the National Honor Society and the National Achievers Society, and to become a Junior Marshal and a North Carolina Scholar. By senior year, she was unapologetic about refusing her peers' invitations to hang out, motivated by the satisfaction she got from her stellar report cards. When asked what she does when she gets her report card, Tanya replied, "I flash it . . . to everybody." Asked what her peers say in response, Tanya replied, "I don't care."

Coming to this stage was a process for Tanya, as it was for other adolescents. Ironically, in Tanya's case, developing confidence and clarity may have been made a little more complicated by her parents' success. Her parents had not attended college, but she and her younger sister seemed to be living a comfortable, middle-class lifestyle. Their parents' annual household income was in the $70,000–$90,000 range, and their well-appointed home, in which they had lived for eight years, was located in a relatively new subdivision featuring large, stately homes.

Tanya's class background may have had some bearing on the types of behaviors she felt it necessary to adopt in order to make black friends in high school. Her perception of black adolescent norms was surprisingly limited, and it was at least partially informed by media images. Adolescents from families of more modest means, particularly those who lived in or near low-income black communities, including Curtis and Gwen, and City High's Courtney and brothers Lynden and Glen (all introduced in chapter 2), expressed very little confusion about what it means to be black and were less uncertain of how one should behave as a black youth. Although Lynden and Glen admitted changing their style of dress to fit the style of other black males at their school, they insisted their new, more urban look had always been their preference, but that their father would not allow it.

Tanya's concerns about how to fit in among fellow blacks as a high-achieving student as she began high school seems surprising, given that she had had black friends in middle school and that she spent holidays and vacations with her extended family in a neighboring Southern state. Still, compared with lower-income students, students from higher SES backgrounds, such as Tanya and Sandra, were more likely to express uncertainty about what it means to be black, particularly in a racially polarized school environment, and to rely on the media for cues.

Carl

Carl was a student at Everton High School. Like Tommy and Tanya, he appeared to have come to know himself much better as he moved from early to later adolescence. Growing concerns about his impending adulthood and about his father's place in his family's life played a central role in Carl's development.

> *Carl*: I mean from the time I got into high school, I knew it was gonna be hard. I paid attention. I was like people are gonna try to influence me and everything. But if I set my eyes to what I want to do and, like, what I want to do when I grow up then nothing shakes, you know, persuades me should I take any drugs or anything.
>
> *Interviewer*: Right. And where'd you get that from, those ideas?
>
> *Carl*: Basically from my folks. My mother was a single parent. My dad, he doesn't do what he's supposed to do. I was like "I'm not gonna be like him." I want to be something when I grow up and I want to come back and help people and everything. And my biggest goal is, like, to be a computer engineer...I just became serious about education, I guess. I mean I was, I did great with my education. I just was doing good to be doing good, just to get by. But I really started to like school and everything, and that's when I didn't know anything about my dad at the time, so I really didn't care. But once I started to figure out, you know, how my dad was and everything I was like, "I'm not gonna be like him."

In middle school, Carl, the oldest of five children living with their single mother in a modest working-class neighborhood, had deliberately limited his classroom participation in order to appear "cool." As he explains above, he dropped that act in high school in order to concentrate on achieving his goals. He said he wanted to attend college and "make that money." Carl had not encountered oppositionality directly, but his observations in middle school led him to fear that he might. Thus, he tried to keep a low profile in the classroom.

He traced the start of his concerns about peer pressure to middle school. There, he said, you stop worrying about "snacks" (a common preoccupation among elementary school children, he explained) and start worrying about girls and about being cool: "being a black person, you sat in the classroom and in order to be cool, you may look like you didn't care about school and everything." Carl was not quite sure where this idea came from, but he recalled noticing differences in behavior between black and white students in the classroom in middle school, and so he decided to "keep [his] mouth shut."

> *Interviewer*: Now, why did that start? Why'd you start doing that in middle school? Did something happen to make you think—?

Carl: That's where stuff starts to matter. In elementary school, you can raise your hand and the kids, you know, they sing along in class and stuff like that. But in middle school, it's different, you know.

Interviewer: Why, what's—?

Carl: You raise your hand if you know it, if you don't—and half the class doesn't raise their hand—so you'll be like, "Well, dang, they'll look at you funny if you did know the answer or not."

Interviewer: Well, did it ever happen or was it just something you thought would happen—?

Carl: Thought, thought.

Interviewer: OK, so where did these thoughts come from, 'cause it didn't happen, you didn't have them in elementary school. So how come all of a sudden in middle school it started to be something that you started to think about? Did you see it happen to someone else and you said, "I don't want that to happen to me"?

Carl: I didn't see it happen to nobody else. I just got the feeling, I was just worried about what people would think. Like what if they think I'm trying to put them down 'cause they don't know the answer. I just got worried about little stuff like that. So, I wanted to be cool and everything.

Interviewer: OK, so you say you wanted to be cool, so you didn't do that. Now, who did that, then? Were those the kids who weren't cool?

Carl: Who raised their hands?... It was mainly, I'm not trying to be racist or anything, but it was mainly white people. I guess that's half the reason why too.

Carl's observations of racial differences in classroom behavior in middle school prompted him to adjust his own behavior, but he eventually developed a clearer self-understanding and clearer goals. At that later point, he was able to let go of his worries about his peers' perceptions of him. When asked about his reaction to his friends' opinions of him as a high school junior, he asserted, "I'm myself. I don't care what nobody say."

Carl's story also reveals details about the transition from a *vulnerable* to a *secure* adolescent. For him, the change was connected to his approaching adulthood, his desire to be a better man than his father was, and his determination to achieve his goal of getting into the college of his choice.

I really want to become a computer engineer. And I know if I want to get into the college I want to, I will need those skills, you know, so far as like the education, grade point average and everything, the scores, in order to get into college and in order to do that computer engineering—in order to make that money, in other words!

Like other *vulnerable* adolescents, as Carl developed a stronger sense of himself and his goals, he had less desire to fit in with what he perceived to be the norm among other black students at his school. It is noteworthy, however, that only study participants at predominantly white and racially diverse schools, such as Everton and Rolling Hills, perceived racial differences in students' achievement behaviors.

CONFORMING TO PEER NORMS

During their early adolescence, many of the study participants seemed to have been concerned about fitting in. By their junior year in high school, however, as we saw with Carl, Tommy, and Tanya, most had ceased worrying about their peers' opinions, whether or not they were consistent with their own firmer self-image, beliefs, goals, and plans for the future. Sandra was different. Unlike most other participants, including other *vulnerable* adolescents, her preoccupation with other people's opinions of her lasted throughout middle school and continued in high school. Moreover, her concerns encompassed both black and white students, and both friends and acquaintances.

Still, for these adolescents, all of whom had been rewarded for their academic efforts and achievements in the past, the goals of going to a good college and getting a good job seemed attainable. This finding is consistent with the results of Mickelson's research on the "attitude-achievement paradox" among black adolescents.[35] Because of their achievements, academically successful students tend to perceive fewer barriers to success; therefore, there is greater consistency between the concrete and the abstract attitudes these youth hold. Once they formulate clear future goals and aspirations and develop strong beliefs and a clear sense of who they are (and are not), these students are likely to be better able, compared to their lower-achieving counterparts, to withstand the pressures to conform to oppositional peer norms. At this stage, they seem to have a better sense of what is at stake and how much they stand to lose. This realization seems to help them reject negative peer influence, even in school environments characterized by racialized tracking.

Other Factors Affecting Adolescents' Response to Peer Pressure

Other factors, including achievement, social class, gender, and parental influence, have been identified in the literature as influencing adolescents' responses to peer pressure. Below, I discuss each in relation to the group of academically successful black students discussed in this chapter. Overall, these factors did not appear to be significantly related to students' responses to oppositional peer cultures.

PARENTAL INPUT AND PEER INFLUENCE

In many cases, *vulnerable* and *secure* adolescents were similarly highly achievement-oriented and, by the time we met them, had assumed almost complete responsibility for their schooling. Curtis, for example, explained that his mother "doesn't feel the need" to be as involved in his schooling at this stage. Once he entered high school, he "took ownership of [his] schooling." Most of our study participants selected rigorous courses without being urged to do so by their parents (at least by junior and senior year). Because their parents had set high standards and expectations for their academic performance "early on," and they did well academically, the students apparently had little difficulty internalizing those standards and expectations. As Marguerite, a Vanderbilt High School senior, explained, "... my parents never expected anything less than my best and I guess now I do that for me too."

Although some of the students set even higher expectations and standards for their achievement than their parents did, all emphasized that their parents were encouraging and supportive of their efforts. According to the students, their parents did not hesitate to intervene, if that seemed necessary. Nevertheless, in contrast to the findings of previous research, I find that parental input is not significant for understanding differences in vulnerability to negative peer influence among these academically successful adolescents.[36]

Students who described their parents as highly involved in their schooling showed no less vulnerability to peer influence than students who considered their parents only marginally involved. This does not mean that parents are unimportant with respect to their children's response to peer pressure. What the findings imply is that parents' influence is indirect. The students' narratives suggest that most eventually internalized their parents' high standards, expectations, and values (or, sometimes, set the bar even higher). Yet for some, there was a time, usually in early adolescence, when their behavior contradicted their parents' expectations, and no amount of parental chastising or punishment seemed effective.

ACADEMIC ACHIEVEMENT

Each of the study participants had a history of high achievement—some longer than others—for which they generally had received institutional recognition and rewards. Each imagined that a successful future, including college and a good-paying job, was within reach and worth striving for. None of these adolescents, regardless of socioeconomic status or neighborhood context, expressed the kind of "alienation and absence of hope for the future," that Elijah Anderson found among the poor inner-city residents in the Philadelphia community he studied.[37]

As high school graduation approached, both *vulnerable* and *secure* adolescents became more future-oriented. They began to seriously consider their options for the future and to think more concretely about college and career plans. Given their academic achievement, the participants all believed college was within reach, and they wanted to make the most of the opportunities available to them. Most were fortunate to have had early experiences of academic success, signaling particular skills and talents, which they were able to draw on to formulate their goals and aspirations for the future. Their prior experiences with success also no doubt gave them confidence in their ongoing ability to achieve. Without that sense of optimism and direction, adolescents like Tommy might have continued along the path of "gang" involvement. Fortunately for him and others like him (e.g., Lori), their prior achievement offered the promise of a good life, with a great career, and nice home. Thus, for most of these students, getting back or staying on track did not require making a huge leap of faith, as they all seemed convinced that education would provide access to the good life they hoped to have. This was especially true for lower-income students like Gwen and Lynden. Lower-achieving students, whose school experiences are generally less favorable, tend to be less confident and optimistic about their futures. This perhaps makes them more vulnerable to the type of peer influence that undermines prospects for a successful future.

SOCIAL CLASS

The relationship between social class and peer influence among black youth is less clear than other relationships found in the data, but social class does seem to matter in important ways. For students from working-class and lower-income families especially, a chance to go to college and possibly get ahead was an opportunity that few in their family or surrounding community had had. Indeed, much was at stake. Academically successful middle-class students expressed a similar sense of urgency, but theirs was based on the fear of being unable to maintain, at the least, the same standard of living their parents had provided for them. Students like Adonis commented that their parents expected them to achieve more than they themselves had. Tanya believed that her parents were "really lucky" to have achieved the standard of living they had without college degrees. Thus, she knew that things would be different for her: "I know now to get the job that's going to pay and support a family, which I want; you have to have a college degree." Middle-class students were inspired by their parents' ability to achieve occupational, financial, or educational success despite humble beginnings. They felt indebted to their parents for the hard work that had made their own comfortable adolescent lifestyles possible.

Whether or not adolescents faced (actual or anticipated) oppositionality did not vary by social class. There were, however, modest social class differences in how students handled racialized and intra-racial oppositionality. Middle-class students in schools characterized by racialized tracking were more likely than working-class and lower-income students and students attending predominantly black schools to express uncertainty about what it means to be authentically black. These students also were more likely to turn to the media for cues. For some lower-income academically successful adolescents, their blackness may have been authenticated by their class background. There is, as J. Martin Favor has pointed out, a long-standing "discourse of blackness" that suggests that "the best way to understand blackness in America is to scrutinize the lower classes, where, in [some people's] view, the most authentic blackness is to be found."[38] While the average black adolescent does not articulate this position, there is an undercurrent of it in the narratives of some of the study participants. These informants looked for ways to show their blackness by mimicking what they believed were mostly the practices of lower-income blacks (e.g., "cussing" or using African American Vernacular English or slang).

Middle- and upper-middle-class black Americans, especially those who do not reside or socialize in black spaces, tend to be more acculturated than lower-income blacks, who are more distant from some of the cultural norms of mainstream America.[39] Hence, the speech, dress, musical tastes, food and leisure preferences, and child-rearing practices of lower-income blacks frequently are considered more authentically black. And, perhaps not surprisingly, television shows often promote images of lower-income blacks as authentic blackness as well. In sum, lower-income blacks' class position provides them ready access to a sense of black authenticity.

Sociologist Sarah Willie has studied the experiences of black adults educated either at predominantly white or historically black colleges and universities. She notes that some of her informants endorsed the view of a link between class standing and racial authenticity. One, Robert, described how as a student at a predominantly white university, he was able to overcome his initial anxieties about venturing outside the boundaries of black organizations once he realized that his background was "what most people expected of black people." As Robert explained, "he grew up in a working-class home, lived in a racially segregated neighborhood, and attended an all-black high school." In short, Willie concluded, he "had an arsenal of associations to respond to any accusation of not being authentically black."[40] Middle-class black students often do not have this kind of "arsenal" at their disposal.[41] Thus, in order to establish their authenticity, some may adopt the vernacular, styles of dress, or, unfortunately, the school-related behaviors and attitudes they perceive as characteristic of the "folk" in post-desegregation America. Since tracking tends to separate students by social class as well as race, it is not surprising that some high-achieving black students (both *secure* and *vulnerable*) attributed the lower achievement and placement of their black peers to the latter's class background.

However, students who reached adolescence with a clearer sense of their black identity or with a greater degree of comfort about how they chose to enact that identity, appeared less vulnerable to the influence of racialized oppositionality. Having clarity in other areas of self did not necessarily protect students from the taunts of peers, as we saw with Sandra. Whether an adolescent's racial identity is positive or negative appears to be less important for vulnerability to racialized oppositionality than the clarity and conviction with which that identity is held. Thus, scales that measure ethnic identity but do not consider the strength of that identity will not be useful for capturing the process of social influence discussed in this chapter.[42] What is needed is research into other factors that might further explain differences in black youth's vulnerability to racialized oppositionality. Psychologists such as Angela Neal-Barnett and Margaret Beale Spencer have studied students' use of the acting white slur in the context of schools, but I am not familiar with any study that has attempted to determine whether particular personality types, for example, make some youth more vulnerable than others to taunts of acting white.[43]

GENDER

One gender difference of note among the *Effective Students* is that males were more likely than females to report that they do not talk to their friends about school. Beyond this, however, my analysis of the students' narratives did not capture any clear gender differences in how adolescents responded to oppositional environments.[44] This is somewhat surprising; other studies have found that black males are more susceptible to negative influence from friends or peers than black females.[45] It may be that a larger sample of black adolescents that includes more males would reveal such differences, or it may be that academically successful students, as a whole, are less likely than less successful students to succumb to negative influence on achievement-related matters.

Conclusion

High-achieving black students face an increased potential for ridicule when the schools they attend are characterized by racialized tracking. However, not all academically successful black adolescents experience ridicule related to achievement—racialized or otherwise. This chapter explored how those who do contend with this kind of oppositionality are able to withstand the pressures to conform. Looking closely at the experiences of six students revealed that as they developed clearer ideas about their identity, beliefs, goals, and aspirations, there was a concomitant change in their response to peer pressure. Among this group of students, the timing of these changes differed, but by their junior year in high school, around age sixteen to seventeen, most adolescents seemed to have come into their own. Some achieved clarity in the key areas earlier than others did, and this enabled them to resist the norms of an oppositional peer culture earlier as well. An examination of how and why some adolescents develop a clear sense of identity earlier than do others is an important area for future research. The data from the *Effective Students* do not and cannot address that topic.

My primary aim in this chapter was to investigate variation in adolescents' vulnerability to the influence of peer cultures oppositional to idealized school and achievement norms, especially in contexts where there is visible racialized tracking. Responses to oppositional peer cultures (whether actual or anticipated) varied, depending on the timing of the encounters and on the students' personal characteristics and individual development trajectories. I identified two general types: the *vulnerable* adolescent, who attempted to adjust her behavior to conform to the perceived norms of peers, and the *secure* adolescent, who rejected those norms. A systematic pattern of statements of indifference to peers' opinions and declarations about who they were and were not distinguished *secure* from *vulnerable* adolescents. Adolescents who had not yet confronted questions such as "Who am I?" "What do I believe?" "What do I want to do in my life?" or who were in the early stages of that process, appeared to be most vulnerable to peer influence, the consequences of which, we know, can be costly.[46] Among this group, there was a consistent pattern of statements expressing desires to "fit in," or at least to not stand out, and to be liked.

Tommy's experiences provided the clearest example of this "window of vulnerability." In an effort to be like the "cool" black kids, he had joined a gang in middle school and had deliberately allowed his grades to slip. His early identity insecurities—complicated by racialized achievement and tracking structures at his school—and lack of direction may have been connected to his experiences growing up in the military and moving frequently, as he pointed out. However, when he finally achieved clarity on his beliefs, goals, and identity, largely through religion, he was able to turn himself around in a way that his parents (and the "whoopings" they administered) had not been able to accomplish. It may be that religion provided Tommy with the sense of belonging he longed for. This in turn may have helped him to develop a desire and an ability to resist negative peer influence.

Other participants besides Tommy explicitly credited a higher power or a particular religious doctrine in explaining their choices and behavior, suggesting that a strong religious foundation may help some adolescents develop clear goals and beliefs. But clarity of purpose and a strong identity do not appear to be dependent on religious conviction. Neither Gwen nor Curtis, for example, made any mention of religion or of God during the time we spent with them, yet both seemed to have discovered their respective core identities and determined their goals earlier, and with less trouble than most of their peers. This kind of early growth seems to have made the school-based aspects of their transition through adolescence smoother and less painful.

Overall, the narratives of these academically successful adolescents indicate that clarity of purpose in terms of goals, and conviction of beliefs, coupled with a firm and well-defined sense of self, protects adolescents from negative peer pressure that could otherwise take them off course academically. High-achieving black students attending schools where a racial hierarchy in achievement exists appear to be most vulnerable to peer pressure. In these schools, the placement of a few black students at the top of a tracking system that is visibly racialized can contribute to resentment and animosity among other black students. This resentment, in turn, can lead to the kind of harassment that Sandra experienced, and which other students feared. Thus, while many students, regardless of race, contend with the kind of general oppositionality that Gwen faced, racialized tracking makes oppositionality more of a threat to black youth who are in the midst of figuring out who they are and where they belong.

Fortunately for our study participants, more fit the profile of *secure* adolescent than *vulnerable* adolescent. This may seem surprising, given that adolescence is a period of rapidly occurring physiological and psychological changes and changing social roles.[47] However, neither the thirty-six members of the subgroup of *Effective Students* whose experiences this chapter drew on, nor the full sample of sixty-five high-achieving North Carolina students, is representative of all black adolescents. Moreover, my analysis focused on just one set of stressors: pressure to conform to the norms of an oppositional peer culture. An examination of other types of stressors may have revealed areas in which our *secure* adolescents were *vulnerable* and/or our *vulnerable* adolescents were *secure*. Thus, these categories are not intended to capture each adolescent's global state of being.

In this chapter, as in chapter 2, I showed that oppositional peer cultures do have the potential to affect high-achieving students' academic behavior. Yet these students generally stayed the course academically. They strove for high grades and continued to take advanced courses, even while struggling with peer ridicule and teasing. In the next chapter, I turn to the topic of course selection and explore the factors—including peer pressure—that shape students' decisions. By drawing on a more racially and academically diverse group for this analysis, I am able to investigate whether the factors that influence course selection differ by students' race or achievement.

Belonging

Course Selection and Race in the Age of "Laissez-Faire" Tracking

Well, I started out taking them because they automatically put me in the schedule for honors classes, like tracking. And then I just followed through it and consistently took honors classes because that was just what I was used to.

> *Jenny*, white female senior, Avery High School
> (85% white; 13% black)

Well, I feel—I thought {AP} was too challenging for me and I wanted to go ahead and see what the regular classes were like.

> *Kala*, black female junior, Clearview High School
> (38% white; 60% black)

WE KNOW FROM PREVIOUS CHAPTERS in this book, and from other studies, that in racially mixed and predominantly white high schools, black students are significantly underrepresented in advanced classes.[1] How this pattern develops is not well understood. There is a widespread perception that where students end up in the high school curriculum is primarily a matter of self-selection. This view prevails because, in most cases, high school students generally are permitted to choose their own courses. Compared to tracking systems of the past, in which students were rigidly and permanently assigned to one overarching curricular track (e.g., vocational or college prep), the structure of tracking in contemporary American high schools is less formal.[2] Students are no longer restricted to one track from which they must take all classes; instead, they are able to select courses from across the curriculum.[3] It seems logical that this newer version of tracking would lead to greater student diversity within classrooms. Yet, as we know, this is not what has occurred.

Many observers, including educators and students, presume that black students and white students do not take a similar approach to academic achievement in general, or to enrollment in advanced courses in particular.[4] For some people, the relative absence of black students in advanced classes is further evidence of black youth's oppositional stance toward school and their fear of acting white.[5] This explanation does not fit very well with the empirical evidence, however. As I have shown in the preceding chapters, academically successful black students continue to enroll in largely white advanced classes, even when doing so exposes them to hostility and racialized ridicule from same-race peers. What, then, does explain why black and white students frequently seem to choose different curricular pathways? Listening to students like Jenny and Kala, quoted above, as they describe their course-selection deliberations provides a basis for developing some more convincing explanations for black high school students' relative absence from high-level courses. The analysis I present in this chapter draws on data from semi-structured, face-to-face interviews with a racially mixed group of sixty-one male and female students (including Jenny and Kala) who were enrolled in selected North Carolina high schools. Table 4.1 lists each school, along with information about the racial composition of its student body, the percent black in selected AP and honors courses, and the number of students interviewed.[6]

My findings may seem surprising. The interviews show that the same principal motivations drive *all* students' course-selection decisions. Indeed, the deliberations are remarkably similar, regardless of students' race, gender, or socioeconomic status, and despite the varied constraints that characterize specific high schools. Jenny and Kala, for instance, select different academic paths, but the reasons they do so are the same. Both students choose classes that they believe will be a good fit for them academically and socially. Jenny explains that she takes advanced classes because she was "automatically" placed in honors classes and has grown accustomed to them. Her response indicates that she is comfortable in the environment of advanced classes and confident enough in her academic ability to be casual about continuing to take them. Kala's decision not to enroll in advanced classes is the opposite of

TABLE 4.1 Selected Characteristics of Participating High Schools (Listed by Percent Black), 1999–2000

High School	Number of Participants: Students	School Racial Composition			Percent Black in Selected Advanced Courses						
		Percent[1] Black	Percent White	Percent Other Minority	AP Biology	AP English	AP Calculus	AP History	Honors Biology	Honors English	Honors History
Banaker	10	88	8	4	64	75	65	84	NA	83	89
Clearview	13	60	38	2	12	0	17	NA	NA	27	30
Franklin	14	54	30	16	NA	46	50	40	NA	46	42
Dalton	7	39	60	2	0	7	0	9	NA	6	12
East	3	27	71	2	17	12	40	10	23	12	11
Avery	14	13	85	2	25	9	NA	5	NA	3	0

[1] *Percentages do not total 100 due to rounding.*

Jenny's, but it arises from the same desire. Kala also wants to continue taking the level of classes to which she has become accustomed and in which she feels comfortable.

These choices described by these two students, one white and "gifted," the other black and "non-gifted," in many ways capture the broader racial pattern found in the data I discuss in this chapter.[7] White participants were more likely to enter high school with a history of having been placed in advanced courses and gifted programs. This prior experience provides two significant benefits. First, and most importantly, their previous experience, particularly of gifted placement, seemed to boost students' academic self-confidence. That confidence was instrumental in the decision to enroll in advanced classes—over and above students' prior academic achievement. Students who lacked academic self-confidence were not willing to enroll in advanced classes, even when teachers and counselors recommended they do so. Second, prior participation in gifted programs and advanced classes gave students access to a network of friends and peers who regularly enrolled in advanced classes. Together, these two factors fostered students' belief that they *belonged* in advanced classes. This made high school advanced courses more appealing to students and the decision to take them a relatively easy one. Table 4.2 presents selected academic and demographic information for the subset of students who are quoted in this chapter.

An analysis of students' course-selection deliberations is useful because their experiences offer an up-close look at the high school course-selection process. Moreover, the narratives of the fifty-five black and white adolescents, many of whom we might expect to be enrolled in advanced classes, make possible detailed comparisons across these two racial groups, as well as comparisons between "gifted" and "non-gifted" students. The discussion in this chapter extends existing research on tracking and race that shows prior placement and achievement as having significant effects on current placement.[8] Previous studies have relied mainly on large-scale surveys to examine the course placements of students at different levels of achievement and of different racial and ethnic backgrounds. The interview data used in this analysis can help us understand how students make course-selection decisions, what factors they consider important, and whether and how those factors differ for blacks and whites. Although I am most interested in factors that contribute to black-white differences in placement, I include all students in my analysis of the overall process of course-selection decision making.

TABLE 4.2 Grade, Gender, Race, and Parent Education and Occupation for Informants Quoted, by School

High School	Informant	Grade	Gifted	Race/Gender	Mother Education	Mother Employment	Father Education	Father Employment
Avery	Terrance	10	No	BM	B.A.	Bank employee	H.S.	Construction
	Paul	11	No	BM	Some college	Secretary	Some college	Butcher
	Zora	11	Yes	BF	B.A.	Accts payable	B.A.	Contractor
	Victor	10	No	AM	H.S.	Service	A.A.	Service
	Maggie	11	Yes	WF	H.S.	Secretary	H.S.	FedEx employee
	Yolanda	9	Yes	WF	H.S.	Housewife	Tech/Voc	Cigarette maker
	Jenny	12	Yes	WF	A.A.	Nurse	B.A.	Tax assessor
	Lila	11	Yes	WF	H.S.	Housewife	Some college	Quality assurance position
	Chris	9	No	WM	H.S.	Teacher	H.S.	Production
	Whitney	12	No	BF	Some college	Nurse's aide	Some college	Service
	Ursala	9	No	WF	B.A.	Teacher	B.A.	Computer programmer

(Continued)

TABLE 4.2 Continued

High School	Informant	Grade	Gifted	Race/Gender	Mother Education	Mother Employment	Father Education	Father Employment
Banaker	Charles	9	Yes	BM	B.A.	Chemist	NA	NA
	Michelle	12	Yes	BF	Tech/Voc	Secretary	H.S.	Truck driver
	Jerrell	12	Yes	BM	Tech/Voc	Self-employed	H.S.	DK
	Kimmi	11	Yes	BF	B.A.	Teacher	B.A.	Laboratory scientist
	Ernest	12	No	BM	Some college	Computers	NA	NA
	Tyler	11	Yes	BM	B.A.	Teacher	Advanced degree	Statistician
	Femea	12	Yes	BM	Tech/Voc	Self-employed	H.S	NA
	Andrea	9	No	BF	H.S.	Retail	NA	NA
Clearview	Kala	11	No	BF	A.A.	Group home aide	H.S.	Grocery distributor
	Shawn	12	Yes	BM	A.A.	Teacher	Tech/Voc	Sheriff
	Hannah	12	Yes	WF	B.A.	Teacher	NA	NA
	Ingrid	12	No	WF	Some college	Textile	Less than H.S.	Carpenter
	Hakim	11	No	BM	H.S.	Machine operator	Tech/Voc	Unemployed
	Gina	12	Yes	WF	B.A.	GED specialist	Advanced degree	Community college position
	Jessica	12	No	BF	A.A.	Film technician	NA	NA

Location	Name							
Dalton	Tamela	11	Yes	BF	A.A.	Unemployed	NA	NA
	Melissa	9	Yes	AF	Less than H.S.	Housekeeper	Less than H.S.	Waiter
	Lexie	12	Yes	WF	H.S.	Lead agent	H.S.	Coordinator
	Kara	10	Yes	WF	Advanced degree	Retail	Advanced degree	Real estate agent
	Tony	12	Yes	WM	B.A.	Teacher's assistant	B.A.	Program director
	Preston	9	No	WM	B.A.	Teacher	Advanced degree	Chemical engineer
East Franklin	Anna Beth	10	Yes	WF	H.S.	Secretary	H.S.	Manager
	Kendra	11	Yes	BF	B.A.	LPN	H.S.	Military
	Greg	11	Yes	WM	Advanced degree	Librarian	NA	NA
	Joyce	12	Yes	WF	H.S.	Refused to answer	H.S.	Refused to answer
	Daniel	11	No	WM	Tech/Voc	Graphic designer	A.A.	Landscape engineer
	Eddie	11	No	HM	B.A.	Executive director	B.A.	Military
	Ned	11	Yes	WM	A.A.	Teacher's assistant	A.A.	Manager
	Shala	11	Yes	BF	B.A.	Correctional officer	H.S.	Technician
	Miki	11	No	BF	Some college	Disabled	NA	NA

Institutional Structure of High School Course Selection

High schools in North Carolina, as in other states, offer a variety of courses in different subject areas at different levels. The six high schools the study participants attended offered a mix of general education (referred to as college prep at Avery High School), honors (which some schools refer to as advanced), AP, IB (available only at Banaker), and dual-enrollment courses.[9] During the 2000–2001 school year, the six schools offered between three (Avery High School) and ten (Banaker High School) AP courses. Each school offered at least one AP course in English, history, and biology. Typically, within a given subject area, students have options with respect to the academic level of the course they select. So, for example, at East High School, in biology, there are different "track" offerings. After completing Earth/Environmental Science, a student could enroll in Biology 1 or Advanced Biology 1, and later, in Biology 2 or AP Biology.[10]

To prepare incoming ninth-grade students for the responsibility of selecting their own courses, high school counselors visited feeder middle schools and met with students individually or in groups. With input from middle school counselors, the high school staff provided guidance to students regarding courses they should or could take. The specific procedures for course enrollment differed across the six schools, but the general process was the same. In each, the course-selection process was relatively open, although in some schools, the rules guiding students' choices were stricter than in others. For example, Franklin High School restricted ninth-grade honors classes to students who fell into at least one of the following three categories: those who were designated as "gifted" (AIG/AG); those who received a teacher's recommendation; or those who scored at the highest levels (a 3 or a 4) on the state's standardized eighth-grade end-of-grade (EOG) tests.

Generally, honors courses were less restrictive than AP courses. The former, depending upon the specific subject, were open to students at all grade levels (except at Franklin, as explained above). AP classes generally were open only to juniors and seniors. Banaker, however, offered at least one AP course as early as ninth grade. Other schools offered one AP course for tenth graders. All schools had prerequisites for enrollment in AP and other advanced courses, but the criteria varied across schools, departments, and courses. Enrollment in some courses required only teacher recommendations; in others, students had to have completed a particular sequence of courses and also must have earned at least the specified minimum grades. For example, in order to enroll in AP Biology at East and Avery, students had to have at least a B average in biology and chemistry, in addition to having completed certain foundational courses. At Dalton, the grade prerequisites for the same course were higher: students had to have at least a 93 in Biology or an 85 in Honors Biology. Banaker, on the other hand, did not restrict access to AP Biology based on grades, although there were prior course requirements.

Despite these differences, students at each school could seek waivers of the school's recommendations and prerequisites for enrollment in advanced classes. But, here too, the process differed from school to school. Some required both parent and student signatures for waivers, while others did not. Avery students were given considerable latitude. They were permitted to select courses that contradicted the recommendations of counselors and teachers and/or ones that did not seem to be the best fit, given the student's academic performance and interests. At Clearview High School, on the other hand, students were closely supervised. There, enrolling in certain advanced courses without having met the requisite criteria required a parent-teacher conference, as well as a waiver that included parent, teacher, and counselor signatures. Even at Clearview, however, not all academic departments imposed the same strict requirements. Some set fixed criteria on minimum grades and test scores for honors and AP enrollment, while others required only teacher recommendations.

To summarize, in contemporary academic placement processes, high school counselors are no longer principally responsible for determining students' course assignments or track placement. Students and parents now play a more active role. Yet counselors, and increasingly teachers, still serve as gatekeepers in the placement process. Their recommendations guide students' selections and their signatures often are required for enrollment in advanced courses. As the next section explains, despite changes that have given today's tracking systems a different appearance, some aspects (and outcomes) remain the same. In particular, input from educators and school administrators continues to play a key role in the courses students take.

Teacher and Counselor Recommendations and Student Choice

The teacher has to sign. Every time we sign up for the schedules, our teachers have to look at our schedule and see what we want to take next semester and they'll initial it—the teacher that you had—and they'll see if it's okay, and if they don't, they won't {initial it}.

Kala, black female junior, Clearview High School (38% white; 60% black)

As Kala explains, teachers at her school are important gatekeepers, without their okay, students' course choices have little meaning. At other schools it is counselors' recommendations that have special weight. Kara, a white sophomore at Dalton, recalled that at her middle school, counselors told students "not to take the honors courses [in high school] because they were too much work, and unless you had a hundred average, not to do it." Not surprisingly, then, during interviews, as students explained how they selected their courses, they often referred first to the recommendations of school personnel. Ingrid, a white senior at Clearview, reported that she enrolled in three honors courses in ninth grade because her counselors and teachers told her that the regular courses would not give her "enough of a challenge." Another student at Clearview, Hakim, a black male in his junior year, said that he had not enrolled in honors English because his tenth-grade English teacher told him, " 'Hakim, I don't want to sign you up for honors English because I don't know who will be teaching it.' That's what he said." "He's a pretty good friend of mine," Hakim added, "I, I think, I let him choose." Banaker junior, Tyler, another black male, signed up for the International Baccalaureate program because the IB coordinator at the school "persuaded" him to. Still, he insisted, "I had a choice. I just chose to take the IB classes."

Yolanda, a white ninth grader at Avery, relied fully on teachers' and counselors' advice. Rather than first selecting her classes and then getting feedback from teachers and counselors, as many other students reported doing, Yolanda said she "let them tell [her] what they thought before" she filled out her course-selection forms. When teachers recommended she take four honors courses, she did not object. She indicated that she would continue to follow her teachers' recommendations, even if they were for the most rigorous courses: "If I'm recommended [for AP courses], and if my teachers tell me I should, I wouldn't have any problem taking those." Previous studies on tracking have found a similar willingness among students to cede course-selection responsibilities to school personnel. Warren Kubitschek and Maureen Hallinan, for example, noted, "The amount of choice students have in their track placement is debatable, but few students exercise any choice they might have. Few students change their placement from that recommended by teachers and counselors."[11]

The data I use, however, which are drawn from talking directly with students about their placements, suggest that they go along with recommendations only to the extent that they feel the recommendations are appropriate. Indeed, not all students followed teacher and counselor recommendations as unquestioningly as Yolanda. Kara, for instance, fought to be placed in an honors class at Dalton, against the school's recommendation.

Algebra, my freshman year was the first year they had ever done an honors algebra course and I had a ninety-three or ninety-four final average in English—or in social studies—and they weren't recommending that we even take algebra at all. They wanted us to go ahead and take world geography over history and take algebra our sophomore year because they thought that it was too hard for us and too much for us to understand. So I begged and I complained, and I moaned and groaned, and got my parents to come down here and put me in honors.

Like many other informants at the six high schools, Kara was aware of tracking and how counselors and teachers guided students' placements. However, some studies suggest that students generally are less conscious of their school's tracking structure and how it influences their course choices. These studies conclude, much as Kubitschek and Hallinan did, that few go against the school's recommendations. For instance, many of the lower-income Mexican American students in Julie Bettie's *Women without Class* did not completely understand tracking until Bettie explained it to them. The young women then recalled how counselors and teachers at their California high school guided them to select the vocational courses in which they were currently enrolled.

In the present study, students were mostly aware of the institutional influence on their course choices. Nevertheless, they were generally satisfied with their school's approach to assigning students to classes. Some students described feeling constrained by the process, but most did not. Even as they acknowledged that the recommendations of teachers and counselors, or the school's formal guidelines, set the parameters for or formed the basis of their decisions, students still believed course decisions ultimately were up to them (in consultation with their parents). When asked whether they had any problems getting assigned to the classes they preferred, students overwhelmingly said no. The comments of Avery junior Zora capture many informants' reported experience and their belief that the course-selection process was open and flexible: "Yeah, I've always got what I wanted.... Like if I wanted to take just a regular class or whatever, [counselors are] like, 'You might want to go a little harder than that.' You know. They'll advise you or whatever. But you can take whatever you want to." The students' beliefs that where they end up is a matter of personal choice is consistent with research reporting that the tracking structure of contemporary schools is less rigid than in the past, with less control in the hands of school counselors and other authorities.

Still, it is somewhat surprising that so few students, including those in lower-level classes, had any complaints about their course assignments. It is possible that the study participants were generally more content with the placement process at their school than were their peers. Since school personnel distributed the study consent forms, it is likely that the students who were given the forms were ones who were in overall good standing with school authorities. Although the participants represent a good range of achievement and course levels, they may not represent the range of experiences with placement or relationships with school personnel.

In any case, it is apparent in this study, as in others, that school personnel continue to have significant input regarding student placement. Control of the course schedules and offerings, and determination of the various prerequisites as well as the procedures for waiving them, all rest with the institution.[12] And although at each of the six high schools parents had the right to veto teacher and counselor recommendations, they rarely did so, according to school personnel. Thus, despite contemporary students' increased freedom to select their own courses, schools are still actively involved in shaping students' choices, whether or not students are aware of it.

High School Students' Course-Selection Deliberations

At all six schools, students' course-selection deliberations were similar. This was true despite the active role school personnel played in shaping students' course selections and despite differences both within and across schools with respect to enrollment criteria for advanced classes. For all informants, making decisions about courses involved considerations related to the level of academic comfort they anticipated in a given course. These considerations usually took priority over teachers' and counselors' recommendations, because students were only willing to accept recommendations if they were consistent with their own perceptions of where they belonged. As Kara's account of her struggle to take honors algebra in ninth grade demonstrates, students rejected the school's recommendations when they contradicted their perceptions of their ability to do well in a course. Kara was completely confident that she could handle the demands of the advanced math class. But Kara's case was not the norm. Students like her, who were designated as "gifted," were usually recommended for higher-level courses, and they usually followed those recommendations. Students who rejected the school's recommendations were more likely to be "non-gifted," and the recommendations were more likely to be for higher-track classes.

OPTING OUT OF ADVANCED CLASSES: A MATTER OF SELF-PROTECTION

Above all else, students seemed to be trying to protect their sense of competence. Thus, they were generally unwilling to take classes in which they did not believe they would be able to do well. Simply put, if they thought they might not pass a higher-level course, they opted for a lower-level one. As Hakim explained, his first priority in selecting a class was to determine how likely he was to pass it.

> OK, even though they add to your grades, honors U.S. history [*pause*], I didn't want to. I just, you know, I felt, you know, it wasn't, that I wouldn't, I didn't—if you don't know what you're getting yourself into, then don't go higher than you can, you know. You do want to pass. I mean, that's the first thing. And then, honors, you know, would be exceeding just passing. But you know, um, I don't want to get myself higher, you know, go for something that I know that maybe I couldn't pass.

For other students, passing was not enough; they wanted to earn good grades. Eddie, a Hispanic junior at Franklin, said he was happy with being in the general education classes he selected, "Because I like that it's easy to have an A or a B, rather than to work hard for a C." Eddie had been encouraged by a teacher to take an honors course. He chose not to because he "didn't want to have to work harder for anything less than" the good grade he earned in his lower-level class. He explained that he had earned a "pretty good grade" in the general education history class, but that he had "worked hard for" it. He was not convinced that he could earn an equally high grade in the honors class, even if he put forth more effort. Therefore, he opted for the lower-level course where he knew he could do well.

Others seemed to share this perspective. According to Victor, an Asian American sophomore at Avery who enrolled exclusively in lower-level, college prep classes, students should take only those courses in which they knew they could get high grades. Other informants were not as forthright, but their resistance to taking classes in which they did not believe they could do well suggests they felt the same way. Even students taking advanced classes admitted that they did so only because they believed they would do well. Charles, for example, a black freshman at Banaker, planned to continue taking honors courses just "so long as I'm doing well in the classes." And, considering that many schools had minimum grade requirements for taking advanced courses, the students' perspective is consistent with the school's message.

Like Victor and Eddie, other students who took only general education classes were content with their course placement, most often because they did not believe they were capable of doing well in more rigorous courses. Paul, a black junior at Avery, expressed satisfaction with his decision to enroll in college prep classes exclusively. He could "do honors," Paul guessed, but he saw that as a risky choice: "I don't know if I could be working that hard." Later in the interview, Paul referred to his twin brother who, he told us, took mostly honors classes, as "the smart one," implying that he himself was not smart. When asked what he thought it would take to be in honors classes, Paul replied, "Smart and hardworking." Ingrid, a white senior at Clearview who began taking honors courses in the ninth grade at the insistence of her teachers and counselors, stopped taking them because she felt the classes were "too much" for her and that she did not belong in them. "I just don't feel in place with them," she said about the students in advanced classes. "I don't feel like I am smart enough to be put in the same category as them." Whatever role the school may have played in these students' placement, the students themselves seemed convinced they were exactly where they belonged. In their own estimation, they were not hardworking or "smart enough" for advanced classes.

When asked if he thought he belonged in the general education/college prep classes he was taking, Victor replied, "Yeah, I think so. I don't think I belong in honors class. [*Why do you say that?*] I think it's kind of hard." Another Avery student, Terrance, a black sophomore, reported that he was not sure if he was ready for more advanced classes, so he "just chose regular" classes. A third Avery student, a white freshman named Chris said he was satisfied with his decision not to take advanced classes. He explained that the classes he was taking were "just easier and they don't expect as much as they do with the AG [gifted] classes." Just as James Rosenbaum found more than thirty years ago among white working-class students, in the current study, students who were taking lower-track classes explained their placement in terms of "their own personal shortcomings."[13]

The students' narratives indicate that taking lower-level courses has little to do with concerns about peers' negative perceptions of academically successful students or of high achievement more generally. Students' main concern was to protect their sense of competence. As students like Terrance explained, by opting out of advanced classes, those who do not believe they are "smart enough" can avoid the frustration and disappointment that result from failure or the failure to meet one's expectations. After commenting that he sometimes feels like "giving up" in his classes, Terrance said, "Well, if I've been really trying hard at a class and I end up not doing as well as I wanted to, especially if it's happened all year, I start to get discouraged." Jessica, a black senior at Clearview, stopped taking honors classes for similar reasons: "Sometimes I felt like I did [belong in honors classes], and sometimes I felt like I didn't. And I guess at times I felt like I didn't because I felt like maybe I was the only one who wasn't catching on to the stuff and that made me feel bad or whatever." Jessica's recollection, strikingly similar to her schoolmate Ingrid's (quoted above), captures precisely the experience that many students hope to avoid. Opting for lower-level classes in which they feel more comfortable academically spares students the possibility of feeling embarrassed or ashamed by failure to succeed. Psychologist William James's observation, "With no attempt there can be no failure; with no failure no humiliation," probably best explains these students' strategy.[14]

These findings about adolescents' concerns with their own competence appear to contradict survey findings such as those Laurence Steinberg reported in *Beyond the Classroom.* Steinberg found that 20 percent of adolescents limit their effort in school because of concerns about their peers' perceptions and few believe their friends think getting good grades in school is important. Students' beliefs about their peers' attitudes may have implications for their own behavior and achievement, but the student narratives I analyzed suggest that even if adolescents believe that their friends do not think highly of high achievers or of academic striving, this may not decrease their own desire to avoid failure.

Adolescents who opted not to take advanced courses conveyed more concern about doing poorly in a course than about their peers' perceptions of students who do well academically. In fact, these students rarely expressed any concerns about their peers' views of academically successful students. Among black students in this group, none expressed concerns about acting white. The primary consideration in students' deliberations was course difficulty. Few adolescents taking only standard academic classes thought of themselves as "smart" or "really bright," words they used to describe their peers enrolled in advanced classes.

It is important to note that some of the younger informants who shied away from advanced classes in their first few years of high school claimed that they would take advanced courses later because they knew doing so would "look good" on their transcript. Thus, plans to attend college could change the equation, making advanced courses seem worth the risk for adolescents who at present did not see themselves as smart enough or as ready for a more challenging curriculum. Adolescents like Terrance and Chris, who thus far had taken only general education courses, indicated that they would enroll in advanced classes in the future. They would do this even if they were not fully confident in their ability to do well in those courses, because, as Chris said, "It would go on my record for when I apply to college." Asked whether there was any other reason he might take advanced classes, Chris replied, "Not really." As the next section explains, Chris's response is indicative of the approach almost all students took with respect to enrolling in advanced classes: the primary value of these classes was understood to lie in their college-related benefits.

ELECTING HIGHER-LEVEL COURSES: MATTERS OF COMPETITION AND CONFIDENCE

Enrollment in advanced courses was a means to an end for students—it would afford them a "competitive social position." Among students enrolled in advanced classes, almost all admitted that they enrolled because they believed such courses were required for college or would provide an advantage in the application process. The extra grade-point weight given to AP and honors courses, and their widespread reputation for being more rigorous than general education and college prep classes, convinced many students that taking these courses would improve their chances of getting into college.

Ned, a white junior at Franklin High taking advanced classes, acknowledged that "at first" he had not wanted to take advanced classes, but he recognized the longer-term "benefits," including a "higher chance for [college] scholarships" and the possibility of earning college credit for the courses. Andrea, too, a ninth-grade black student at Banaker, admitted that at first she did not "want to be in" an honors class. Despite her concerns that the course might be too hard, however, she agreed to take it on her mother's recommendation that "it would look good on [her] record." "So the main reason why you chose to take the honors English class was because it would look good on your record?" the interviewer asked Andrea. "Uh-hum," she replied casually. Similarly, when asked about the courses she took, Whitney, a black senior at Avery, was adamant that she would not have taken honors courses "just for the heck of it." She did so, she explained, only to meet a requirement of the North Carolina Scholars Program, which allowed her to graduate with honors and to be eligible for scholarships from local businesses. Other comments such as "colleges look at honors"; "it would look better on [my] college transcript"; "it looks good on applications and stuff"; and "I want to get into a good college," were voiced repeatedly.

Comments about learning more in advanced courses or gaining strong academic preparation for college, on the other hand, were much less frequent. Students who noted that preparing for college was an important consideration in their decision to take advanced courses did so by pointing to the competitive advantage these courses would provide. As Banaker junior Tyler put it: "I wanted to stay ahead academically, you know, having a, have an edge on the competition. I wanted to make sure I would be prepared for college." Melissa, an Asian American ninth grader at Dalton, was clear that the sole reason for taking advanced courses was to fulfill the "challenge" requirement: "The only reason that I'm taking [advanced classes] is that you have to have a challenge to go to college." Students believed that a transcript showing advanced courses and a high GPA would improve their chances of getting into the school of their choice, so they planned accordingly.

A focus on college was not the only thing students taking advanced classes had in common. These students were strikingly similar in the degree of academic self-confidence they expressed. Perhaps what makes this characteristic stand out so sharply is its contrast to the lack of confidence expressed by students like Victor and Terrance and others who were taking only lower-level courses. A consistent comment among those in higher-level courses was that they required an academic "challenge." With predictable frequency, those in higher-level courses cited the appeal of the level of the curriculum as among their primary reasons for enrolling in an advanced class: "it's a challenging class"; "it's more of a challenge"; "I just feel like I want a challenge"; "mainly for a challenge"; "it's something that challenges me." This desire to be challenged academically may seem contradictory to the students' emphasis on the benefits of advanced courses for college goals, but the two are consistent. In many cases, students' desire for "a challenge" was directly related to their understanding that "you have to have a challenge to go to college," as Melissa said. However, while most study participants, regardless of achievement level, were aware of the college-related benefits of taking advanced classes, not all, as we learned from students like Chris and Terrance, felt ready or were willing to take on the challenge of those courses.

Most of the students taking advanced classes viewed these classes as simply the "right fit" for them, as Jerrell, a black senior at Banaker, put it; thus, the decision to enroll in advanced classes did not usually involve much deliberation or concern. For example, when asked how she felt about being recommended for advanced classes, Yolanda replied, "I had made good grades all of my life; it wasn't a surprise. I wasn't worried about the courses or anything. It was just kind of normal." Similarly, Tony, a white senior at Dalton who is dyslexic, felt he belonged in the advanced classes. Describing himself as "really, really smart," and echoing other informants, Tony said he decided to take AP and honors courses because, "They're harder and they give me more of a challenge, which I need." His school's special education department "didn't have the resources to help" him, he said. The teachers in the advanced classes, however, were able to work with him to provide the modifications he needed. Another white student, Greg, a junior at Franklin High, accounted for his enrollment in AP classes by noting that, "I'm a lot more intelligent than just your average person." For highly confident students like these, the anticipated risk of failure was minimal; therefore, advanced courses were a safe bet. And the payoffs—possible college credit and a more competitive transcript—made the challenge of advanced courses worthwhile. Perceived competence, then, was as much of a factor in the decision making of students who selected higher-level courses as it was of the students who opted to take only lower-level courses.

The few students who described their decision to take an advanced course as less casual or "automatic" also seemed, initially, to have been less confident in their academic abilities. Shala, a black junior at Franklin, admitted that "at the beginning I really didn't want to do it [take honors courses], but I was like, I should do it because it'll help me out and it'll make me work harder. . . . I was like, I'm not going to be able to do all this work in this set amount of time, because they give a criteria sheet, I didn't think I could do it, but I did." Banaker senior Michelle, like Shala, also risked taking advanced classes after careful deliberation, and in spite of initial anxiety: "At first I did, I was like, 'I don't know if I can do this.' Because it seemed so hard. But now, um, I think I belong in those classes. . . . I was still nervous. My friends were like, 'Oh Lord, you're taking all these honors classes.' So I was like, 'I don't know if I can do it.' But, the kind of person I am, if I want something and it doesn't matter how hard it is, I'm going to try to do it to the best of my ability, so I said, 'Just gotta do it.' " Note that, like their peers taking lower-level classes, Michelle and Shala were anxious about taking advanced classes not because they feared their friends might ridicule or ostracize them, but because they feared they might not be able to handle the work. Michelle's friends, it seems, were similarly afraid for her.

It is not clear how these two students were able to get over their initial insecurities and muster the confidence to take on the challenge of advanced courses, but they shared a distinguishing characteristic with many other informants enrolled in advanced classes: they both had "gifted" status. Thirty-seven of the fifty (74%) students enrolled in advanced classes had been identified as "gifted." Interestingly, Michelle and Shala notwithstanding, informants who expressed the need to be challenged as a reason for taking advanced classes overwhelmingly were "gifted" students. Of the twenty-one students citing the need for a "challenge," only four, all of whom were black, had not been identified as gifted. I return to the topic of self-confidence later in the context of my discussion of the effects of being labeled as gifted.

Gifted Status and High School Course-Taking

The effects of gifted status are substantial for the students in this study. As table 4.3 shows, students identified as gifted were significantly more likely to take advanced courses, especially AP courses. Among the juniors and seniors, twenty-three of twenty-seven (85%) who had taken at least one AP course had been identified as gifted. On the other hand, among the juniors and seniors taking only general academic (or college prep) courses, none had been identified as gifted. The pattern is less clear for juniors and seniors taking only honors; half of those in this group reported gifted identification. Among the ninth- and tenth-grade students, eight of the eleven taking AP, IB, or honors classes reported gifted placement, whereas just one of the six taking only general education or college prep courses was "gifted."

TABLE 4.3   High School Course Enrollment by Grade, Race, and Gifted Status

	Highest Level Courses Taken and Gifted Status					
	AP	Gifted	Honors	Gifted	General Ed/ College Prep	Gifted
Juniors and Seniors (44)	27	23	12	6	5	0
Black (23)	11	9	9	4	3	0
White (16)	13	11	3	2	0	0
Native American (1)	0	0	0	0	1	0
Hispanic (2)	1	1	0	0	1	0
Asian (2)	2	2	0	0	0	0
Freshmen and Sophomores (17)	4	3	7	5	6	1
Black (8)	4	3	2	1	2	0
White (8)	0	0	5	4	3	1
Asian (1)	0	0	0	0	1	0

To put this another way, among the students who had never taken an advanced class in high school, only one was "gifted." And among those who had taken at least one advanced class during high school, only about one-quarter were "non-gifted." Although some informants who had never taken an advanced class indicated that they planned to do so in the future, the current pattern indicates that "gifted" students begin taking advanced courses earlier than "non-gifted" students.

To further explore the effect of gifted status, my colleagues and I analyzed existing statewide data (2002–2003) for more than 43,000 North Carolina high school students.[15] Using logistic regression to predict the odds of taking an AP class, we found that even after controlling for students' race, parent education, and previous achievement (measured using grades 3–8 math and reading test scores), the odds of taking an AP course were significantly higher for students who had been identified as gifted (see table 4.4). "Gifted"

TABLE 4.4   Effect of Gifted Status on Odds of Enrollment in Advanced Placement Course

	Model 1	Model 2
Gifted ID	2.122***	2.155***
Asian	2.496***	
Black	2.010***	2.056***
Hispanic	1.256	
American Indian	1.071	
Other	1.166	
Female	1.090**	1.096***
Prior achievement (grades 3–8 average math and read EOGs)	1.102***	1.103***
Parent education		
Less than HS	0.761*	0.709*
Some education beyond HS	1.325***	1.308***
Trade or business school	1.213	1.224
Community/technical/two-year degree	1.331***	1.336***
Four-year college degree	2.025***	2.032***
Advanced degree	2.431***	2.386***
Black*AG interaction	0.717***	0.697***
Constant	0.000***	0.000***
N	43145	41353

* $p<0.05$, ** $p<0.01$, *** $p<0.001$

students were twice as likely as "non-gifted" students to have taken an AP course. We also found that the odds of taking an AP course increase for students the longer they participate in the gifted program.

These findings indicate that gifted placement in elementary or middle school is a gateway to higher-level courses in high school. There are a number of possible reasons for this relationship between gifted identification and later enrollment in advanced courses. First, as the learning opportunities hypothesis suggests, exposure to rigorous academic materials and instruction in the early grades may better prepare students to master challenging material later and to perform well on standardized tests.[16] Thus, students may get a boost in confidence from their actual academic performance and proven ability to excel. Second, the teacher expectations literature indicates that teachers and counselors may be more likely to steer "gifted" students toward advanced classes because they hold higher expectations for these students than they do for "non-gifted" ones.[17]

A third possibility is that students who are identified as "gifted" gain a boost in confidence from the label itself, what my colleague William Darity Jr. calls an "anointment effect." This explanation is consistent with the "expectations states" literature. That literature posits that children develop ideas about themselves consistent with the evaluations they receive, and that these ideas lead them to behave in ways that make the initial evaluations appear accurate.[18]

The "gifted" students' accounts of their course-selection deliberations and responses to their gifted identification support the anointment effect interpretation. When students discussed how they felt when they learned they would be placed in the gifted program, they often remembered feelings of enhanced ability and competence. Hannah, a white senior at Clearview, recalled, "I felt smart, really smart," and Kara described her reaction to the experience as "an ego boost." Anna Beth, a white freshman at East High School, reported being happy about her gifted placement because she had "always wanted to be kinda smart." When Greg learned that he would be placed in the gifted program, he recalled thinking, "Hey, neat. I'm, like, I've like proven I'm smarter than most other people. I'm smarter than most of my peers." The power of the gifted label to enhance children's self-perception is unmistakable in these students' remarks. Interestingly, black students' recollections of how they felt when they were invited to participate in the gifted program did not include statements about feeling like they were smarter or more intelligent than their peers. This may reflect a greater hesitance on the part of black adolescents to make statements that might appear haughty or superior.

As might be expected, "gifted" students were more likely than "non-gifted" students to make comments suggesting that selecting higher-level courses was an obvious or natural choice in light of their above-average intelligence and/or prior achievement. These students often also explicitly mentioned their gifted (AG/AIG) placement as a part of their course-selection deliberations. When asked whether he belonged in the honors courses he was taking at Banaker, Jerrell answered, "Yeah.... Because, you know, I've been like in AG for a while. Plus, you know, I think I made, you know, pretty good grades too. So I think it's, it's the right fit for me." Lexie, a white senior at Dalton High School said she made the decision to take honors and AP courses on her own, without input from her parents or counselors: "Since I've been taking AG courses early on," she explained, "it was kind of expected [of me] to continue." Asked why she chose honors classes, Maggie, a white junior at Avery High, replied: "Well, just because my teachers recommended me, and I felt like I've been doing it (gifted program) since fifth grade, so I could keep it up." Banaker senior Femea gave a similar explanation for how he came to be in honors courses: "I just signed up for it. And 'cuz I was like in like the more advanced classes, so I just been taking 'em ever since."

These students' explanations of their enrollment in advanced courses reflect a sort of nonchalance, a taken-for-granted notion that they belonged in advanced classes, because, owing to their early identification as gifted, they believed they were "really smart" and had always been placed in higher-level classes. Jenny's comments perhaps best capture the importance of gifted identification for advanced course-taking in high school. When asked whether she belonged in the AP courses she was taking, Jenny responded, "Yeah. But it's because I've known it for so long that I don't think I could go to, I don't think I fit in anywhere else.... Now we're all kind of nonchalant about it, because we feel we have to just follow through and go from honors to AP to college—that's how we're tracked to be, and so we're just kind of following with the system." The centrality of the gifted label (and other prior experience with advanced placements) for high school course selection cannot be overstated. Students identified as "gifted" may have been more capable than others to begin with, but as the evidence in table 4.4 suggests, that does not preclude an anointment effect. The "gifted" effect is an independent one; it is not due simply to differences in prior performance between "gifted" and "non-gifted" students.

As with other tracking and ability grouping practices, gifted programs send two equally powerful messages, one about who is smart and the other about who is not. This seems to contribute to students' tendency to talk about themselves (and others) as if they believe intelligence is a fixed trait;

you have it or you do not, and in either case, there is not much you can do about it.[19] Students' accounts of their course-selection deliberations suggest that they internalize these institutional messages about who is smart and who is not and judge their own abilities and where they belong accordingly. When students are told they are gifted, they begin to think of themselves as such. They also expect more of themselves academically than do other students and, as we have seen, they believe they need a more challenging curriculum than that offered in regular courses.

In general, black students and males were less likely than whites and females, respectively, to report gifted placement. Of the sixty-one informants, nearly three-quarters of the females reported gifted placement compared to less than half of the males. With respect to race, 75 percent of white informants reported gifted placement compared to 52 percent of blacks. Blacks and males were also less likely to express academic self-confidence and to take advanced classes.

Race and Gifted Placement in North Carolina

Whatever the causes of the higher academic self-confidence of "gifted" students, the contrast with "non-gifted" students is obvious, and the consequences for students' course-selection decisions are clear. Unfortunately, in North Carolina the rate of black and other minority (with the exception of Asian Americans) participation in gifted programs is significantly below that of whites' rate. For the cohort of North Carolina public high school students graduating in 2003, for example, 18 percent of whites compared to just 3.8 percent of blacks were identified as gifted. White students made up close to 90 percent of the population of gifted students in North Carolina in 2002, although they composed just 59 percent of the state's overall student population.

Analyses of 1999–2000 data obtained for the larger NCDPI study of minority underrepresentation in rigorous courses and programs showed that minority students were identified as gifted in elementary and middle schools at less than half the rate of their presence in the general student population.[20] This pattern is consistent with information obtained from the school mail-in surveys.[21] For example, the survey data showed that white students were overrepresented in gifted programs (relative to their proportion in the overall student body) in 93 percent of the 517 elementary schools reporting in the state. In one-third of the 517 schools, students of color (mostly black) made up the majority of the student body. Yet there were only thirty-eight schools

(7%) in which students of color (black, Hispanic, and American Indian) were not underrepresented in gifted programs relative to their enrollment in the student body. In fifteen of those thirty-eight schools, black, American Indian, and Hispanic students made up more than half of the school population; and in nine schools, they represented more than 90 percent of the student body. This suggests that in order for students of color to achieve at least proportional representation in a school's gifted program, the student body had to be predominantly minority or consist almost exclusively of students of color.

This scenario is not unique to North Carolina. Particularly with respect to black-white differences, race-based underrepresentation in gifted programs occurs nationwide. According to Jacqueline Jordan Irvine, compared to white students, black students across the country are "only one-half as likely to be in a class for the gifted or talented."[22] Previous studies have reported similar patterns for black students in cities in Pennsylvania, California, New York, Maryland, Florida, and Louisiana.[23] It seems that in many areas of the country the dismantling of formal tracking systems has been accompanied by the emergence of other practices that have a similar stratifying effect, channeling students from certain backgrounds into particular curriculum tracks and ability groups. As the student narratives quoted in this chapter suggest, the new system of "laissez-faire" tracking produces effects similar to the older, more formal system of tracking.

BECOMING "GIFTED"

Students' accounts of how they achieved their gifted status also show an interesting racial pattern. The specific criteria for gifted placement in North Carolina,[24] including test score and IQ cut-offs, varied. For instance, in some schools, students had to score at the 95th percentile, at others, the 98th. The instruments schools used to identify giftedness also varied (there were more than one hundred in use). Although the study participants were identified as gifted between three and nine years earlier, most recalled a straightforward process of gifted placement based on their test scores from statewide EOG tests or on some other achievement or IQ test results.[25] Some believed teacher recommendations were definitive. A few informants, on the other hand, described a process that involved parents pushing and complaining in order to secure placement, even though the student had not met the school's formal criteria. Interestingly, this awareness of their parents' intervention did not prevent these students from considering themselves "gifted" or otherwise deserving of placement. Instead, they implied that adverse circumstances at the time of their assessment had skewed the initial results. While the students' recollections of these events may be imprecise, it is noteworthy that only white students believed their parents had been responsible for their placement.[26]

A white senior at Franklin, Joyce, recalled failing the test for the gifted program in middle school: "I don't know why I didn't pass it, but then my mom was like, 'You better make her take that test again.' So then the woman [test proctor], I remember the woman gave me a brownie and a little juice before I took my test and then I passed it that time." Similarly, Daniel, a white junior at Franklin, reported that although he had not "passed" the AG test in middle school, he was allowed to take the advanced classes anyway because his mother came to school and complained, "It's like you have to get your parents to go up and complain, that's what my mom did because she wanted me to have like the best education, so she had to complain to them about getting me into those classes."

Tony's case is especially interesting. As a senior, he was taking a mix of AP, honors, and special education classes at Dalton. He reported that his dyslexia had been diagnosed in the third grade, the same year he and the rest of his class took the test for placement in the gifted program. Despite his disability, which affected his reading, Tony was later placed into the gifted program, although he did not recall if he had met the formal criteria for placement. He did recall, however, that it was a "confusing time" for him, because he "wasn't sure he belonged [in AG]." According to Tony, his disability was, and has continued to be, a "big" problem: "I'm not just a little bit, I don't have just a minor learning disability, I'm, like, off the charts, you know?" The magnitude of his problem had led Tony to decide to "drop out of AP English" in his senior year. Throughout his school career, however, as Tony explained, his mother would "fight for things" and "have battles" with the special education department to make sure that he received all available services.

Hannah, a Clearview senior, claimed to have been one of the first few students placed into the gifted program at her elementary school, "before they let other people in." According to Hannah, these "others" gained admittance because their "parents griped about it a lot.... That's just how it is around here," she explained. "If parents gripe, they get what they want." Interestingly, Hannah's elementary school, Holt, was included in the larger study of minority underrepresentation in rigorous courses and programs conducted for the NCDPI. At the time of that study, Holt exhibited one of the most significant cases of underrepresentation of black students in the gifted program in the state. As mentioned in chapter 2, Holt's student body was 71 percent black, but the gifted program was 100 percent white. Either Holt's black parents were not among those "griping" about their children not being in the gifted program or they were not among those who "get what they want." That is, black parents either were not as proactive or not as powerful as white parents.

Still, these examples support Amy Stuart Wells and Irene Serna's assertion that the " 'gifted' label may be more a form of symbolic capital than a true measure of innate student ability."[27] But the value of the gifted label is not only in the honor and prestige it bestows on the labeled children and their parents. The "gifted" label also provides real advantages for children, including access to a more rigorous curriculum and, in later grades, access to advanced classes. Thus, parents who push for their children to be placed in gifted programs are no doubt also trying to ensure that their children are afforded some of those advantages. The comments of the white "gifted" students in this study are in keeping with much of the available evidence on the way in which white and middle-class parents secure educational advantages for their children, including work by Lee Hubbard and Hugh Mehan, Annette Lareau, Jeannie Oakes and her colleagues, and Timothy Sieber.[28] In *Shades of White*, a study of racial identities among white high school students, Pamela Perry recalls being told by a school counselor that "she gets pressure from white parents to have their children placed in the accelerated classes and, given the difficulty of assigning so many students, she often succumbed to the parents' wishes."[29] In Ellen Brantlinger's research on middle-class school advantage, she describes how the mothers in her study, all of whom are white, "believe that advocating for school advantage for their children is integral to being a good parent."[30] The mothers' recollections of lobbying for their children to ensure that they did not miss any available educational opportunity, share many of the same features of the recollections of the adolescents quoted above.

In contrast, the black students reported few such incidents of parents lobbying to secure increased opportunities for their children. None of the sixteen black "gifted" students mentioned their parents pushing for their placement in the program or in advanced classes. In fact, in one incident in which an opportunity to be placed in an advanced class did not materialize for a black middle school student, he did not even bother to involve his parents. According to Hakim, during middle school, his teacher "said that she was going to squeeze [him] up from pre-algebra to algebra," but it "never happened."

Interviewer: And when she didn't put you in, what happened? Did you ask, did anybody ask...?

Hakim: I just let it go. She said it *might* happen, you know, you can't go by that.

Interviewer: Right. And what did you think about it? Did you—do you have any idea why it didn't happen?

Hakim: No, no. Mm-mm [no].

Interviewer: And you never asked?

Hakim: Naw, I just let it go, you know.

Interviewer: Did your parents know about it at all?

Hakim: No, no.

Note the difference between Hakim's response to this incident and Kara's account of fighting for placement in honors algebra in ninth grade. Kara, a white "gifted" student, refused to accept the school's recommendation for her lower-level course placement. Instead, she got her "parents to come down [to the school] and put me in honors." Hakim, a black "non-gifted" student, seemed resigned to his current placement, because as he explained, the higher-level placement was not promised. Kara thought she belonged in the higher-level course, and her parents made sure she ended up there. Hakim was not certain where he belonged, and his parents, who never knew that he might have been able to take a more advanced class, did not intervene.

Students' recollections of their initial placement as gifted, as well as their parents' actions to help them secure such placements, suggest that the label itself confers important advantages to those who have it. The next section, which explores the academic and social benefits of taking classes with friends, traces the link between gifted students' course selections and the composition of their friendship groups. Students with gifted status have the advantage of rarely having to decide between a course in which they are likely to be comfortable socially versus one where they are likely to be comfortable academically. For them, these two course-selection criteria overlap.

Friends in High Places

Having friends in class was an important consideration in all students' course-selection deliberations because friends provided an additional source of comfort, and, by extension, strengthened the sense of belonging. Students often indicated that they felt more comfortable, both socially and academically, in classes in which they knew and were friends with others. This is a scenario, which, as one informant put it, "breaks down the walls." Under these conditions, students reported that they were more engaged in class, and participated more often and openly. Clearview senior Ingrid explained that she is usually "really quiet" in class, "unless one of my good friends are in there," in which case she will "talk a lot." Miki, a black student at Franklin, also reported that she and one of her friends "talk[ed] more than everybody else" in their honors English class and that she generally was more "talkative" and sociable in classes in which she had friends.

Ernest, a black senior at Banaker, said that the black and white students in his pre-calculus class are "tight" and that they tend to be more actively engaged in the class compared to other students. He explained that because there were so few Asian American students in the class, for example, they tended to be "somewhat conservative."

> *Ernest*: Like in class we're like fired up to answer questions and fired up, you know, to shout out—
> *Interviewer*: The blacks and the whites do?
> *Ernest*: And I think it's because it's not, like, a whole lot of Asian people who actually go to this school, and it's not a whole lot of Asian people in the class, so they'll stand up and go to the board and stuff like that, but it just seems as if, you know, we're more comfortable, and we're able to just go ahead and, you know, call it out and . . . [*He laughs.*]

Preston, a white freshman at Dalton, explained that, for him, honors courses provide "a better learning environment" because "first," you are "in there with everybody you know." When asked later in the interview why he liked being in honors classes, Preston again focused on having friends in the class: "Well, because you're in there with your friends, it's easier to relate and you always have something to talk about and look forward to, and the teacher knows that we know each other, so that breaks down the walls even with the new ones."

For Kimmi, a black junior at Banaker, the advantage of having friends in the class had more to do with academic support: "If you don't understand, like me and my friends, we'll discuss, even if on the phone three-way or something, we all talking about something and then somebody will be like, 'I didn't understand such and such today.' You should have two people or two friends that can say, 'Well, this is what I got out of it.' So then you're going to have your friends as your backbone." Other informants echoed these sentiments about the importance of having friends in class and also mentioned that they study with friends, talk about class-related topics outside of class, "give each other ideas," and generally "help each other out."

All students generally felt more comfortable in classes in which they had friends, but white students were more likely than others were to explicitly cite "friends" as an appeal of advanced classes. Adolescent friendship groups are most likely to be intra-racial (same race) and advanced classes tend to be predominantly white.[31] As a result, white students were less likely than others to feel conflicted about where they belonged academically and where they belonged socially. This was particularly true for white "gifted" students, for whom advanced classes evoked the strongest sense of belonging. After he had commented that "some of my best friends are in-class mates" and "most of my friends are in AP and honors classes," the interviewer asked Tony, the dyslexic "gifted" student, how he felt about taking those classes. He responded, "That's where I'm supposed to be. That's where everybody, all my peers are." Not surprisingly, "gifted" students routinely reported that their friends did not have any reaction to their course placements. As Preston explained, "mainly we're in there together, so you'd expect them to be in there with you."

For students whose friends were not in their classes, the classroom experience was less enjoyable. Ursala, a middle-class white student taking general education classes exclusively, was isolated in some of her classes at Avery because, as she explained, "Most of my friends are in honors classes." Ursala reported that she did not like some of her classes because of "the people that are in them." Her experience of isolation from her friends, though unusual among the twenty-four white informants, was comparable to the experience of a number of black informants enrolled in advanced classes. With the exception of students at Banaker and those with interracial friendships, such as Zora, black students in advanced classes tended to feel isolated and uncomfortable.

Zora included among her close friends at Avery many of her basketball teammates, almost all of whom were white. When asked about her experience in advanced classes, her response was nearly identical to white informants'. She reported that she was comfortable in her classes and that her friends never teased her about taking advanced classes because they were enrolled in the same classes. Only black students at Banaker reported a similar or higher degree of comfort in their advanced classes. In fact, the only black students to cite "friends" as an appeal of advanced classes were those attending Banaker, such as Ernest. Other informants in that school's IB program described their relationships with IB classmates as "a family-type thing." Many of these students had been together in the IB program since middle school.

Having friends in class was no less important to black students at racially diverse and predominantly white schools. However, because there were so few blacks enrolled in advanced courses at these schools (see table 4.1), many who wished to take advanced classes had to give the importance of friends in class less priority in their decision making. The black students at these schools were aware of the racial imbalance in their advanced classes (it was they, rather than the interviewer, who initiated the discussion about how many black students were in their advanced classes), but many claimed that they were unaffected by it, at least academically. As the students explained, they were accustomed to the situation, and while many were not close friends with their white classmates, they usually were acquainted with one another. In a discussion about the students in his honors classes, for example, Shawn, a black senior at Clearview, mentioned that there were only "a few blacks." Yet, when asked about that experience, he responded, "Most of my honors classes are like that. . . . I don't let it affect me, I'm just there to get my studies off, but most of the white people, they're cool, it really don't bother me in a sense."

Kendra, who also was a senior, maintained that the racial isolation she experienced in her advanced classes at Franklin "didn't stop [her] from learning," but she acknowledged that she initially felt uncomfortable with the situation. While explaining that at her school whites are most likely to be in honors and AP classes, she reported, ". . . there are only three black people in that whole [AP English] class," and "my honors chemistry, there weren't but like two of us in that one." Describing how she felt in that situation, Kendra said, "At first, like my AP class, when I first got in that class I was like, I felt intimidated at first. After that I just felt like myself, whatever, you know. So, it doesn't really matter to me. At first it did, though, because I was like, 'Oh my gosh! They'll be looking at me, making sure I say everything this way, and everything that way.'" Kendra's response to the experience of being one of the few black students in an advanced class is not unusual, as black students in this situation often are initially anxious and self-conscious.[32]

Although comfortable in her advanced classes academically and accustomed to the isolation, Dalton junior Tamela wished it could be different. She imagined she would have more fun and feel more comfortable socially if other black students were enrolled in the classes she was taking:

Interviewer: OK, do you like being in the honors and AP classes?
Tamela: I mean I would like it for the education-wise thing but, it's, like, in my AP U.S. history course, I'm the only black person in there, right. And, I mean, as far as talking to the other people and whatnot, but I'll—But, it's, they don't really relate to me, you know what I'm saying? If I could, like, if I could just have, like, the other [black] girl

from, that I met in sixth grade. She's in AP U.S. history too, but she's in first period. And so like if she was in my class, I mean, I would, I mean it would be more fun for me. I'm sayin', not that it's not fun now, but it would just be—better. I would feel more comfortable.

Note the similarities here to the experiences of the academically successful black students described in chapters 2 and 3. These students' accounts reinforce the point that enrollment in advanced classes in racially diverse and predominantly white schools often entails social isolation for black students.

At Avery, Dalton, Clearview, East, and Franklin high schools, black students were underrepresented in most advanced courses relative to their enrollment at the school, and sometimes significantly so (see table 4.1). This was especially true at Dalton (Tamela's school), where blacks were 39 percent of the total student body but no more than 12 percent of those enrolled in any of the seven advanced courses included in the analysis. In two courses, AP Biology and AP Calculus, there were no black students enrolled. As Tamela's comments confirm, these conditions can make taking advanced courses an alienating experience for black students because they are isolated from their friends, who are most likely to be other black students. The same is often true for Latino students. For example, a Latino student in Annegret Staiger's ethnography of a racially diverse California high school explained to her that he would not want to be in the mostly white gifted program because, "If a Latino gets in, he won't see no more Latinos. . . . I wouldn't see no Hispanics in there. I wouldn't relate to nobody out there."[33] White middle-class students, in particular, rarely seem to face a choice between being with friends and taking advanced courses.[34] For them, one choice does not necessarily preclude the other.[35]

Of course, students can have interracial friendships, but generally, student friendship groups are racially segregated. As Robert Crosnoe notes, friendships are "guided by opportunities to meet and by forces that increase attraction."[36] Thus, as long as young people continue to experience racially segregated classrooms, schools, and neighborhoods, racial divisions are likely to persist. Indeed, although schools can potentially provide many opportunities for young people to meet, those opportunities are limited, directly and indirectly, by racialized tracking and related placement decisions. Gifted programs, found in many public elementary and middle schools, contribute to the initial sorting process that sets black and white students on different academic paths as very young children.[37] By high school, gifted students typically have been together for a long period of time. Repeatedly sharing classroom experiences and "giftedness," as well as racial and social class characteristics increases the chances that these students will form friendships with one another. Previous research confirms that assignment to the same class, program, ability group, or track is a primary means by which students meet and become friends with one another.[38]

In fact, informants often mentioned that they had been in advanced classes or gifted programs with many of the same students since elementary or middle school. Lila, a white junior at Avery, said of her honors and AP classes, it is "the same people over and over." Franklin junior Ned reported that he hangs out with "a mix of AP and honors students," adding that "a lot of [my] friends are from sixth-grade AG." The following exchange between Gina, a white senior at Clearview, and the interviewer underscores the longevity of these associations and friendships:

> *Interviewer*: And who are those people [in your advanced classes]? Are those people that you've been in school—?
> *Gina*: Yeah, I've been in classes with them basically my whole life.
> *Interviewer*: Since elementary school?
> *Gina*: Yeah, some of them.
> *Interviewer*: And are those students who were in AG with you?
> *Gina*: Yeah, some of them are.
> *Interviewer*: Would you say that the majority of them were, or not?
> *Gina*: The majority of them were in AG; they may not have been in there with me, because they were from different elementary schools, but we were all in the AG classes in junior high, so yeah.

For these students, long-term gifted placement may not necessarily provide the same "family-type" environment in advanced classes that black students at Banaker described in their IB classes, but it does guarantee them a certain level of familiarity and comfort with their classmates. For white students, especially, it also seems to guarantee that they will be among friends.

As I described above, selecting advanced courses was an obvious choice for many gifted students; these classes were simply where they felt they belonged. Because black students are afforded fewer opportunities for gifted participation, they are more likely to find themselves isolated in advanced classes if they elect to take them in racially diverse and predominantly white high schools. This kind of isolation is particularly likely for black students in advanced classes if these students lack the "gifted" label, since that would mean that they had not had the opportunity to develop friendships over time with their classmates.

Conclusion

In the formal tracking systems of the past, race and social class were among the key criteria used to allocate students to curriculum tracks. Today, this approach has been replaced by one in which, theoretically, students select the courses they wish to take. Given this change, the uneven distribution of students by race (and class) in curriculum tracks in high schools is perplexing. My objective in this chapter was to shed light on the factors responsible for contemporary racial patterns in track location by investigating how students make course-selection decisions. Some researchers have suggested that black students avoid taking advanced classes because they fear they will be perceived to be acting white and consequently will be ostracized by their black peers. Yet my analysis of transcripts of individual interviews conducted with sixty-one high school students showed that all students' deliberations center, in large part, on their assessments of where they belong; that is, where they believe they will be most comfortable both academically and socially.

For all students, the ability to do well in a given course was a first-order consideration. Students chose courses in which they expected to do well and avoided those they considered academically risky. They sought course options they believed would provide opportunities to feel competent. The comments of lower-achieving students quoted in this chapter make clear students' preference for successful academic experiences. They also provide additional insight into the link between a sense of academic incompetence and disengagement from school that scholars such as Claude Steele and Jomills Braddock have stressed.[39] Whereas students with a history of prior high academic achievement, and gifted identification, in particular, were likely to elect advanced courses, other students avoided those courses. They opted instead for the lower-level classes, where they expected to feel comfortable because the chances for failure were lower.

As other studies have found, prior placement and achievement are part of the explanation for students' location in the tracking structure of the contemporary high school. But prior placement and achievement involve more than differences in ability; they also create psychological and social effects that persist over time. Even as tracking has become less formal and rigid and high school teachers and counselors have ceded some of the control over placement to students and parents, old patterns of racial imbalance have persisted. It is achievement trajectories that are laid out in elementary and middle school that now restrict students to a higher or lower track when they reach high school. Indeed, the students' narratives show how the new "laissez-faire" system of tracking operates to produce outcomes not unlike the older, more formal system. Researchers studying tracking have long noted how little "choice" students really have in track placement. As Joan Spade, Lynn Columba, and Beth Vonfossen contend, "By the time a student reaches high school, many social and interpersonal forces converge to make it appear that the process of course selection is based on personal choice."[40]

One of the more powerful forces influencing students' "choice" in course selection is gifted identification, or the lack of it. Students who had been identified as gifted were significantly more likely to enroll in advanced courses than students who had not been so labeled; the former expressed greater confidence in their abilities and believed that as a result of their "superior" intellect, they required more challenging educational material. "Non-gifted" students, on the other hand, were more likely to shy away from courses they considered challenging. Many did not believe they were "smart enough" or capable of doing the level of work required in advanced courses. They believed that the lower-level classes they selected were where students with their shortcomings belonged.

"Gifted" students, too, believed that they were where they belonged based on their talents and needs. But once formally identified as gifted, students are set on a trajectory of achievement that includes exposure to challenging curricular materials and placement in advanced classes as they progress through primary and secondary school, as well as access to learning opportunities that can lead to higher test scores. According to psychologist Lauren Resnick, this "system is a self-sustaining one in which hidden assumptions are continually reinforced by the inevitable results of practices that are based on those assumptions." She argues that, "Children who have not been taught a demanding, challenging, *thinking curriculum* do not do well on tests of reasoning or problem solving, confirming our original suspicions that they did not have the talent for that kind of thinking."[41] My investigation of students' course-selection decision making suggests that exposure to a more challenging curriculum as well as the confidence gained from the gifted label itself facilitates the mobility of gifted students. The mobility of other students, on the other hand, is often restricted by their failure to achieve gifted status and, subsequently, their lack of exposure to a "demanding, challenging, thinking curriculum."

More problematic still is the racial variation in gifted identification in North Carolina (and elsewhere). This long-standing imbalance only exacerbates the divide, both academic and social, between black and white students. The disparity in placement may well be implicated in the persistence and widening of the test score gap between whites and blacks over the course of children's schooling.[42] In fact, Robert Dreeben and Adam Gamoran have found that "when black and nonblack first graders are exposed to similar instruction, they do comparably well."[43] Furthermore, more recent research by Angel Harris and Keith Robinson shows that students' prior skills explain significantly more of the black-white achievement gap than behaviors.[44] The results of the present analysis suggest that increasing the competence, confidence, and comfort of blacks and other students of color through exposure to more rigorous curricular materials and instruction may be a particularly effective solution for narrowing the achievement gap.

Additionally, as long as tracking and grouping structures continue to divide students along racial lines in elementary and middle school, interracial interaction will be limited and racial divisions in friendships will persist through high school and beyond. Although many youth today are attending racially diverse schools, there is little evidence that they are benefiting from that diversity, because, as the experiences of the students in this book show, their classrooms remain largely segregated.

Formed primarily within classrooms, friendship networks supply comfort and support, benefits that many students prioritized in their course-selection deliberations. Taking classes with friends increased students' comfort levels and enhanced their academic and social experience, thus heightening the appeal of these courses. Students relied on friends for help with class work, studying, and missed assignments, and they participated more in classes they shared with friends.

When considering advanced courses, however, students may give comfort and support even greater priority because of the presumed difficulty of the courses. They may reason that the course load and work in advanced classes is challenging enough without the additional stress of social isolation and having to make new friends. Thus, those whose friendship networks include few "gifted" students or others likely to enroll in advanced classes may be less willing to consider enrolling in advanced classes. In general, race will matter in these deliberations insofar as (1) one group is overrepresented among the school's gifted and high-achieving students and others are underrepresented among these groups, and (2) high school students have few cross-racial friendships.

In explaining their decisions to enroll in advanced courses, most white students mentioned that their friends were in the same classes. Thus, for these students, enrolling in advanced courses usually did not involve a choice between friends and academic striving. By contrast, black students were less likely to cite the presence of friends as an appeal of advanced courses, because few high-achieving blacks shared advanced courses with same-race peers. As a result, black informants were more likely to downplay or disregard the importance of friends when they made their course decisions. Academically successful black students acknowledged that few of their peers were enrolled in advanced classes, and that the absence of same-race friends sometimes made them uncomfortable. Nevertheless, they did not avoid enrolling in these classes. When black students considered race in their decisions, it was primarily with respect to deliberations on the degree of racial and social isolation they expected to experience in a particular course. In other words, they made their decisions in light of particular institutional constraints, and these included race-based factors. In schools with racialized tracking, black students must be especially achievement-oriented and willing to sacrifice their own social comfort in order to take advanced classes in which they are likely to be isolated from their friends, who are most likely to be black. Given the high number of academically successful students in this study, my analysis likely underestimates the extent to which this situation negatively influences the course-taking decisions of blacks and other students of color.

Being ridiculed by peers for high academic achievement is a concern for some black students, as I showed in chapters 2 and 3. However, the findings in this chapter suggest that for most students, this is not the primary consideration when selecting courses. In opting out of advanced courses, students' desire to avoid feelings of incompetence that accompany failure is the more important consideration. As documented in the previous chapters, most high-achieving students found ways to offset their peers' negative perceptions when that was an issue, and they continued to strive to do well. Thus, I would argue that where matters of school achievement are concerned, in making decisions, the weight adolescents give to peers' and friends' perceptions varies depending on the individual adolescent's level of achievement and self-perceptions of ability. Relative to their less academically successful peers, academically successful students, because they are more likely to have plans to attend college, tend to believe that they have more at stake than the possibility of being ridiculed or ostracized.

Finally, this chapter also revealed that for most students, the decision to take higher-level courses is motivated less by an interest in gaining particular knowledge and skills and more by a desire to gain a competitive advantage. The danger in this, according to David Labaree, is that it "reinforces the value of tokens of educational accomplishment (grades, credits, and degrees) at the expense of substance (the acquisition of useful knowledge and skill), turning education into little more than a game of 'how to succeed in school without really learning.' "[45] We can hardly fault the students for this, though, because American society has long promoted schooling as little more than a path to upward social mobility and material wealth.

Restoring
The Promise of *Brown*

M UCH OF THE EVIDENCE I have presented in the preceding chapters
tells a rather disheartening story of broken promises. More than fifty
years after the Supreme Court outlawed the doctrine of "separate but equal,"
curriculum tracking leaves many North Carolina public schools officially
desegregated but far from integrated. Generally, in the literature about school
segregation, concerns have centered on the overall racial composition of the
student body and the startling rate at which schools are resegregating.[1] The
racial composition of the student body, however, tells only part of the story
about equality of educational opportunity in the post-*Brown* era. Blacks and
whites may have access to the same schools, but as we observed and heard
from students in numerous schools in North Carolina, they often do not have
access to the same curriculum. Black students are disproportionately underrepresented in gifted programs and in advanced courses, especially in predominantly white and racially diverse schools. These racialized placement
patterns, which are not unique to North Carolina, present various challenges
for black students.

In examining some of these challenges, I paid particular attention to the
phenomenon of students casting academic achievement as acting white. Two
concerns prompted this focus. First, there is mounting evidence of a connection between the emergence of racialized tracking structures in the aftermath
of desegregation and the use of the acting white slur with respect to academic
achievement. Yet, relatively little attention has been paid to this relationship.[2]
Second, the topic of acting white continues to arise in scholarly, journalistic,

and lay debates about black students' academic underperformance, but there is still no consensus on its meaning or impact. Surprisingly few studies have attempted to provide answers to why and how achievement-related behaviors have come to be defined as acting white, and how this affects black students. So, although we have known for a long time that we have a problem, we have remained uncertain about what the problem is and why it exists.

The consequences of this kind of lack of understanding are nicely captured in the upstream/downstream fable. The fable centers on a village called Downstream whose inhabitants have for years contended with the problem of spotting people being swept along in the river. At first the village was so ill-equipped to deal with the problem that most of the people caught in the currents drowned. However, over time, the village's response to the crisis improved and many lives were saved. The villagers built a hospital close to the river; they had many expert swimmers living in the village, ready to respond when victims were seen; and they had a fleet of boats on hand for the rescues. Equipped with the best facilities and an effective set of procedures, the Downstreamers eventually were well prepared to respond to the large numbers of people they saw in the river as it flowed by their village. Although they were not always able to save all the people who ended up in the water each day, they did save many. And while the costs were enormous, the villagers were proud of their system and pleased that they were able to save so many lives. The fable ends with this passage: "Oh, a few people in Downstream have raised the question now and again, but most folks show little interest about what's happening Upstream. It seems there's so much to do to help those in the river, that nobody's got time to check how all those bodies are getting there in the first place. That's the way things are, sometimes."[3] In writing *Integration Interrupted*, my goal was to look upstream to return us to the fundamental question of why black students define academic achievement as acting white in the first place.

The Connection between Tracking and the New Meaning of Acting White

As the preceding chapters have shown, when schools visibly and unmistakably sort students by race, academic placement can become a part of youth's own boundary making. This occurs especially during adolescence, when black youth are actively working on, as psychologist Beverly Daniel Tatum writes, "finding the answer to questions such as, 'What does it mean to be a black person? How should I act? What should I do?'"[4] Some have argued that such questions reify race. But racially segregated classrooms exist, as do other racially segregated private and public spaces in American life. These realities buttress the idea of race and the notion that race is what makes us fundamentally different. As long as such stark patterns of racial segregation persist questions about racial identity may be inevitable, especially among African American adolescents. Philosophers Lionel McPherson and Tommie Shelby make this point, noting that, "The preoccupation of African Americans with their racial identity seems largely, if not entirely, the result of the historical and contemporary obsession of other groups, especially whites, with the heritable characteristics of those of African descent."[5]

Thus, as I showed in chapter 2, for black youth who attend schools in which the racial disparity in tracking and achievement is glaring, particular achievement-related behaviors are more likely to become part of the repertoire of things that define what it means to be a black person and what blacks do. Like other institutional structures, tracking shapes students' experiences. It does more than set students on a particular path, however. It also contributes to the kinds of situations with which students must contend and colors how they view the educational system and their place in it. The findings presented throughout this book demonstrate that repeated exposure to racialized tracking creates beliefs about a relationship between race and achievement (and intelligence) that black and white students recognize and act on. There is no question that tracking continues to contribute to the "stereotyping of students," as James Rosenbaum found more than thirty years ago.[6] If it seems as though equating high achievement with whiteness has become entrenched, it is because racialized achievement hierarchies are part of many black youth's experience in school. The historical relationship between blacks and whites in America, on its own, has little bearing on the way black students today *initially* approach schooling and academic achievement. What happens to black students as they spend time within schools does more to activate feelings of distrust and "otherness" than does knowledge of the history of blacks in America or the experiences of significant others in black students' lives.

The student narratives quoted in this book make clear that responses to the peculiar experience of racialized tracking vary. For example: Sandra was "devastated." Juliana laughingly reminded her black peers, "I'm still the same person, ain't nothing different." Curtis dismissed his peers' comments, remarking disdainfully, "I never let it get to me because their opinion really doesn't matter." Black youth are not an undifferentiated mass. They are located throughout the economic and social class structure, as well as throughout the achievement structure. They have different religious affiliations and belong to groups of various kinds. Each and all of these affiliations may affect how they make sense of their schooling experiences. Some students may rely on the dominant achievement ideology to understand the racial disparities they observe. Thus, they may interpret black students' underrepresentation in advanced classes as an indication that most black students do not work as hard as other students do or that they are in some way deficient. Other students may seek alternative explanations to account for the racial disparities they observe. All students, though, are likely to try to make sense of what they see and experience in ways that will "preserve, protect, and defend" their essential selves. As John Hewitt explains, "We want to feel positively toward ourselves, to value what we are."[7] Thus, lower-achieving black students, in particular, may draw on the African American cultural tool kit for particular discourses of race that will allow them to dismiss the visible hierarchy of achievement and "feel positively" about themselves.

The acting white slur, which has a long history among African Americans, can be thought of both as youth's "in vivo" coding of the repeated manifestation of achievement as white that they observe in school, and as an expression of resentment of these daily reminders of their own low status. In each high-achieving black student's account of being accused of acting white because of achievement-related behaviors, there was evidence that others perceived (rightly or wrongly) him or her as arrogant or snobbish. Thus, I argue that youth are drawing on the acting white slur both as a means of retaliation and as a means to make sense of the tracking patterns they observe in ways that shield them (individually and as a group) from painful negative stereotypes and evaluations. Ridiculing their peers for acting white lets them capture the meaning of racialized tracking in ways that, if only symbolically, restore their sense of power and control in school. They are simultaneously able to reject those who reject them and deny that they want what the school has to offer.

The Impact of Oppositionality on Black Academic Achievement

Only a small number of participants in any study reported on in this book experienced ostracism or taunts of acting white because of their academic achievement or achievement-related behaviors. Therefore, it is important to stress that every black student who attends a school in which students are racially segregated within the curriculum *does not* come to associate achievement with whiteness or to experience dissonance when she excels. Many high-achieving black students reported some teasing, but it was the type of generic name calling (e.g., "geek" or "nerd") that most high-achiev-ing American adolescents face. Indeed, in the typical American high school, studious, hardworking students are rarely part of the popular or leading crowd (unless they also participate in sports or some other "normal" extra-curricular activity).[8]

American adolescents are quite conscious of the potential for studious, high-achieving students to be ridiculed at school. Thus, similar to their white counterparts, many of the high-achieving black adolescents discussed in this book were careful to negotiate a balance between excelling academi-cally and conforming to peer norms. In chapter 3, I described how, for some adolescents, the period of negotiation was relatively short and uncompli-cated. This group of adolescents, whom I called *secure*, expressed a greater degree of clarity and firmness regarding their identity, goals, and beliefs than others did. And, if confronted with oppositional peer cultures, they seemed better able to resist pressures to conform. *Secure* adolescents were quick to dismiss other people's perceptions of them. As Yvette put it, "I don't really care what other people think about me. I'm going to try to do good. If you don't want to do good, that's on you." Gwen had a similarly dismissive response to her peers' perceptions: "I look at it as, this is my future I'm working on, so, nothing else really matters." *Secure* adolescents asserted that they knew who they were, where they were headed, and what it would take to get there. As might be expected, these students easily rejected or ignored racialized and other peer pressure that might have taken them off course academically.

Other high-achieving adolescents had a more difficult time ignoring the norms and expectations of peers at their schools. These students, whom I called *vulnerable*, expressed more insecurity and uncertainty about their iden-tities, beliefs, and/or goals. They were more concerned with being liked and accepted by others. When they encountered oppositional peer cultures, they made greater attempts to adjust their behavior to fit in among their peers. Keisha summed up this strategy succinctly, saying, "Try not to know every-thing. Try to make people like you." For *vulnerable* adolescents, racialized tracking proved to be especially threatening, because it increased the poten-tial for racialized ridicule and contributed to greater concerns about fitting in with the black crowd. Many of the students I labeled *vulnerable* recalled them-selves being most susceptible to the opinions of their peers during middle school and the first two years of high school. As juniors and seniors, these adolescents often also described more recent experiences in which they seemed to have developed greater self-awareness and a better sense of direction. For *vulnerable* adolescents, the process of becoming *secure* seemed to take longer, and was at times intense. Over time, however, fitting in became less important to most of the high-achieving black adolescents I studied, as they began to look ahead to the future and to focus more intently on their post–high school goals.

My findings suggest that concerns about the impact of oppositional peer cultures on black students' academic achievement may be overstated, particularly for students with a history of high academic achievement. Even when they were bothered by peer pressure, most high-achieving adolescents did not substantially alter their behavior. The adjustments they made either were short-lived or had little direct bearing on academic achievement. For example, most *vulnerable* adolescents devised positive ways of fitting in with their black peers. Some made a conscious effort to "hang out" with fellow blacks more often and/or to dress in a fashion similar to the "normal black" crowd. Such strategies were socially effective and at the same time did not negatively influence these adolescents' achievement-related behaviors or their achievement. It is unfortunate, though, that at the time in the life course when young people struggle most with fitting in, school structures effectively require them to choose between friends and opportunities to learn. This is a predicament which, as explained in chapter 4, disproportionately affects black (and other racial and ethnic minority) students. Yet these students persisted in advanced classes despite, at times, their own reluctance and discomfort. Unquestionably, study participants sometimes felt frustrated and distressed in school environments characterized by visible hierarchies in track placement and achievement. Academically successful students, however, were generally resilient; many persevered in the face of racial isolation and other difficult situations at school.

None of the students featured in this book reported dropping out of or avoiding advanced courses solely or in part because of their frustration with racial isolation in those courses. Their determination and persistence is laudatory, but it may not be generalizable. It may be a result of an overrepresentation of "gifted" students and others with a history of high academic achievement. It may be that the focus of the studies or the methods used to recruit participants did not allow us to capture the experiences of a broad enough range of black students.[9] A black student in one of my undergraduate classes noted that he had dropped out of advanced classes in high school because he "wanted to be in the same track" as the group of friends he had had since elementary school. Isolated from his friends and excluded by his new classmates, most of whom were white and female, this student reported that he recalled feeling "as if I were an outsider in my own school." It is not hard to imagine that other similarly positioned students may make the same decision to opt out of advanced classes. Therefore, my analysis may have underestimated the extent to which racialized tracking negatively affects the achievement trajectory of otherwise capable black students. This is certainly an area in which more research is warranted. There is also a need for better measures to capture the effects of the acting white slur and other racialized ridicule on black students' academic achievement. Research on oppositional peer cultures and on student track placement must also pay greater attention to the racial composition of both schools and classrooms.

Shifting the Responsibility of Racial Progress from Generation to Generation

The issue of racialized tracking deserves far more attention than it has received, not only from the courts and school officials, but from all American adults. Most of the high-achieving adolescents I studied took their separation from other blacks at school in stride. Even as they acknowledged their own concerns and insecurities, they were prepared to do what they deemed necessary to achieve the goal of attending college. Is this fair? Why do we expect these young people to dismiss their concerns about being excluded or having their presence and performance excessively scrutinized when many adults remain unable or unwilling to overcome their own concerns about crossing racial boundaries? American adults continue to oppose integration in their neighborhoods and leisure activities, and in their places of worship and work sites. Why do we expect the youth of this nation to address race-related issues more effectively than many of their elders do? Why should they be capable of meaningful interracial relationships when we neither encourage such relationships nor systematically provide the space required for them to develop? Why should the nation's young people be expected to take the risks that adults regularly avoid? Compared to adolescents, whose identities are in flux, adults should feel more psychically secure crossing racial boundaries. But even a cursory look at American public and private spaces suggests that we do not. What responsibility do adults have to the next generation with respect to real integration? How long will we continue to pass to the next generation the burden of what we cannot or will not do in the present? Despite a tremendous improvement in race relations in this country since 1954, each succeeding generation nevertheless has inherited a nation marked by deep-seated racial divisions and lingering hostility. The system of tracking I have described in this book helps to promote rather than prevent these problems.

No institution in our society brings together as many diverse young people for as much time over an extended period as schools do. Thus, schools have a unique opportunity to lead the movement toward a truly integrated society. Aside from promoting multiracial sports teams and athletic programs, however, schools are doing little to foster and cultivate healthy and meaningful cross-racial relationships. More than half a century after *Brown*, many schools continue to fall short of the goals of integration. Rather than bringing students of different racial and social class backgrounds together as equals, schools now separate them by establishing unequal status through race and class hierarchies. This kind of institutionalized sorting breeds animosity and resentment among students and leaves some high-achieving black students feeling frustrated and alone. Thus, we have eliminated one system of school segregation only to replace it with another. Moreover, racialized tracking presents an image that continues to send the same messages about racial difference and black intellectual inferiority propagated during the eras of slavery and Jim Crow segregation, albeit now in a more subtle and covert manner. Consequently, tracking, as it is currently practiced in North Carolina and other parts of the country, compounds the problem of race for the next generation. It negates the goals of an integrated society and adds yet another aspect to the various ways in which black and white youth perceive themselves to be different from one another.

The Larger Problem of Social Inequality

Tracking in the aftermath of desegregation should not be understood as simply an issue of racial intolerance, however. The findings in this book support previous research that has shown that tracking is another tool in an intense competition over scarce goods and resources (e.g., quality education, access to good colleges and universities, and high-paying, high-status jobs).[10] In this post-desegregation era, many middle-class, white Americans perceive their privileged position as being increasingly encroached upon and challenged by other racial and ethnic groups and working-class whites. In K–12 public education, tracking is one strategy middle-class whites have used in their fight to preserve their standing. Yet as David Labaree reminds us, one of the consequences of treating education as a private good, as a tool to "enhance the competitive social position of the degree holder," is that it "leaves no one watching out for the public interest in education—no one making sure that education is providing society with the competent citizens and productive workers that the country's political and economic life requires."[11] As parents push to secure advantages for their children through gifted programs and other stratifying and divisive practices, without regard for the children who are left behind, they undermine the larger goals of public education.

As I showed in chapter 4, participation in gifted programs boosted young people's achievement and confidence, and those benefits persisted through high school. Indeed, gifted identification had a significant positive influence on these students' high school course choices. Having met with early academic success and been formally designated as "gifted," they were determined to continue on that path. By high school, "gifted" students had come to see themselves as smart. They expected to do well. Other students were also influenced by their early academic experiences and placements. "Non-gifted" students and those who had had fewer experiences of success were less certain of their paths and were more cautious in their academic choices. They preferred to take "easy" courses in which they were confident they could do well rather than more challenging courses. The early separation of students into "gifted" and "non-gifted" allows for a less rigid high school tracking system, as the labels relieve schools of the full responsibility for sorting students into their "appropriate" positions in the curriculum.

Struggles between school districts and parents and communities over diversity initiatives continue, with some playing out in widely publicized court cases.[12] Meanwhile, within-school segregation seems to go largely unnoticed by all but a few concerned and outspoken parents and educators.[13] Much of the public awareness of the problem of within-school segregation is focused on social segregation. For example, some observers have questioned why black students set themselves apart from whites and other racial and ethnic groups by sitting together in the cafeteria and in other social spaces at school. Educators and parents seem less concerned about the fact that black and white students are also segregated in the curriculum. Recognition of within-school segregation as a significant problem is complicated by the widespread perception that students' segregation is self-imposed, a matter of free choice. Because this view appears consistent with people's experiences and with what they have come to believe about black peer culture, it is powerful and difficult to alter. Yet, as the findings in this book demonstrate, this perception is flawed.

The effort to make sense of the association between achievement and race they observe in school is the first step in a process that leads some black youth to racialized oppositionality. As it stands now, black students are left to contend with this situation on their own.[14] But the responsibility to change racialized and other peer cultures oppositional to school norms and expectations rightfully belongs to adults. Similar expressions of oppositionality, particularly a culture of anti-intellectualism, pervade American society. The 2008 presidential election season provided a recent and dramatic example. Qualities such as intellectualism and an Ivy League education were often derided and framed as liabilities—for the job of president of the United States, no less. While the rhetoric of the American dream and the American achievement ideology tout these qualities and accomplishments as ideals to which all Americans should strive, contradictory messages are regularly communicated in American public life. A society can hardly expect its young people to live up to its highest ideals if adults express ambivalence about those standards, lauding them one day and denigrating them the next. This ambivalence underscores, again, the very real tensions that exist in this country between the haves and the have nots, and the latter's distrust and resentment of the former. Schools that sanction the system of racialized tracking, either by promoting it or ignoring it, must bear some responsibility for the growth of inter- and intra-group resentment. When schools are polarized by tracking, peer relations among and between groups become increasingly complicated.

Everyone hopes for upward social mobility, but we do not all achieve it. Adolescents who see themselves left behind seem to fear that their upwardly mobile peers will soon come to scorn them and treat them with the same contempt that other privileged people sometimes do. As some of the experiences of high-achieving black students in this research showed, and as studies of Latino and working-class white students have reported, lower-achieving peers often are offended by what they perceive to be high achievers' arrogance and haughtiness.[15] Some academically able youth may attempt to avoid such criticisms by figuring out how to cultivate and maintain relationships with their same-race and -class peers, even if doing so may mean jeopardizing their own achievement. By leaving racialized tracking unchallenged, we require some students to negotiate and devise strategies to minimize the fallout from a system that they neither created nor consented to, a system that demonstrably determines winners and losers based on their race and class. As one student, Shelly, said of this kind of tracking, "It's like they give you a target on your chest and then they give [other] people arrows to shoot at you." The behaviors of contemporary black students have to be understood within this context.

Making Good on the Promise of Brown

There are strategies that schools could pursue to dismantle the institutional structures that establish and maintain the type of environment Shelly described. Such strategies range from detracking,[16] to eliminating gifted programs and replacing them with a rigorous core curriculum for all students, to examining current placement practices and criteria to assess whether and how they contribute to racialized patterns and making changes where necessary.[17] Schools should work to abolish the repeated expression of achievement as white by, at a minimum, ensuring that ability groups, gifted programs, and individual classes are better integrated and that more than a token number of students of color are recognized as high achievers. These changes would help erode the perception that doing well in school is acting white. If that perception were to disappear, the cultural meaning of the term would shift.

To be most effective, the main goal of whatever strategy, or combination of strategies, schools embrace should be to do away with policies and practices that mark and visibly separate students in the curriculum. Although tracking ostensibly sorts on the basis of intellectual ability, it too often also categorizes students by race, social class, gender, neighborhood, and so forth. Such practices, whether they are intentional or not, reflect institutional racism and must be addressed. Most sorting practices convey powerful messages about who is smart, and more unfortunately, about who is not. They also signal what smartness looks like and sounds like. These are the messages students draw on as they construct views of themselves and others; these are the ideas and images that shape where they believe they and others fit within the school hierarchy. Most problematic, however, is how the practices that stratify students in the curriculum undermine the goals of public education as a common good. Thus, efforts to dismantle the institutional structures that lead to the achievement hierarchies based on race (and class) found at many of the schools described in this book would go a long way toward making good on the promise of *Brown*.

Schools have a dual responsibility. They should provide all children with a high-quality education that adequately prepares them for full participation in American society. They also should help children reach their highest potential, regardless of their race, family income, or parents' education. All children would benefit from early opportunities to build academic competence and confidence. Fully integrated schools would be a step in that direction. As the data and analysis in this book confirm, desegregated schools are not enough to achieve integration. We must also desegregate classrooms and provide more opportunities for young people to have meaningful interracial interactions within those classrooms. Doing so is not just for the good of African Americans and other youth of color; it is for the good of the entire society. My hope is that the research findings I have presented in this book will contribute to greater understanding of the consequences of within-school segregation and better position schools to restore the promise of *Brown*.

Introduction

1. U.S. Department of Education, National Center for Education Statistics, National Assessment of Educational Progress (NAEP), NAEP 2004 Trends in Academic Progress; unpublished tabulations, NAEP Data Explorer. Rev. March 29, 2010. Available: http://nces.ed.gov/nationsreportcard/nde/.

2. This argument is found in published research monographs, editorials, and the public comments of educators and high-profile commentators such as Bill Cosby and Spike Lee. For a detailed discussion of some of the comments made by black leaders and other public figures, see O'Connor, Horvat, and Lewis, "Framing the Field," 1–24.

3. "Transcript: Illinois Senate Candidate Barack Obama," *Washington Post*, July 27, 2004. Rev. October 17, 2005. Available: http://www.washingtonpost.com/wp-dyn/articles/A19751-2004Jul27.html. For similar remarks made while Obama was campaigning for president in 2007, see Bacon, "Obama Reaches Out with Tough Love."

4. "Speaking English Properly Is No Cause for Derision." Rev. January 4, 2006. Available: http://query.nytimes.com/gst/fullpage.html?res=9401EFDE1639F 933A25750C0A960958260. Similar teacher comments are also found in the research literature, including O'Connor, "Premise of Black Inferiority"; Tyson, Darity, and Castellino, "It's Not a Black Thing."

5. For more on this research, see Tyson, "Weighing In."

6. McWhorter, *Losing the Race.*

7. Throughout this book, I use the terms "high- and low-achieving" to describe students. These designations are based on judgments, mostly in the form of grades, rendered by schools. See the preface for information on the study of high-achieving students, which I refer to as *Effective Students.*

8. Student reports of similar experiences are found in the scholarly literature and the popular press. An example of the former is Mickelson and Velasco, "'Bring It On!'" An example of the latter is included among the recollections of Yma Johnson, the daughter of an African-born University of Michigan professor, published in the magazine *Michigan Today*. Johnson describes how in school she was made to feel that "if [she] ever wanted to have Black friends [she] would have to change." She recalls that "the majority of these encounters happened in the hallway because other Black students were almost never in advanced placement classes, another difference held against me. All the way through middle and high schools I was usually the only Black person in my Latin, French and Humanities classes." Johnson, "Travels in Mind and Space."

9. A recent study by Charles Clotfelter, Helen Ladd, and Jacob Vigdor found that classroom-level segregation in North Carolina was modest. However, the researchers focused on English classes. As I show in chapter 2, these tend to be less segregated than math and science classes. "Classroom Level Segregation and Resegregation in North Carolina," 70–86.

10. Other studies involving black students in predominantly black schools find similar results. See Akom, "Reexamining Resistance as Oppositional Behavior."

11. Prudence Carter also finds that black and Latino youth's most frequent use of the acting white slur is "in reference to speech and language styles." See "Intersecting Identities," 116.

12. Numerous other studies have reported similar effects of classroom racial composition on the experiences of high-achieving black students. See Butterfield, "To Be Young, Gifted, Black, and Somewhat Foreign," 133–155; Carter, *Keepin' It Real*; Horvat and Lewis, "Reassessing the 'Burden of Acting White,'"; Mickelson and Velasco, "'Bring It On!'"

13. Kunjufu, in *To Be Popular or Smart*, vii, has cautioned against attributing this phenomenon "solely to integration." He argues that, "There are schools that only African-American students attend, there are *no* white students, and they still say to be smart is to be white." Yet I know of no evidence, including that which Kunjufu presents, that supports his assertion. Kunjufu begins his book with ten African American students from a variety of Illinois high schools discussing their experiences with achievement in school. The only student who clearly indicates that black peers equated positive school achievement behaviors with whites was a student attending a desegregated school that Kunjufu described only as "very liberal on racial balance." In every other case, the experiences the students discussed had more to do with the anti-intellectualism that pervades American culture in general. I do not mean to imply that this is not a problem for black students. What I am arguing is that it is not a uniquely black phenomenon.

14. There are a few notable exceptions. Some scholars have suggested this connection in their work. See Carter, *Keepin' It Real*; Mickelson, "Subverting *Swann*";

Mickelson and Velasco, "'Bring It On!'"; O'Connor, "Premise of Black Inferiority."

15. See Welner, "Ability Tracking."

16. I had a similar reaction in an honors classroom at another school, but I later learned that the class was not actually an honors class. The teacher explained to me that due to a "scheduling mess" that "took five weeks to straighten out," the class contained students who were taking the course for general education credit and three, including the participant I was shadowing, who were taking it for honors credit.

17. This was the only advanced class I saw like that during my time observing three students at Earnshaw and it was never clear why.

18. See Diamond, "Still Separate and Unequal."

19. Clotfelter, *After* Brown.

20. Lucas and Berends, "Sociodemographic Diversity."

21. Important studies of within-school segregation include Clotfelter, *After* Brown; Lucas, *Tracking Inequality*; Lucas and Berends, "Sociodemographic Diversity"; Meier, Stewart, and England, *Race, Class and Education*; Oakes, *Keeping Track*; Orfield and Eaton, *Dismantling Desegregation*; Welner, *Legal Rights, Local Wrongs*.

22. See Brantlinger, *Dividing Classes*; Mickelson and Velasco, "'Bring It On!'"; Oakes, "Two Cities' Tracking"; Oakes and Guiton, "Matchmaking"; Ogbu, *Black American Students in an Affluent Suburb*; Staiger, *Learning Difference*; Tyson, Darity, and Castellino, "It's Not a Black Thing."

23. For more on this topic, see Ansalone, "Tracking"; and Meier, Stewart, and England, *Race, Class and Education*.

24. Reports that black and white students sit apart from one another in the cafeteria and other social spaces at school have persisted for many years. See Tatum, *"Why Are All the Black Kids Sitting Together in the Cafeteria?"*

25. The *Brown v. Board of Education, Topeka, Kansas* (347 U.S. 483) decision overturned the "separate-but-equal" doctrine legalized in 1896 in *Plessy v. Ferguson* (163 U.S. 537). In 1955, in *Brown II* (349 U.S. 294), the Supreme Court attempted to clarify its position on when and how desegregation should occur with the mandate that schools desegregate "with all deliberate speed."

26. See Clotfelter, *After* Brown; Donelan, Neal, and Jones, "The Promise of *Brown*"; Frazier, "Wrong Side of the Track"; Kozol, *Savage Inequalities*; Mickelson, "Incomplete Desegregation"; Oakes, "Two Cities' Tracking"; O'Connor, "Premise of Black Inferiority"; Perry, *Shades of White*; Staiger, *Learning Difference*; Steinhorn and Diggs-Brown, *By the Color of Our Skin*; Tatum, *"Why Are All the Black Kids Sitting Together in the Cafeteria?"*

27. Rosenbaum, *Making Inequality*, 165. For more on the salience of the categories tracking creates, see Bettie, *Women without Class*; Lee, *Unraveling the "Model Minority" Stereotype*; Staiger, *Learning Difference*.

28. See Bettie, *Women without Class*; Perry, *Shades of White*.

29. McArdle and Young, "Classroom Discussion of Racial Identity."

30. See Bergin and Cooks, "High School Students of Color"; Neal-Barnett, "Being Black"; Peterson-Lewis and Bratton, "Perceptions of 'Acting Black' among African American Teens."

31. See Griswold, *Cultures and Societies in a Changing World*.

32. Anne Galletta and William Cross make a similar argument about the importance of integration to understanding "oppositionality" among black students. See "Past as Present."

33. Annegret Staiger draws on her research at a California high school to argue that giftedness is a "racial project," and that "[m]agnet programs are devices in the arsenal of school desegregation." See "Whiteness as Giftedness," 161. See also Meier, Stewart, and England's *Race, Class, and Education* for a discussion of the use of tracking and disciplinary policies in efforts to resist desegregation.

34. See Katznelson and Weir, *Schooling for All*; Lucas, *Tracking Inequality*; Oakes, *Keeping Track*; Persell, *Education and Inequality*; Tyack, *One Best System*.

35. See Clotfelter, *After Brown*; Katznelson and Weir, *Schooling for All*.

36. See Katznelson and Weir, *Schooling for All*; Oakes, *Keeping Track*.

37. See Coleman, *Adolescent Society*; Rist, "Student Social Class and Teacher Expectations"; Sennett and Cobb, *Hidden Injuries of Class*; Stinchcombe, *Rebellion in a High School*.

38. Sennett and Cobb, *Hidden Injuries of Class*, 82.

39. See Campbell, *When a City Closes Its Schools*; Gates, *Making of Massive Resistance*; Muse, *Virginia's Massive Resistance*.

40. Andrews, "Movement-Countermovement Dynamics."

41. In the 1970s, this "white flight" was legally challenged. In 1974, in *Milliken v. Bradley* (418 U.S. 717), the Supreme Court rejected a plan that would have allowed busing across district lines to integrate heavily minority central city school districts with largely white suburban districts.

42. See Clotfelter, *After Brown*; Orfield and Eaton, *Dismantling Desegregation*; Meier, Stewart, and England, *Race, Class and Education*; Ogletree, *All Deliberate Speed*; Persell, *Education and Inequality*; Walters, "Educational Access and the State."

43. See Chemerinsky, "Segregation and Resegregation"; Clotfelter, *After Brown*; Jennifer Hochschild, *The New American Dilemma*; Mickelson, "Subverting Swann."

44. See Clotfelter, *After Brown*, 2004; Meier, Stewart, and England, *Race, Class and Education*, 1989; Mickelson, "Incomplete Desegregation"; Mickelson and Heath, "Effects of Segregation"; Oakes, *Keeping Track*; Persell, *Education and Inequality*; West, "Desegregation Tool."

45. See Staiger's *Learning Difference*, an ethnographic case study of a California high school that used a gifted program to accommodate "the demands for

desegregation," which shows some of the consequences of this strategy. See also Epstein, "After the Bus Arrives."

46. Meier, Stewart, and England, *Race, Class, and Education*, 6.

47. *People Who Care v. Rockford Board of Education, School District # 205*, 851 F. Supp.905, 1026 (1994).

48. Clotfelter, *After* Brown, 131.

49. Quoted in West, "Desegregation Tool," 2575. For more on the findings of the *Rockford* case, see Oakes, "Two Cities' Tracking."

50. One example is *Hobson v. Hansen*, 269 F. Supp. 401 (D.D.C. 1967). For discussion of other cases see Hochschild, *New American Dilemma*; Persell, *Education and Inequality;* and Welner, "Ability Tracking." Also, Georgia's Screven County school district ended the use of tracking after a group filed a complaint with the U.S. Department of Education and the agency agreed to investigate tracking and segregation in the district's three high schools. And a case is currently pending in Monroe County, Alabama, where the ACLU filed a discrimination lawsuit against school officials, citing numerous violations of black students' rights, including subjecting them to racially segregated classrooms. Available: http://www.wkrg.com/news/article/racial_lawsuit_filed_against_monroe_county_school_officials/14161/.

51. Racialized tracking may help explain why desegregation has not had a greater impact on the achievement gap. See Jencks and Phillips, *Black-White Test Score Gap*, for discussion of the black-white achievement gap and desegregated schools. See also Burris and Welner, "Closing the Achievement Gap by Detracking"; Oakes, "Two Cities' Tracking."

52. See Lucas and Berends, "Race and Track Location"; Mickelson, "Incomplete Desegregation"; Oakes, "Two Cities' Tracking."

53. In earlier studies using national data, researchers found a black advantage in track location when prior achievement, SES, and school factors were controlled. See Gamoran and Mare, "Secondary School Tracking."

54. Meier, Stewart, and England, *Race, Class and Education*, 51.

55. As Erwin Chemerinsky, a legal scholar, notes, in later decisions the Supreme Court concluded that "proof of discriminatory impact is not sufficient to show an equal protection violation," because the Constitution guarantees equal opportunity, but not equal results. "Segregation and Resegregation," 35. Other scholars also attribute much of the current pattern of within-school segregation to decreasing judicial oversight. See Clotfelter, Ladd, and Vigdor, "Classroom-Level Segregation."

56. *Thomas County Branch of the NAACP v. City of Thomasville School District*, 299 F. Supp. 2d 1340, 1367 (M.D. Ga. 2004).

57. Fordham and Ogbu, "Black Students' School Success"; Ogbu, "Variability in Minority School Performance"; Ogbu, "Origins of Human Competence."

One

1. Shelly's remarks are part of her response to a question about how she was doing in school compared to other black students. She began by saying that very few of her black peers were working really hard in school.

2. For more detailed descriptions of previous explanations of black students' use of the acting white slur in schools, see Galletta and Cross, "Past as Present, Present as Past"; Mickelson and Velasco, " 'Bring It On!' "; O'Connor, Horvat, and Lewis, "Framing the Field."

3. For more on this perspective, see Ogbu, "Variability in Minority School Performance." See also Fordham and Ogbu, "Black Students' School Success."

4. Galletta and Cross refer to this as the "legacy" argument, which they contend "underestimates the power of certain integration policies and practices and exaggerates the role of black culture, in explaining the origins of black student oppositional attitudes." See "Past as Present, Present as Past," 20.

5. Fordham and Ogbu, "Black Students' School Success"; Ogbu, "Variability in Minority School Performance"; Ogbu, "Origins of Human Competence." See also McWhorter, *Losing the Race*; Norwood, "Blackthink's Acting White Stigma in Education."

6. For more discussion on culture as an explanation for black underachievement, see Carter, *Keepin' It Real*; Darity, "Intergroup Disparity"; Gould, "Race and Theory"; Norguera, *City Schools and the American Dream*.

7. The percent of blacks graduating from high school increased from 31 percent in 1970 to more than 70 percent in 2000. The figures for college attainment, while less impressive, also show a steady increase over the same period, from 4.4 percent in 1970 to 14.3 percent in 2000. *U. S. Census Bureau*, rev. January 22, 2010. Available: http://www.census.gov/population/www/socdemo/education/phct41.html

   (Tables 3 and 4). For more on the black professional and middle classes, see Lacy, *Blue-Chip Black*.

8. In fact, according to most survey findings, African Americans generally express a strong belief in the efficacy of education. See Mickelson, "Attitude-Achievement Paradox"; Cook and Ludwig, "Burden of Acting White."

9. See Bettie, *Women without Class*; Carter, *Keepin' It Real*; MacLeod, *Ain't No Makin' It*.

10. See Carbonaro, "Tracking, Students' Effort, and Academic Achievement," especially the conceptual model on page 30.

11. For more on the foundational literature about the self and social influence, see Cooley, *Human Nature and the Social Order*; Mead, *Mind, Self, and Society*. For more on expectancy effects, see Babad, "Pygmalion 25 Years After Interpersonal Expectations in the Classroom"; Cooper, "Pygmalion Grows Up"; Jussim, "Social Reality and Social Problems."

12. For additional student comments on this issue drawn from each of the studies, see Tyson, "The Making of a 'Burden.'"

13. Marguerite rarely mentioned her parents in the context of this discussion of her achievement. In fact, she downplayed their role. When asked where her motivation and expectation to do well came from she responded: "Well, none of it was from my parents. It was mostly me."

14. Bettie, *Women without Class*; Clark, *Family Life and School Achievement*. See also Lewis, *Race in the Schoolyard*; Rosenbaum, *Making Inequality*; Sennett and Cobb, *Hidden Injuries of Class*.

15. Carol Dweck's work also has shown that how students interpret their prior achievement experiences depends on their understanding of intelligence. Students who believe that intelligence is a fixed trait are more likely to avoid tasks on which they previously have not done well or to exert less effort on those tasks in the future. Students who believe that intelligence is malleable are more likely to take on tasks on which they have not done well in the past and to continue to exert effort in an attempt to improve their skills and master the material. See Dweck, "Messages That Motivate"; Dweck, "Development of Ability Conceptions."

16. Clark, *Family Life and School Achievement*, 175–176.

17. See Clark, *Family Life and School Achievement*; Lee, "In Their Own Voices"; MacLeod, *Ain't No Makin' It*; Williams and Kornblum, *Growing Up Poor*; Young, "Navigating Race."

18. MacLeod, *Ain't No Makin' It*, p. 121.

19. As will become clear in chapters 2 and 3, Curtis was not a favorite, either among his peers or his teachers. He was seen by many as arrogant, and he conceded that that perception was probably accurate.

20. For similar examples, see also Diamond, Lewis, and Gordon, "Race, Culture, and Achievement Disparities."

21. A doo-rag is a head wrap. "Bling" is a hip-hop term that refers to flashy diamond-studded jewelry.

22. Informant was a participant in the NCDPI *Understanding Minority Underrepresentation* study.

23. Informants were participants in the study *In Their Own Words II: Linwood*, hereafter referred to as *Linwood*.

24. Three of the four studies I draw on in this book include parent interviews (*Understanding Minority Underrepresentation* is the exception). However, most of these interviews were with parents (mainly mothers) of children who were attending predominantly or all-black elementary schools. In the *Effective Students* study, which involved adolescents, only a small number of parents participated in interviews.

25. Ogbu, *Black American Students in an Affluent Suburb*, 53.

26. Many white middle-class Americans assert similar claims. Ellen Brantlinger documents how middle-class parents rationalize their advantage by attributing

negative qualities (e.g., less intelligence, less respect for education) to low-income families. See *Dividing Classes*.

27. See Feagin and Sikes, *Living with Racism*; Lacy, *Blue-Chip Black*.
28. Du Bois, *The Souls of Black Folks*.
29. Young, "Navigating Race"; Carter, *Keepin' It Real*; O'Connor, "Race, Class, and Gender in America." See also Fergus, *Skin Color and Identity Formation*.
30. Staiger, *Learning Difference*, 59.
31. Bettie, *Women without Class*; MacLeod, *Ain't No Makin' It*; Newman, *No Shame in My Game*. See also Steinberg, Dornbusch, and Brown, "Ethnic Differences in Adolescent Achievement."
32. Willis, *Learning to Labor*, 14.
33. Corsaro, "Interpretative Reproduction," 164.
34. Adler and Adler, *Peer Power*; Carter, "Intersecting Identities"; Sennett and Cobb, *Hidden Injuries of Class*; Willis, *Learning to Labor*.
35. Fordham and Ogbu, "Black Students' School Success," 194.
36. See Bettie, *Women without Class*; Carter, *Keepin' It Real*.
37. Bettie, *Women without Class*, 90.
38. Brantlinger, *Dividing Classes*, 38.
39. Sennett and Cobb, *Hidden Injuries of Class*; Stinchcombe, *Rebellion in a High School*.
40. Stinchcombe, *Rebellion in a High School*, 107.
41. Scholars would later define similar student behavior as resistance. See Willis, *Learning to Labor*.
42. The process Stinchcombe describes is similar to the process of disidentification that Claude Steele and Jason Osborne have identified among students. However, Osborne argues that disidentification is a "group-level response to stigma, rather than a response to poor performance" (728). Osborne, "Race and Academic Disidentification"; Steele, "Race and the Schooling of Black Americans."
43. Hewitt, *Self and Society*.
44. Imagine a situation in which an American adolescent from a black immigrant family is reprimanded by her high school teacher for questioning a grade she received on an assignment. The girl walks away upset, trying to understand the teacher's response. She considers that perhaps her behavior toward the teacher was rude. She was raised according to the idiom "children should be seen and not heard." Her parents and grandparents have always taught her that it is inappropriate for a child to challenge any adult or authority figure. On the other hand, recalling what she has learned about racism and discrimination since coming to America, the girl thinks that the teacher, who is white, may have responded to her harshly because he does not like foreigners or black people. She considers, too, that American teens of her age are expected to have developed a sense of autonomy and independence from their parents. She also knows that many American teenagers regularly challenge authority. She concludes that the teacher must be prejudiced. To be sure, incidents like these are

often much more complicated. They involve many nuances related to tone of voice, body language, and gestures, for example. However, for the sake of simplicity, I limit the details.

45. Swidler, "Culture in Action," 273.

46. Patterson, "Taking Culture Seriously," 203.

47. Swidler, "Culture in Action," 273. Other scholars, however, contend that culture shapes both "the means and the ends of action." See Blair-Loy, *Competing Devotions*, 222.

48. Swidler, "Culture in Action," 277.

49. See Ferguson, *Bad Boys*; Irvine, *Black Students and School Failure*; Lareau, *Unequal Childhoods*; Lareau, "Social Class Differences"; Lewis, *Race in the Schoolyard*; Rist, "Student Social Class and Teacher Expectations"; Roscigno and Ainsworth-Darnell, "Race, Cultural Capital, and Educational Resources"; Valenzuela, *Subtractive Schooling*.

50. Lareau, "Social Class Differences"; Lareau, *Unequal Childhoods*.

51. Heath, *Ways with Words*.

52. See Bowles and Gintis, *Schooling in Capitalist America*. For criticisms of purely structural arguments, see Bourdieu and Passeron, *Reproduction in Education, Society, and Culture*; Carnoy and Levin, *Schooling and Work in the Democratic State*; Giroux, *Theory and Resistance in Education*.

53. Anyon, "Social Class and the Hidden Curriculum of Work"; Willis, *Learning to Labor*; MacLeod, *Ain't No Makin' It*.

54. Sennett and Cobb, *Hidden Injuries of Class*, 88.

55. Meyer, "Effects of Education as an Institution," 60.

56. Lareau and Weininger, "Cultural Capital in Educational Research," 568.

Two

1. Shelby, *We Who Are Dark*; Patterson, "Taking Culture Seriously".

2. Favor, *Authentic Blackness*, 3. The Harlem Renaissance refers to a period during the 1920s (and '30s by some accounts) in which African American literature, art, and music flourished. The movement reflected a new race pride and recognition of black Americans' connection to Africa and people of African descent across the globe.

3. Eugene Genovese's examination of black life in America under slavery and Jim Crow reveals evidence of this long history. *Roll, Jordan, Roll*.

4. Painter, *Creating Black Americans*.

5. Published records show no specific reference to acting white with respect to academic achievement prior to desegregation. A search for the term acting white in online databases containing scholarly and popular literature (e.g., Econ Lit, ERIC, Sociological Abstracts), and in ones that index newspapers and magazines (e.g., ProQuest, Lexis-Nexis), yields many citations. However, prior to the 1980s, none of these publications contain acting white used in reference to school achievement.

6. For example, in a January 2000 *New York Times Magazine* article entitled "Schools Are Not the Answer," James Traub wrote, "And prominent black figures have to weigh in against the antiacademic and even oppositional peer culture that [Edmund] Gordon and others say is retarding black progress." See also McWhorter, *Losing the Race*.

7. Signithia Fordham and John Ogbu first made these claims in their article, "Black Students' School Success."

8. See Carter, *Keepin' It Real*; Horvat and Lewis, "Reassessing the 'Burden of Acting White'"; Tatum, *"Why Are All the Black Kids Sitting Together in the Cafeteria?"*; Tyson, Darity, and Castellino, "It's Not a Black Thing."

9. For more on preadolescents' attitudes toward school and use of the acting white slur see Tyson, "Weighing In."

10. It is important to note that the total number of gifted students in a school can be small, sometimes as few as four or five. In North Carolina in 2000–2002, roughly 10 percent of students were designated as gifted. In 2002, nearly 15 percent of whites were designated as gifted compared to just 4 percent of blacks. *Digest of Education Statistics*. Rev. October 4, 2009. Available: www. nces.ed.gov./programs/digest/do6/tables/dto6_051.asp.

11. When our research team arrived on site at Holt to conduct interviews for this state-mandated study, a black male had been added to the gifted program. An adult informant reported that this was done about a month prior to our visit in response to the upcoming visit.

12. Staiger, "Whiteness as Giftedness."

13. Ferguson, *Bad Boys*, 94.

14. Ibid.

15. Ferguson, *Bad Boys*; Irvine, *Black Students and School Failure*; Lewis, *Race in the Schoolyard*; Staiger, *Learning Difference*.

16. For more on preadolescents' response to gifted programs, see Tyson, "Making of a 'Burden.'"

17. The only other students who mentioned race were two mixed-race students who did so in response to the interviewer's inquiry about their racial background. Both explained that one parent is black and the other is white.

18. We did not ask students which classroom they were in or to identify their teachers by name.

19. See Dyer, *White*; Lewis, *Race in the Schoolyard*.

20. Spencer, "Black Children's Race Awareness"; Tatum, *"Why Are All the Black Kids Sitting Together in the Cafeteria?"*

21. Sniderman and Piazza, *Scar of Race*, 12.

22. One exception I am aware of is a study of a mixed-race group of elementary school children's use of various language resources at school. The researcher found that it was not unusual for children to talk about race spontaneously. Dyson, *Social Worlds of Children*.

23. Lewis, *Race in the Schoolyard*.

24. In the formal interview protocol, only one question specifically mentioned race. That question asked informants how they thought they were doing in school compared to other black students at their school.

25. When the number of blacks in the class was noticeably low (three or fewer), we confirmed the number with the informant. Thus, although these figures are based on counts obtained during our visits, and generally do not account for students who were absent, we are relatively confident that they are accurate.

26. Sandra decided to remain at Earnshaw after visiting a small private school and finding that it also seemed cliquish.

27. We observed Juliana in just two classes, neither of which was advanced, thus we were not able to substantiate her specific experience of racial isolation. However, in her Food and Nutrition class, Juliana was one of ten black students in a class of twelve (80%).

28. Staiger, *Learning Difference*, 55.

29. Tatum, *"Why Are All the Black Kids Sitting Together in the Cafeteria?"* 56.

30. Karabel and Halsey, *Power and Ideology in Education*, 25.

31. Schofield and Sagar, "Social Context of Learning," 171.

32. Bettie, *Women without Class*; Rosenbaum, *Making Inequality*; Tyson, Darity, and Castellino, "It's Not a Black Thing."

33. Immigrant youth are common targets of peer ridicule and taunting. See Lopez, *Hopeful Girls and Troubled Boys*.

34. When we observed Adonis at school the following year, the situation had improved slightly. Although he was the only black student in his pre-calculus math class of twenty-seven (4%), he was one of three black males in his advanced English class of thirty students (10%).

35. Adonis seemed happy with his group of white friends, despite his belief that he was "like a foreign exchange student to them," and the boys' racist jokes, and the fact that they called him "whitey" because he did not "wear [his] hat backwards and ... sag [his] pants and smoke weed and ... carry guns." Adonis was friendly and outgoing, and although most of his friends were white, he did not intentionally distance himself from his black peers.

36. Previous studies have shown that other students of color also commonly used strategies such as these to fit in among their same-race peers, and to challenge each other's racial authenticity when they appeared to be adopting the cultural styles of other racial and ethnic groups. See Bettie, *Women without Class*; Carter, *Keepin' It Real*; Lee, *Unraveling the "Model Minority" Stereotype*.

37. Had Shelly not described her style of dress as a conscious effort at impression management, I probably would have overlooked it as a strategy. Therefore, it is likely that, in this analysis, I missed other similar strategies of impression management that participants did not make explicit.

38. The boys had had a practice of changing clothes after leaving the house, but after their parents separated and their father no longer lived with them, they were free to wear their hip-hop gear to school.

39. Selina is another of the foreign-born participants. Her family is from the West Indies.

40. For more on the importance of this sense of community and connectedness among African Americans, see Charles, "Can We Live Together?"; Dawson, *Behind the Mule*; Shelby, *We Who Are Dark*.

41. Black youth culture was not necessarily the same at each school, but there were some common features in the youth's styles of dress (e.g., "the Black People's Uniform"), musical tastes (hip-hop and R&B), and the slang they used.

42. It is interesting to note that students such as Shawnie who report social problems (e.g., accused of acting white, trouble fitting in) in high school, also recall similar problems in elementary school.

43. Fordham, "Racelessness as a Factor."

44. See also Horvat and Lewis's (2003) study of high-achieving black students. According to the authors, these students did not sacrifice their racial identity in order to succeed. "Reassessing the 'Burden of Acting White.'"

45. All of the black students in AP European History were participants in the study.

46. See Clotfelter, *After* Brown; Lucas and Berends, "Sociodemographic Diversity"; Lucas and Berends, "Race and Track Location."

47. Additionally, only a few years earlier, a local newspaper reported that just 13 percent of the black students in area schools were "enrolled in honors or advanced sections of high school courses such as English, algebra or biology" compared to 40 percent of white students. See Simmons, "Color of Their Skin."

48. Only two other schools were as small.

49. City High is in a school district that participates in a national organization whose mission is to find ways to improve the academic achievement of students of color, particularly African Americans and Latinos.

50. See *Minority Underrepresentation* (also discussed in chapter 4). For a more detailed discussion of the study's findings regarding acting white, see Tyson, Darity, and Castellino, "It's Not a Black Thing."

51. Second-generation black Caribbean youth in Nancy Lopez's study of race and gender disparities in education, most of whom attended segregated minority schools in inner-city New York, were similarly perplexed when Lopez asked them "whether they had ever heard of any academically successful co-ethnics being accused of acting White." See *Hopeful Girls, Troubled Boys*.

52. See Carter, *Keepin' It Real*; Horvat and Lewis, "Reassessing the 'Burden of Acting White'"; Mickelson and Velasco, "'Bring It On!'"; Tyson, Darity, and Castellino, "It's Not a Black Thing."

53. I have not seen any evidence showing that black students actually believe that academic success is the prerogative of whites. Studies report the experiences of academically successful students who have been accused of "acting white," but

none have offered direct accounts from the students who make such accusations. No participant in the studies I have conducted has ever admitted to accusing a peer of "acting white" because of academic success.

54. Bettie, *Women without Class*, 181. Note that tracking was highly racialized at Waretown; white students were significantly overrepresented in the advanced classes and Mexican-Americans were underrepresented.

55. In *We Who Are Dark*, Tommie Shelby points out that most groups in a similar position to that of African Americans would respond this way. In *Blue-Chip Black*, Lacy finds that many middle-class black parents actively work to ensure that their children have opportunities to develop an "authentic" black identity.

56. David Snow and Leon Anderson discuss this general process in their study of identity construction among homeless individuals. See "Identity Work among the Homeless."

57. Black immigrants not raised in America are often baffled by Americans' preoccupation with racial difference, but over time they come to understand it and adopt perceptions similar to other Americans'. See Waters, *Black Identities*.

58. See Lacy's *Blue-Chip Black* for more on how middle-class black Americans define blackness.

59. See Dawson, *Behind the Mule*.

60. Carter, "Intersecting Identities," 116.

61. For some examples of positive and negative ways in which commonalities among blacks matter, see Annette Hemmings's study of high-achieving black students, "Conflicting Images?"

62. Horvat and Lewis, "Reassessing the 'Burden of Acting White.'"

63. In *To Be Popular or Smart*, Kunjufu argues that even black students in all-black settings equate being smart with being white. And although Fordham spends a considerable amount of time in her book *Blacked Out* defining and providing examples of behavior deemed acting white, there is no evidence that any of the students in her study used the term with respect to achievement-related behaviors. In the examples she provides, Fordham applies the acting white concept to the data, but the students do not make any reference to race. With respect to the students' discussion of teasing for achievement, again, there is no reference to race. Thus, there is no evidence that acting white is at issue for informants in these cases.

64. Fordham, *Blacked Out*, 284.

65. Fine, *Gifted Tongues*, 222.

66. For examples, see Adler and Adler, *Peer Power*; Kinney, "From Nerds to Normals"; Perry, *Shades of White*; Sennett and Cobb, *Hidden Injuries of Class*; Steinberg, *Beyond the Classroom*.

67. Steinberg, *Beyond the Classroom*, 146.

68. Ibid., 19. How the "geeky crowd" is defined may be different across schools, but in many schools, as David Kinney found in his study of students' transition from middle to high school, "geek" can be synonymous with "nerd." See "From Nerds to Normals."

69. See also Eckert, *Jocks and Burnouts.*

70. Adler and Adler, *Peer Power*, 47.

71. The full blog can be found online: http://www.huffingtonpost.com/mitchell-bard/vp-debate-apparently-not_b_131601.html. Rev. October 4, 2008. See also Kristof, "Obama and the War on Brains." Rev. November 10, 2008. Available: http://www.nytimes.com/2008/11/09/opinion/09kristof.html.

72. At most schools, some combination of academic criteria (e.g., minimum GPA) and teacher or counselor recommendation is required for placement in advanced classes. See chapter 4 for more discussion of the high school placement process.

73. See Farkas, Lleras, and Maczuga, "Does Oppositional Culture Exist in Minority and Poverty Peer Groups?"; Cook and Ludwig, "Burden of Acting White."

74. Fryer and Paul, "Empirical Analysis of 'Acting White.'"

Three

1. Fine, *Gifted Tongues*, 222. See also Adler and Adler, *Peer Power*; Harter, "Self and Identity Development"; Kinney, "From Nerds to Normals"; Perry, *Shades of White*; Sennett and Cobb, *Hidden Injuries of Class*; Steinberg, *Beyond the Classroom.*

2. Harter, "Self and Identity Development"; Tatum, *"Why Are All the Black Kids Sitting Together in the Cafeteria?"*

3. Hewitt, *Self and Society*, 104. See also Steinberg, Dornbusch, and Brown, "Ethnic Differences in Adolescent Achievement." Note, however, that Carola Suárez-Orozco and Marcelo Suárez-Orozco suggest that this may not be true for adolescents of other cultures and nationalities. See *Transformations.*

4. See Alexander and Campbell, "Peer Influence"; Coleman, *Adolescent Society*; Duncan, Haller, and Portes, "Peer Influences on Aspirations."

5. See Crosnoe, "Friendships in Childhood and Adolescence"; Crosnoe, Cavanagh, and Elder, "Adolescent Friendships"; Epstein, "Friends among Students in Schools"; Maxwell, "Friends."

6. For examples of studies showing the positive benefits of academically oriented peers, see Crosnoe, Cavanagh, and Elder, "Adolescent Friendships"; Epstein, "Friends among Students in Schools"; Mounts and Steinberg, "Ecological Analysis." For examples of studies showing the negative consequences of membership in delinquent friendship networks, see Maxwell, "Friends"; Miller-Johnson et al., "Peer Social Structure."

7. Giordano, "Wider Circle of Friends in Adolescence."

8. For more on this type of social influence, see also Fine and Kleinman, "Rethinking Subculture."

9. Biddle, Bank, and Marlin, "Parental and Peer Influence on Adolescents"; Crosnoe, Kristan Erickson, and Dornbusch, "Protective Functions of Family Relationships."

10. Mounts and Steinberg, "Ecological Analysis."

11. Ibid.

12. Biddle, Bank, and Marlin, "Parental and Peer Influence on Adolescents."

13. Cheng and Starks, "Racial Differences"; Hout and Morgan, "Race and Sex Variations"; Steinberg, Dornbusch, and Brown, "Ethnic Differences."

14. It is important to note that lower-performing students can also be *secure* adolescents. In other words, any adolescent with a firm identity and strong and clear goals, aspirations, and beliefs is likely to be relatively insulated from peer pressure.

15. I do not categorize adolescents who did not face ridicule or teasing related to achievement as *vulnerable* or *secure* because their narratives offer few instances in which their resolve in the face of peer pressure was tested.

16. Any number of things can happen in a young person's life to make her feel less certain about herself, or prompt her to question her sense of self, beliefs, or goals and aspirations.

17. Tyson, Darity, and Castellino, "It's Not a Black Thing."

18. Distinguishing between the two categories can be difficult if information on either the intended meaning or each party's class background is not known. When white students use the acting "high and mighty" slur, it usually signifies a class-based injury (i.e., why the insulter felt put down). When the slur is used by other racial groups, it is not always clear whether the injury is one of class, race, or both.

19. See McArdle and Young, "Classroom Discussion of Racial Identity"; McWhorter, *Losing the Race*; Willie, *Acting Black*.

20. Kinney, "From Nerds to Normals," 32.

21. Notable exceptions are the student-athletes, such as Massey basketball player Karen, whose comments began the section on *secure* adolescents. Not only was Karen well known because of both her participation on the team, she was also personable.

22. Gwen had hoped to become a member of the National Honor Society, but she did not meet the criteria. The National Achievers Society requires that members earn at least two A's and no C's, submit a written report on community service completed, and show proof of recognition for "artistic and cultural talents."

23. See Horvat and Lewis, "Reassessing the 'Burden of Acting White.'"

24. Thoits and Virshup, "Me's and We's."

25. Mickelson and Velasco, "'Bring It On!'" 41.

26. Adonis's concerns about fitting in seemed directed mainly toward his close friends, most of whom were white. They often made rather racist jokes about blacks, which Adonis called them on when they seemed "over the top."

27. Steve Urkel, the exaggerated "nerd" character from the popular 1990s television show *Family Matters*, was a common referent for adolescents as they discussed how nerds look and behave and how they are treated by others.

28. Hitlin, "Values as the Core of Personal Identity."

29. In this episode of *Fresh Prince*, the character Carlton, who grew up in a wealthy black family in Bel Air, faces similar issues trying to fit in with black fraternity

members. In the end, he decides, as Tommy recalls, that he was "too much of a brother to be a brother."

30. See Tatum, *Why Are All the Black Kids Sitting Together in the Cafeteria?*

31. Crosnoe, "Friendships in Childhood and Adolescence."

32. See Lacy, *Blue-Chip Black*.

33. Among the students, Wicca was considered a religion or system of beliefs associated with witchcraft.

34. Sandra did not mention the race of this student.

35. Mickelson, "Attitude-Achievement Paradox."

36. Biddle, Bank, and Marlin, "Parental and Peer Influence on Adolescents"; Mounts and Steinberg, "Ecological Analysis."

37. Anderson, *Code of the Streets*, 32.

38. Favor, *Authentic Blackness*, 4.

39. See Pinkney, *Black Americans*, 169.

40. Willie, *Acting Black*, 135.

41. See also Lacy's *Blue-Chip Black* for a discussion of the dilemmas of authentic blackness facing middle-class black Americans.

42. For a scale that does capture the intensity of identity, see Phinney, "Multigroup Ethnic Identity Measure."

43. Neal-Barnett, "Being Black." Spencer, Noll, Stolzfus, and Harpalani, "Identity and School Adjustment."

44. I suspect there may be gender differences in how boys and girls are able to negotiate being smart *and* cool (as Carter found in *Keepin' It Real*), because males were more likely than females to introduce this topic. However, only a few study participants discussed the issue at all.

45. For example, see Cheng and Starks, "Racial Differences"; Crosnoe, "Friendships in Childhood and Adolescence."

46. See MacLeod, *Ain't No Making It*; Maxwell, "Friends."

47. Zimmer-Gembeck and Collins, "Autonomy Development during Adolescence."

Four

1. Many studies have documented the uneven distribution of students by race in American secondary schools. See, for example, Blau, *Race in the Schools*; Diette, "Algebra Obstacle"; Gamoran and Mare, "Secondary School Tracking and Educational Inequality"; Gamoran, "Access to Excellence"; Kelly, "Increased Levels of Parental Involvement"; Lucas, *Tracking Inequality*; Oakes, "Two Cities' Tracking"; Oakes, *Keeping Track*.

2. Lucas, *Tracking Inequality*.

3. Warren Kubitschek and Maureen Hallinan argue that this new form of tracking should properly be referred to as ability grouping. "Curriculum Differentiation and High School Achievement."

4. For example, see Lee, *Unraveling the "Model Minority" Stereotype*; O'Connor, "Premise of Black Inferiority"; Tyson, Darity, and Castellino, "It's Not a Black Thing."

5. See Fordham, *Blacked Out*.

6. See the preface for a more detailed discussion of the data used in this chapter.

7. For the sake of brevity, I refer to students who were identified as gifted as "gifted" and those who were not as "non-gifted." I do not mean to suggest that giftedness inheres in those who have been so labeled.

8. See Hallinan and Kubitschek, "Curriculum Differentiation and High School Achievement."

9. In dual-enrollment courses, students simultaneously earn high school and college credits, and the classes they attend usually are held at a local community college.

10. I refer to AP, honors/advanced, and IB courses as advanced, higher-level, or rigorous courses interchangeably. General education classes I refer to as lower-level.

11. Kubitschek and Hallinan, "Tracking and Students' Friendships," 13.

12. See also Oakes and Guiton, "Matchmaking"; Riehl, Pallas, and Natriello, "Rites and Wrongs."

13. Rosenbaum, *Making Inequality*, 167.

14. James, *Principles of Psychology*, I:310.

15. These data were obtained from the North Carolina Education Research Data Center at Duke University. See the preface for more on the larger NCDPI study of the underrepresentation of minority students in rigorous courses and programs in North Carolina public schools.

16. See McPartland and Schneider, "Opportunities to Learn and Student Diversity."

17. See Babad, "Pygmalion—25 Years After Interpersonal Expectations in the Classroom"; Good and Brophy, *Looking in Classrooms*; Cooper, "Pygmalion Grows Up"; Ferguson, "Teachers' Perceptions and Expectations"; Jussim and Eccles, "Teacher Expectations II."

18. See Entwisle and Hayduk, *Too Great Expectations*; Wittrock, "Teachers' Thought Processes."

19. Hong, Chui, and Dweck, "Implicit Theories of Intelligence."

20. William Darity Jr. et al., 2001, "Increasing Opportunity to Learn via Access to Rigorous Courses and Programs: One Strategy for Closing the Achievement Gap for At-Risk and Ethnic Minority Students." Available upon request from author.

21. See the preface for more detailed information on the *Minority Underrepresentation* study and the mail-in surveys.

22. Irvine, *Black Students and School Failure*, xiv.

23. For a discussion of gifted programs and race in New York City, see deMause, "Looking a Gifted Horse in the Mouth"; and Saulny, "Lighting Rod for Fury Over School's Gifted Programs," 7. Studies identifying racial disparities in gifted programs in California schools include Ferguson, *Bad Boys*; Lewis, *Race in the Schoolyard*; and Staiger, *Learning Difference*. At the California high school

Annegret Staiger studied, white students accounted for less than 20 percent of the total student body, but made up more than half of the students in the school's gifted program. The district required a parent or teacher referral in order for students to be tested for "giftedness."

24. We did not collect information on the formal procedures or criteria for gifted identification at the participants' elementary and middle schools.

25. In North Carolina, as in other states, students could be identified as gifted based on school assessments or on the evaluation of an outside psychologist. Some parents opted for an outside evaluation when their child did not qualify as gifted according to the school's assessment.

26. Other studies find evidence of black parents going outside of the school to secure gifted placement for their children. For example, in her study of the impact of social class on children's life experiences, Annette Lareau describes a situation in which a middle-class black parent takes "prompt action" to have her two children placed in their school's gifted program when they did not meet the minimum IQ requirement. She had them both tested privately and they were subsequently admitted to the program. *Unequal Childhoods*, 176. Also, a black administrator interviewed in the NCDPI study on which I report in this chapter, described how years earlier she had pushed to have her child included in the gifted program by having her retested by a private psychologist.

27. Wells and Serta, "The Politics of Culture," 105.

28. Hubbard and Mehan, "Race and Reform"; Lareau, *Unequal Childhoods*; Oakes, Wells, Jones, and Datnow, "Detracking"; Sieber, "Politics of Middle-Class Success."

29. Perry, *Shades of White*, 58.

30. Brantlinger, *Dividing Classes*, 41.

31. Kubitschek and Hallinan, "Tracking and Students' Friendships."

32. Jasmine, a participant in the study of high-achieving black students (see chapter 2), explained that although she is no longer uncomfortable being the only black student in advanced classes, initially, she was self-conscious: "It doesn't, no, it doesn't make me uncomfortable. It did at first. It did at first 'cause, like, I mean, like, not to sound judgmental but, like, when you're in a room and you're, like, the only black person you're going to notice that. But, I mean it's nothing that I focus on every day."

33. Staiger, *Learning Difference*, 57. See also Carter, *Keepin' It Real*.

34. In previous research, we found that in some schools, lower-income whites faced teasing and ridicule from peers when they ventured to take advanced classes, which were populated largely by middle-class whites. See Tyson, Darity, and Castellino, "It's Not a Black Thing."

35. In fact, in Pamela Perry's (2002) study of racial identity among high school students, some white students in the higher track believed that they had been

placed in advanced classes, even though they did not request that placement, because their friends were there. See *Shades of White*.

36. Crosnoe, "Friendships in Childhood and Adolescence," 381.
37. In New York City, for example, gifted classes begin in first grade.
38. Hallinan and Williams, "Interracial Friendship Choices"; Kubitschek and Hallinan, "Tracking and Students' Friendships"; Rosenbaum, *Making Inequality*.
39. Jomills Henry Braddock, House Subcommittee on Select Education of the Committee on Education and Labor, Improving the Education and Achievement of African American Males: Hearing Before the Subcommittee on Select Education of the Committee on Education and Labor, House of Representatives (Washington, DC: U.S. Government Printing Office, 1990); Steele, "Race and the Schooling of Black Americans," 68–78. See also Clark, *Family Life and School Achievement*.
40. Spade, Columba, and Vonfossen, "Tracking in Mathematics and Science," 110.
41. Resnick, "From Aptitude to Effort," 57. Emphasis in original.
42. Entwisle and Alexander, "Entry into School"; Phillips, Crouse, and Ralph, "Does the Black-White Test Score Gap Widen after Children Enter School?" 229–272.
43. Dreeben and Gamoran, "Race, Instruction, and Learning," 667.
44. Harris and Robinson, "Schooling Behaviors or Prior Skills?"
45. Labaree, "No Exit," 112.

Conclusion

1. See Clotfelter, *After Brown*; Boger and Orfield, *School Resegregation*; Orfield and Eaton, *Dismantling Desegregation*; Street, *Segregated Schools*.
2. Notable exceptions include Bettie, *Women without Class*; Carter, *Keepin' It Real*; Mickelson, "Subverting *Swann*"; O'Connor, "Premise of Black Inferiority"; Staiger, *Learning Difference*; Tatum, *"Why Are All the Black Kids Sitting Together in the Cafeteria?"*
3. Ardell, *High Level Wellness*.
4. Tatum, *"Why Are All the Black Kids Sitting Together in the Cafeteria?"* 60.
5. McPherson and Shelby, "Blackness and Blood," 185.
6. Rosenbaum, *Making Inequality*, 164.
7. Hewitt, *Self and Society*, 93.
8. See Fine, *Gifted Tongues*; Adler and Adler, *Peer Power*; Kinney, "From Nerds to Normals"; Perry, *Shades of White*; Sennett and Cobb, *Hidden Injuries of Class*; Steinberg, *Beyond the Classroom*.
9. Interestingly, most of the research I am aware of on black students' course taking focuses not on lower-achieving students and their decision making, but on higher-achieving students who are enrolled in advanced classes. The latter are often asked to speculate on the decisions of the former. See for example, Ogbu, *Black American Students in an Affluent Suburb*; Mickelson and Velasco, "'Bring It On!'"

10. Wells and Serta, "The Politics of Culture," 105.

11. Labaree, "No Exit," 112.

12. See *Parents Involved in Community Schools v. Seattle School District No. 1 et al.* 551 U.S. (2007); *Belk v. Charlotte-Mecklenburg Board of Education* 535 U.S. 986 (2002).

13. Education researchers have been attentive to within-school segregation for more than two decades.

14. Some schools, such as Dalton High School (see chapter 4), have attempted to help high-achieving black students deal with racialized oppositionality. Dalton created a club for these high achievers so that they would feel less isolated from one another. This strategy, however, left the underlying problem intact. See Tyson, Darity, and Castellino, "It's Not a Black Thing."

15. See Bettie, *Women without Class*; Carter, *Keepin' It Real*, 2005; Tyson, Darity, and Castellino, "*It's Not a Black Thing*."

16. Detracking has its detractors, including Maureen Hallinan, who has published extensively on tracking. Hallinan has argued that in the absence of certain conditions at a school, eliminating tracking may not produce the desired outcomes. See Hallinan, "Tracking from Theory to Practice." However, I propose detracking here as one option among others, understanding that eliminating tracking without making other adjustments, such as increasing the teaching staff or providing additional supports for lower-achieving students, may create other problems or exacerbate existing ones. Detracking would force schools to address racial and social class inequities in curricular placement and reduce a key form of social comparison that breeds animosity among students. For more on the debate over tracking and detracking efforts, see Burris and Welner, "Closing the Achievement Gap by Detracking"; Loveless, *Tracking Wars*; Oakes et al., "Detracking"; Wells and Oakes, "Potential Pitfalls of Systemic Reform"; Wells and Oakes, "Tracking, Detracking and the Politics of Educational Reform"; Wells and Serna, "Politics of Culture."

17. See Tyson, "Providing Equal Access to 'Gifted' Education."

REFERENCES

Adler, Patricia A., and Peter Adler. *Peer Power: Preadolescent Culture and Identity*. Brunswick, NJ: Rutgers University Press, 1998.

Ainsworth-Darnell, James W., and Douglas. B. Downey. "Assessing the Oppositional Culture Explanation for Racial/Ethnic Differences in School Performance." *American Sociological Review* 63 (1998): 536–553.

Akom, A. A. "Reexamining Resistance as Oppositional Behavior: The Nation of Islam and the Creation of a Black Achievement Ideology." *Sociology of Education* 76 (2003): 305–325.

Alexander, Norman, and Ernest Campbell. "Peer Influence on Adolescent Educational Aspirations and Attainments." *American Sociological Review* 29 (1964): 568–575.

Anderson, Elijah. *Code of the Streets: Decency, Violence and the Moral Life of the Inner City*. New York: W.W. Norton and Company, 1999.

Andrews, Kenneth. "Movement-Countermovement Dynamics and the Emergence of New Institutions: The Case of White Flight in Mississippi." *Social Forces* 80 (2002): 911–936.

Ansalone, George. "Tracking: A Return to Jim Crow." *Race, Gender and Class* 13 (2006): 144–153.

Anyon, Jean. "Social Class and the Hidden Curriculum of Work." *Journal of Educational Psychology* 162 (1980): 67–92.

Ardell, Donald. *High Level Wellness: An Alternative to Doctors, Drugs and Disease*. Emmaus, PA: Rodale, 1977.

Babad, Elisha. "Pygmalion – 25 Years after Interpersonal Expectations in the Classroom." In *Interpersonal Expectations: Theory, Research, and Applications*, ed. Peter David Blanck, 125–153. New York: Cambridge University Press, 1993.

Bacon, Perry, Jr., "Obama Reaches Out with Tough Love." *Washington Post*, May 3, 2007. Available: http://www.washingtonpost.com/ac2/wp-dyn/e mailafriend?contentId=AR2007050202813&sent=no&referrer=emailart icle.

Belk v. Charlotte-Mecklenburg Board of Education 535 U. S. 986 (2002).

Bergin, David, and Helen Cooks. "High School Students of Color Talk about Accusations of 'Acting White.' " *The Urban Review* 34 (2002): 113–134.

Bettie, Julie. *Women without Class: Girls, Race, and Identity*. Berkeley: University of California Press, 2003.

Biddle, Bruce, Barbara Bank, and Marjorie Marlin. "Parental and Peer Influence on Adolescents." *Social Forces* 58 (1980): 1057–1079.

Blair-Loy, Mary. *Competing Devotions: Career and Family among Women Executives*. Cambridge, MA: Harvard University Press, 2003.

Blau, Judith. *Race in the Schools: Perpetuating White Dominance?* Boulder, CO: Lynne Rienner, 2003.

Boger, Charles, and Gary Orfield. *School Resegregation: Must the South Turn Back?* Chapel Hill: University of North Carolina Press, 2005.

Bourdieu, Pierre, and Jean Claude Passeron. *Reproduction in Education, Society, and Culture*. London: Sage Publications, 1977.

Bowles, Herbert, and Samuel Gintis. *Schooling in Capitalist America: Educational Reform and the Contradictions of Economic Life*. New York: Basic Books, 1976.

Brantlinger, Ellen. *Dividing Classes: How the Middle Class Negotiates and Rationalizes School Advantage*. New York: RoutledgeFalmer, 2003.

Brown v. Board of Education of Topeka 347 U.S. 483 (1954)/ *Brown II* 349 U.S. 294 (1955).

Burris, Carol, and Kevin Welner. "Closing the Achievement Gap by Detracking." *Phi Delta Kappan* 86 (2005): 594–598.

Butterfield, Sherri-Ann. "To Be Young, Gifted, Black, and Somewhat Foreign." In *Beyond Acting White: Reframing the Debate on Black Student Achievement*, ed. Erin McNamara Horvat and Carla O'Connor, 133–155. Lanham, MD: Rowman & Littlefield, 2006.

Campbell, Ernest Q. *When a City Closes Its Schools*. Chapel Hill: University of North Carolina Press, 1960.

Carbonaro, William. "Tracking, Students' Effort, and Academic Achievement." *Sociology of Education* 78 (2005): 27–49.

Carnoy, Martin, and Henry M. Levin. *Schooling and Work in the Democratic State*. Stanford, CA: Stanford University Press, 1985.

Carter, Prudence. "Intersecting Identities: 'Acting White,' Gender, and Academic Achievement." In *Beyond Acting White: Reframing the Debate on Black Student Achievement*, ed. Erin McNamara Horvat and Carla O'Connor, 111–132. Lanham, MD: Rowman & Littlefield, 2006.

———. *Keepin' It Real: School Success Beyond Black and White.* New York: Oxford University Press, 2005.

Charles, Camille Zubrinsky. "Can We Live Together? Racial Preferences and Neighborhood Outcomes." In *The Geography of Opportunity: Race and Housing Choice in Metropolitan America*, ed. Xavier de Souza Briggs, 45–80. Washington, DC: The Brookings Institution, 2005.

Chemerinsky, Erwin. "The Segregation and Resegregation of American Public Education: The Courts." In *School Resegregation: Must the South Turn Back?* ed. John Boger and Gary Orfield, 29–47. Chapel Hill: University of North Carolina Press, 2005.

Cheng, Simon, and Brian Starks. "Racial Differences in the Effects of Significant Others on Students' Educational Expectations." *Sociology of Education* 75 (2002): 306–327.

Clark, Reginald M. *Family Life and School Achievement: Why Poor Black Children Succeed or Fail.* Chicago: The University of Chicago Press, 1983.

Clotfelter, Charles. *After Brown: The Rise and Retreat of School Desegregation.* Princeton, NJ: Princeton University Press, 2004.

Clotfelter, Charles, Helen Ladd, and Jacob Vigdor. "Classroom-level Segregation and Resegregation in North Carolina." In *School Resegregation: Must the South Turn Back?* ed. John Boger and Gary Orfield, 70–86. Chapel Hill: University of North Carolina Press, 2005.

Coleman, James S. *The Adolescent Society: The Social Life of the Teenager and Its Impact on Education.* New York: Free Press, 1961.

Cook, Philip J., and Jens Ludwig. "The Burden of Acting White: Do Black Adolescents Disparage Academic Achievement?" In *The Black-White Test Score Gap*, ed. Christopher Jencks and Meredith Phillips, 375–400. Washington, DC: Brookings Institution Press, 1998.

Cooley, Charles Horton. *Human Nature and the Social Order.* New York: Scribners, 1902.

Cooper, Harris. "Pygmalion Grows Up: A Model for Teacher Expectation Communication and Performance Influence." *Review of Educational Research* 49 (1979): 389–410.

Corsaro, William. "Interpretive Reproduction in Children's Peer Cultures." *Social Psychology Quarterly* 55 (1992): 160–177.

Crosnoe, Robert. "Friendships in Childhood and Adolescence: The Life Course and New Directions." *Social Psychology Quarterly* 63 (2000): 377–391.

Crosnoe, Robert, Shannon Cavanagh, and Glen H. Elder. "Adolescent Friendships as Academic Resources: The Intersection of Friendship, Race, and School Disadvantage." *Sociological Perspectives* 46 (2003): 331–352.

Crosnoe, Robert, Kristan Glasgow Erickson, and Sanford Dornbusch. "Protective Functions of Family Relationships and School Factors on the

Deviant Behavior of Adolescent Boys and Girls." *Youth and Society* 33 (2002): 515–544.

Darity, William, Jr. "Intergroup Disparity: Why Culture Is Irrelevant." *The Review of Black Political Economy* 29 (2002): 70–90.

Dawson, Michael C. *Behind the Mule: Race and Class in African-American Politics*. Princeton, NJ: Princeton University Press, 1994.

deMause, Neil. "Looking a Gifted Horse in the Mouth: Parents Say Standardized Tests No Way to Pick Kids for Advanced Classes." *The Village Voice* (July 30 - August 5, 2008): 6, 8–9.

Diamond, John. "Still Separate and Unequal Examining Race, Opportunity, and School Achievement in 'Integrated' Suburbs." *The Journal of Negro Education* 75 (2006): 495–505.

Diamond, John, Amanda Lewis, and Lamont Gordon. "Race, Culture, and Achievement Disparities in a Desegregated Suburb: Reconsidering the Oppositional Culture Explanation." *International Journal of Qualitative Studies in Education*, Special Issue: Free Spaces: Excavating Race, Class, and Gender among Urban Schools and Communities, 20 (2007): 655–680.

Diette, Timothy. "The Algebra Obstacle: Access, Race, and the Math Achievement Gap." Ph.D. diss., University of North Carolina, Chapel Hill, 2005.

Donelan, Richarde, Gerald Neal, and Deneese Jones. "The Promise of *Brown* and the Reality of Academic Grouping: The Tracks of My Tears." *The Journal of Negro Education* 63 (1994): 376–387.

Dreeben, Robert, and Adam Gamoran. "Race, Instruction and Learning." *American Sociological Review* 51 (1986): 660–669.

Du Bois, W. E. B. *The Souls of Black Folks*. 1903. Reprint, New York: Penguin Books, 1989.

Duncan, Otis Dudley, Archibald Haller, and Alejandro Portes. "Peer Influences on Aspirations: A Reinterpretation." *The American Journal of Sociology* 74 (1968): 119–137.

Duster, Troy. "Comparative Perspectives and Competing Explanations: Taking on the Newly Configured Reductionist Challenge to Sociology." *American Sociological Review* 71 (2006): 1–15.

Dweck, Carol. "The Development of Ability Conceptions." In *The Development of Achievement Motivation*, ed. A. Wigfield and J. Eccles, 57–91. New York: Academic Press, 2002.

———. "Messages That Motivate: How Praise Molds Students' Beliefs, Motivation, and Performance (in Surprising Ways)." In *Improving Academic Achievement*, ed. Joshua Aaronson, 38–58. Amsterdam: Academic Press, 2002.

Dyer, Richard. *White*. New York: Routledge, 1997.

Dyson, Anne Haas. *Social Worlds of Children Learning to Write in an Urban Primary School*. New York: Teachers College Press, 1993.

Eckert, Penelope. *Jocks and Burnouts: Social Categories and Identity in High School*. New York: Teachers College Press, 1989.

Entwisle, Doris R., and Karl L. Alexander. "Entry into School: The Beginning School Transition and Educational Stratification in the United States." *Annual Review of Sociology* 19 (1993): 401–423.

Entwisle, Doris, and Leslie A. Hayduk. *Too Great Expectations: The Academic Outlook of Young Children*. Baltimore: Johns Hopkins University Press, 1978.

Epstein, Joyce. "After the Bus Arrives: Resegregation in Desegregated Schools." *Journal of Social Issues* 41 (1985): 23–43.

———. "Friends among Students in Schools: Environmental and Developmental Factors." In *Friends in School: Patterns of Selection and Influence in Secondary Schools*, ed. Joyce Levy Epstein and Nancy L. Karweit, 3–18. New York: Academic Press, 1983.

Farkas, George, Christy Lleras, and Steve Maczuga. "Does Oppositional Culture Exist in Minority and Poverty Peer Groups?" *American Sociological Review* 67 (2002): 148–155.

Favor, J. Martin. *Authentic Blackness: The Folk in the New Negro Renaissance*. Durham, NC: Duke University Press, 1999.

FDCH E-Media. "Transcript: Illinois Senate Candidate Barack Obama." *Washington Post*, July 27, 2004. Rev October 17, 2005. Available: http://www.washingtonpost.com/wp-dyn/articles/A19751-2004Jul27.html.

Feagin, Joe R., and Melvin P. Sikes. *Living with Racism: The Black Middle-Class Experience*. Boston: Beacon Press, 1994.

Fergus, Edward. *Skin Color and Identity Formation: Perceptions of Opportunity and Academic Orientation among Mexican and Puerto Rican Youth*. New York: Routledge, 2004.

Ferguson, Ann Arnett. *Bad Boys: Public Schools in the Making of Black Masculinity*. Ann Arbor: University of Michigan Press, 2000.

Ferguson, Ronald. "Teachers' Perceptions and Expectations and the Black-White Test Score Gap." In *The Black-White Test Score Gap*, ed. Christopher Jencks and Meredith Phillips, 273–317. Washington, DC: Brookings Institution Press, 1998.

Fine, Gary Alan. *Gifted Tongues: High School Debate and Adolescent Culture*. Princeton, NJ: Princeton University Press, 2001.

Fine, Gary Alan, and Sherryl Kleinman. "Rethinking Subculture: An Interactionist Analysis." *American Journal of Sociology* 85 (1979): 1–20.

Fordham, Signithia. *Blacked Out: Dilemmas of Race, Identity and Success at Capital High*. Chicago: University of Chicago Press, 1996.

———. "Racelessness as a Factor in Black Students' School Success: Pragmatic Strategy or Pyrrhic Victory?" *Harvard Educational Review* 58 (1988): 54–84.

Fordham, Signithia, and John U. Ogbu. "Black Students' School Success: Coping with the 'Burden of Acting White.' " *The Urban Review* 18 (1986): 176–206.

Frazier, Herb. "Wrong Side of the Track." *Southern Exposure* 23 (1995): 27–32.

Fryer, Roland, and Paul Torelli. 2005. "An Empirical Analysis of 'Acting White.' " *Journal of Public Economics* 94 (2010): 380–396.

Galletta, Anne, and William E. Cross. "Past as Present, Present as Past: Historicizing Black Education and Interrogating 'Integration.' " In *Contesting Stereotypes and Creating Identities: Social Categories, Social Identities, and Educational Participation*, ed. Andrew Fuligni, 15–41. New York: Russell Sage Foundation, 2007.

Gamoran, Adam. "Access to Excellence: Assignment to Honors English Classes in the Transition from Middle to High School." *Educational Evaluation and Policy Analysis* 14 (1992): 185–204.

Gamoran, Adam, and Robert Mare. "Secondary School Tracking and Educational Inequality: Compensation, Reinforcement or Neutrality?" *American Journal of Sociology* 94 (1989): 1146–1183.

Gates, Robbins. *The Making of Massive Resistance*. Chapel Hill: University of North Carolina Press, 1962.

Genovese, Eugene D. *Roll, Jordan, Roll: The World the Slaves Made*. New York: Random House, 1972.

Giordano, Peggy. "The Wider Circle of Friends in Adolescence." *American Journal of Sociology* 101 (1995): 661–697.

Giroux, Henry. *Theory and Resistance in Education: A Pedagogy for the Opposition*. South Hadley, MA: Bergin & Garvey, 1983.

Good, Thomas L., and Jere E. Brophy. *Looking in Classrooms*, 6th ed. New York: HarperCollins, 1994.

Gould, Mark. "Race and Theory: Culture, Poverty, and Adaptation to Discrimination in Wilson and Ogbu." *Sociological Theory* 17 (1999): 171–200.

Griswold, Wendy. *Cultures and Societies in a Changing World*. Thousand Oaks, CA: Pine Forge Press, 1994.

Hallinan, Maureen. "Tracking from Theory to Practice." *Sociology of Education* 67 (1994): 79–91.

Hallinan, Maureen, and Richard Williams. "Interracial Friendship Choices in Secondary Schools." *American Sociological Review* 54 (1989): 67–78.

Harris, Angel, and Keith Robinson. "Schooling Behaviors or Prior Skills? A Cautionary Tale of Omitted Variable Bias within Oppositional Culture Theory." *Sociology of Education* 80 (2007): 139–157.

Harter, Susan. "Self and Identity Development." In *At the Threshold: The Developing Adolescent*, ed. S. Shirley Feldman and Glen R. Elliott, 352–387. Cambridge, MA: Harvard University Press, 1990.

Heath, Shirley Brice. *Ways with Words: Language Life and Work in Communities and Classrooms*. New York: Cambridge University Press, 1983.

Hemmings, Annette. "Conflicting Images? Being Black and a Model High School Student." *Anthropology and Education Quarterly* 27 (1996): 20–50.

Hewitt, John P. *Self and Society: A Symbolic Interactionist Social Psychology*. Boston: Allyn and Bacon, 1984.

Hitlin, Steven. "Values as the Core of Personal Identity: Drawing Links between Two Theories of Self." *Social Psychology Quarterly* 66 (2003): 118–137.

Hochschild, Jennifer L. *The New American Dilemma: Liberal Democracy and School Desegregation*. New Haven, CT: Yale University Press, 1984.

Horvat, Erin McNamara, and Kristine Lewis. "Reassessing the 'Burden of Acting White': The Importance of Peer Groups in Managing Academic Success." *Sociology of Education* 76 (2003): 265–280.

Horvat, Erin McNamara, and Carla O'Connor, eds. *Beyond Acting White: Reframing the Debate on Black Student Achievement*. Lanham, MD: Rowman & Littlefield, 2006.

Hout, Michael, and William Morgan. "Race and Sex Variations in the Causes of the Expected Attainments of High School Seniors." *The American Journal of Sociology* 81 (1975): 364–394.

Hubbard, Lea, and Hugh Mehan. "Race and Reform: Educational 'Niche Picking' in a Hostile Environment." *Journal of Negro Education* 68 (1999): 213–226.

Irvine, Jacqueline Jordan. *Black Students and School Failure: Policies, Practices, and Prescriptions*. Westport, CT: Greenwood Press, 1990.

James, William. *Principles of Psychology*. New York: Dover Publications, 1950.

Jencks, Christopher, and Meredith Phillips. *The Black-White Test Score Gap*. Washington, DC: Brookings Institution, 1998.

Johnson, Yma A. "Travels in Mind and Space." *Michigan Today*, 2003. Available: http://www.umich.edu/news/MT/03/Sum03/travels.html.

Jussim, Lee. "Social Reality and Social Problems: The Role of Expectancies." *Journal of Social Issues* 46 (1990): 9–34.

Jussim, Lee, and Jacquelynn Eccles. "Teacher Expectations II: Construction and Reflection of Student Achievement." *Journal of Personality and Social Psychology* 63 (1992): 947–961.

Karabel, Jerome, and A. H. Halsey, eds. *Power and Ideology in Education*. New York: Oxford University Press, 1977.

Katznelson, Ira, and Margaret Weir. *Schooling for All: Class, Race, and the Decline of the Democratic Ideal*. New York: Basic Books, 1985.

Kelly, Sean. "Do Increased Levels of Parental Involvement Account for Social Class Differences in Track Placement?" *Social Science Research* 33 (2004): 626–659.

Kinney, David A. "From Nerds to Normals: The Recovery of Identity among Adolescents from Middle to High School." *Sociology of Education* 66 (1993): 21–40.

Kozol, Jonathan. *Savage Inequalities: Children in America's Schools*. New York: Crown, 1991.

Kristof, Nicholas. "Obama and the War on Brains." *New York Times*, November 9, 2008. Available: http://www.nytimes.com/2008/11/09/opinion/09kristof.html.

Kubitschek, Warren N., and Maureen Hallinan, "Curriculum Differentiation and High School Achievement." *Social Psychology of Education* 3 (1999): 41–62.

———. "Tracking and Students' Friendships." *Social Psychology Quarterly* 61 (1998): 1–15.

Kunjufu, Jawanza. *To Be Popular or Smart: The Black Peer Group*. Chicago: African American Images, 1988.

Labaree, David F. "No Exit: Public Education as an Inescapably Public Good." In *Reconstructing the Common Good*, ed. Larry Cuban and Dorothy Shipps, 110–129. Stanford, CA: Stanford University Press, 2000.

Lacy, Karyn. *Blue-Chip Black: Race, Class, and Status in the New Black Middle Class*. Berkeley: University of California Press, 2007.

Lareau. Annette. "Social Class Differences in Family School Relationships: The Importance of Cultural Capital." *Sociology of Education* 60 (1987): 73–85.

———. *Unequal Childhoods: Class, Race and Family Life*. Berkeley: University of California Press, 2003.

Lareau, Annette, and Elliot Weininger. "Cultural Capital in Educational Research: A Critical Assessment." *Theory and Society* 32 (2003): 567–606.

Lee, Patrick. "In Their Own Voices: An Ethnographic Study of Low-Achieving Students within the Context of School Reform." *Urban Education* 34 (1999): 214–244.

Lee, Stacey. *Unraveling the "Model Minority" Stereotype: Listening to Asian American Youth*. New York: Teachers College Press, 1996.

Lewis, Amanda E. *Race in the Schoolyard: Negotiating the Color Line in Classrooms and Communities*. Piscataway, NJ: Rutgers University Press, 2003.

Lopez, Nancy. *Hopeful Girls, Troubled Boys: Race and Gender Disparity in Urban Education*. New York: Routledge, 2003.

Loveless, Tom. *The Tracking Wars: State Reform Meets School Policy*. Washington, DC: Brookings Institution Press, 1999.

Lucas, Samuel R. *Tracking Inequality: Stratification and Mobility in American High Schools*. New York: Teachers College Press, 1999.

Lucas, Samuel R., and Mark Berends. "Race and Track Location in U.S. Public Schools." *Research in Social Stratification and Mobility* 25 (2007): 169–187.

———. "Sociodemographic Diversity, Correlated Achievement, and De Facto Tracking." *Sociology of Education* 75 (2002): 328–348.

MacLeod, Jay. *Ain't No Making It: Leveled Aspirations in a Low-Income Neighborhood*. 1987. Reprint, Boulder, CO: Westview Press, 1995.

Maxwell, Kimberly. "Friends: The Role of Peer Influence across Adolescent Risk Behaviors." *Journal of Youth and Adolescence* 31 (2002): 267–277.

McArdle, Clare, and Nancy Young. "Classroom Discussion of Racial Identity or How Can We Make It Without 'Acting White.'" *American Journal of Orthopsychiatry* 41 (1970): 135–141.

McPartland, James, and Barbara Schneider. "Opportunities to Learn and Student Diversity: Prospects and Pitfalls of a Common Core Curriculum." *Sociology of Education* 69 (1996): 66–81.

McPherson, Lionel K., and Tommie Shelby. "Blackness and Blood: Interpreting African American Identity." *Philosophy and Public Affairs* 32 (2004): 171–192.

McWhorter, John. *Losing the Race: Self-Sabotage in Black America*. New York: Free Press, 2000.

Mead, George Herbert. *Mind, Self, and Society: From the Standpoint of a Social Behaviorist*. Chicago: University of Chicago Press, 1934.

Meier, Kenneth J., Joseph Stewart Jr., and Robert E. England. *Race, Class and Education: The Politics of Second-Generation Discrimination*. Madison: University of Wisconsin Press, 1989.

Meyer, John. "The Effects of Education as an Institution." *American Journal of Sociology* 83 (1977): 55–77.

Mickelson, Roslyn. "The Attitude-Achievement Paradox among Black Adolescents." *Sociology of Education* 63 (1990): 44–61.

———. "The Incomplete Desegregation of the Charlotte-Mecklenburg Schools and Its Consequences, 1971–2004." In *School Resegregation: Must the South Turn Back?* ed. John Boger and Gary Orfield, 87–110. Chapel Hill: University of North Carolina Press, 2005.

———. "Subverting Swann: First- and Second-Generation Segregation in the Charlotte-Mecklenburg Schools." *American Educational Research Journal* 38 (2001): 215–252.

Mickelson, Roslyn, and Damien Heath. "The Effects of Segregation on African American High School Seniors' Academic Achievement." *Journal of Negro Education* 68 (1999): 566–586.

Mickelson, Roslyn, and Anne Velasco. "Bring It On! Diverse Responses to 'Acting White' among Academically Able Black Adolescents." In *Beyond Acting White: Reframing the Debate on Black Student Achievement*, ed. Erin McNamara Horvat and Carla O'Connor, 27–56. Lanham, MD: Rowman & Littlefield, 2006.

Miller-Johnson, Shari, Philip Costanzo, John Coie, Mary Rose, Dorothy Browne, and Courtney Johnson. "Peer Social Structure and Risk-Taking Behaviors among African American Early Adolescents." *Journal of Youth and Adolescence* 32 (2003): 375–384.

Mounts, Nina, and Laurence Steinberg. "An Ecological Analysis of Peer Influence on Adolescent Grade Point Average and Drug Use." *Developmental Psychology* 31(1995): 915–922.

Muse, Benjamin. *Virginia's Massive Resistance.* Bloomington: Indiana University Press, 1961.

Neal-Barnett, Angela M. "Being Black: New Thoughts on the Old Phenomenon of Acting White." In *Forging Links: Clinical Developmental Perspectives*, ed. Angela M. Neal-Barnett, Josefina M. Contreas, and Kathryn A. Kerns, 75–88. Westport, CT: Praeger Publishers, 2001.

Newman, Katherine S. *No Shame in My Game: The Working Poor in the Inner City.* New York: Vintage and Russell Sage Foundation, 2000.

Norguera, Pedro. *City Schools and the American Dream.* New York: Teachers College Press, 2003.

Norwood, Kimberly. "Blackthink's Acting White Stigma in Education and How It Fosters Academic Paralysis in Black Youth." *Howard Law Journal* 50 (2007): 711–754.

Oakes, Jeannie. *Keeping Track: How Schools Structure Inequality.* New Haven, CT: Yale University Press, 1985.

———. "Two Cities' Tracking and Within-School Segregation." *Teachers College Record* 96 (1995): 681–690.

Oakes, Jeannie, and Gretchen Guiton. "Matchmaking: The Dynamics of High School Tracking Decisions." *American Educational Research Journal* 32 (1995): 3–33.

Oakes, Jeannie, Amy Stuart Wells, Makeba Jones, and Amanda Datnow. "Detracking: The Social Construction of Ability, Cultural Politics, and Resistance in Reform." *Teachers College Record* 98 (1997): 482–510.

O'Connor, Carla. "The Premise of Black Inferiority: An Enduring Obstacle Fifty Years Post *Brown*." *Yearbook of the National Society for the Study of Education* 105 (2006): 316–336.

———. "Race, Class, and Gender in America: Narratives of Opportunity among Low-Income African American Youths." *Sociology of Education* 72 (1999): 137–157.

O'Connor, Carla, Erin McNamara Horvat, and Amanda E. Lewis. "Framing the Field: Past and Future Research on the Historic Underachievement of Black Students." In *Beyond Acting White: Reframing the Debate on Black Student Achievement*, ed. Erin McNamara Horvat and Carla O'Connor, 1–24. Lanham, MD: Rowman & Littlefield, 2006.

Ogbu, John U. *Black American Students in an Affluent Suburb: A Study of Academic Disengagement*. Berkeley, CA: Lawrence Erlbaum, 2003.

———. "Origins of Human Competence: A Cultural-Ecological Perspective." *Child Development*, 52 (1981): 413–429.

———. "Variability in Minority School Performance: A Problem in Search of an Explanation." *Anthropology and Education Quarterly* 18 (1987): 312–334.

Ogletree, Charles, Jr. *All Deliberate Speed: Reflections on the First Half-Century of* Brown v. Board of Education. New York: Norton, 2004.

Orfield, Gary, and Susan E. Eaton. *Dismantling Desegregation: The Quiet Reversal of* Brown v. Board of Education. New York: New Press, 1996.

Painter, Nell Irvin. *Creating Black Americans: African-American History and Its Meanings, 1619 to the Present*. New York: Oxford University Press, 2006.

Parents Involved in Community Schools v. Seattle School District No. 1 et al. 551 U.S. (2007).

Patterson, Orlando. 2000. "Taking Culture Seriously: A Framework and an Afro-American Illustration." In *Culture Matters: How Values Shape Human Progress*, ed. Lawrence E. Harrison and Samuel P. Huntington, 202–218. New York: Basic Books, 2000.

Pattillo-McCoy, Mary. *Black Picket Fences: Privilege and Peril among the Black Middle Class*. Chicago: University of Chicago Press, 1999.

Perry, Pamela. *Shades of White: White Kids and Racial Identities in High School*. Durham, NC: Duke University Press, 2002.

Persell, Caroline Hodges. *Education and Inequality: A Theoretical and Empirical Synthesis*. New York: The Free Press, 1977.

Peterson-Lewis, Sonja, and Lisa Bratton. "Perceptions of 'Acting Black' among African American Teens: Implications of Racial Dramaturgy for Academic and Social Achievement." *The Urban Review* 36 (2004): 81–100.

Phillips, Meredith, James Crouse, and John Ralph. "Does the Black-White Test Score Gap Widen after Children Enter School?" In *The Black-White Test Score Gap*, ed. Christopher Jencks and Meredith Phillips, 229–272. Washington, DC: Brookings Institution Press, 1998.

Phinney, Jean. "The Multigroup Ethnic Identity Measure: A New Scale for Use with Diverse Groups." *Journal of Adolescent Research* 7 (1992): 156–176.

Pinkney, Alphonso. *Black Americans*. Englewood Cliffs, NJ: Prentice-Hall, 1993.

Resnick, Lauren. "From Aptitude to Effort: A New Foundation for Our Schools." *Daedalus* 124 (1995): 55–62.

Riehl, Carolyn, Aaron Pallas, and Gary Natriello. "Rites and Wrongs: Institutional Explanations for the Student Course-Scheduling Process in Urban High Schools." *American Journal of Education* 107 (1999): 116–154.

Rist, Ray C. 1970. "Student Social Class and Teacher Expectations: The Self-Fulfilling Prophecy in Ghetto Education." *Harvard Educational Review* 40 (3): 411–450.

Rosenbaum, James E. *Making Inequality: The Hidden Curriculum of High School Tracking*. New York: John Wiley and Sons, 1976.

Roscigno, Vincent, and James Ainsworth-Darnell. "Race, Cultural Capital, and Educational Resources: Persistent Inequalities and Achievement Returns." *Sociology of Education*, 72 (1999): 158–178.

Salzano, Rachel. "Speaking English Properly Is No Cause for Derision." *New York Times*, March 10, 1996, Available: http://query.nytimes.com/gst/fullpage.html?res=9401EFDE1639F933A25750C0A960958260.

Saulny, Susan. "Lightning Rod for Fury Over Schools' Gifted Programs." *New York Times*, March 22, 2006, Available: http://www.nytimes.com/2006/03/22/nyregion/22gifted.html.

Schofield, Janet Ward, and H. Andrew Sagar. "The Social Context of Learning in an Interracial School." In *Desegregated Schools: Appraisals of an American Experiment*, ed. Ray Rist, 155–199. New York: Academic Press, 1979.

Sennett, Richard, and Jonathan Cobb. *The Hidden Injuries of Class*. New York: Vintage, 1972.

Shelby, Tommie. *We Who Are Dark: The Philosophical Foundations of Black Solidarity*. Cambridge, MA: Harvard University Press, 2005.

Sieber, Timothy. "The Politics of Middle-Class Success in an Inner-City Public School." *Boston University Journal of Education* 164 (1982): 30–47.

Simmons, Timm. "A Crisis out of Hiding: Color of Their Skin Guides Destiny of Black Schoolchildren." *Raleigh News and Observer* (November 21, 1999): A1.

Sniderman, Paul M., and Thomas Piazza. *The Scar of Race*. Cambridge, MA: Harvard University Press, 1993.

Snow, David, and Leon Anderson. "Identity Work among the Homeless: The Verbal Construction and Avowal of Personal Identities." *American Journal of Sociology* 92 (1987): 1336–1371.

Spade, Joan, Lynn Columba, and Beth Vonfossen. "Tracking in Mathematics and Science: Courses and Course-Selection Procedures." *Sociology of Education* 70 (1997): 108–127.

Spencer, Margaret Beale. "Black Children's Race Awareness, Racial Attitudes and Self-Concept: A Reinterpretation." *Journal of Child Psychology and Psychiatry* 25 (1984): 433–441.

Spencer, Margaret Beale, Elizabeth Noll, Jill Stolzfus, and Vinay Harpalani. "Identity and School Adjustment: Revisiting the 'Acting White' Assumption." *Educational Psychologist* 36 (2001): 21–30.

Staiger, Annegret. *Learning Difference: Race and Schooling in the Multiracial Metropolis*. Stanford, CA: Stanford University Press, 2006.

———. "Whiteness as Giftedness: Racial Formation at an Urban High School." *Social Problems* 51 (2004): 161–181.

Steele, Claude. "Race and the Schooling of Black Americans." *Atlantic Monthly* 269 (1992): 68–78.

Steinberg, Laurence. *Beyond the Classroom: Why School Reform Has Failed and What Parents Need to Do*. New York: Simon & Schuster, 1996.

Steinberg, Laurence, Sanford M. Dornbusch, and Bradford B. Brown. "Ethnic Differences in Adolescent Achievement: An Ecological Perspective." *American Psychologist* 47 (1992): 723–729.

Steinhorn, Leonard, and Barbara Diggs-Brown. *By the Color of Our Skin: The Illusion of Integration and the Reality of Race*. New York: Dutton, 1999.

Stinchcombe, Arthur L. *Rebellion in a High School*. Chicago: Quadrangle Books, 1964.

Street, Paul. *Segregated Schools: Educational Apartheid in Post–Civil Rights America*. New York: Routledge, 2005.

Suárez-Orozco, Carola, and Marcelo Suárez-Orozco. *Transformations: Migration, Family Life, and Achievement Motivation among Latino Adolescents*. Stanford, CA: Stanford University Press, 1995.

Swidler, Ann. "Culture in Action: Symbols and Strategies." *American Sociological Review* 51 (1986): 273–286.

Tatum, Beverly Daniel. *"Why Are All the Black Kids Sitting Together in the Cafeteria?" and Other Conversations about Race*. New York: Basic Books, 1997.

Thoits, Peggy, and Lauren Virshup. "Me's and We's: Forms and Function of Social Identities." In *Self and Identity: Fundamental Issues*, ed. Richard D. Ashmore and Lee Jussim, 106–133. New York: Oxford University Press, 1997.

Traub, James. "Schools Are Not the Answer." *New York Times Magazine*, January 16, 2000.

Tyack, David. *The One Best System: A History of American Urban Education*. Cambridge, MA: Harvard University Press, 1974.

Tyson, Karolyn. "The Making of a 'Burden': Tracing the Development of a 'Burden of Acting White' in Schools." In *Beyond Acting White: Reframing the Debate on Black Student Achievement*, ed. Erin McNamara Horvat and Carla O'Connor, 57–88. Lanham, MD: Rowman & Littlefield, 2006.

———. "Providing Equal Access to 'Gifted' Education." In *Everyday Antiracism: Getting Real about Race in School*, ed. Mica Pollock, 126–131. New York: New Press, 2008.

———. "Weighing In: Elementary-Age Students and the Debate on Attitudes toward School among Black Students." *Social Forces* 80 (2002): 1157–1189.

Tyson, Karolyn, William Darity Jr., and Domini Castellino. "It's Not 'a Black Thing': Understanding a Burden of Acting White and Other Dilemmas of High Achievement." *American Sociological Review* 70 (2005): 582–605.

U.S. Department of Education, National Center for Education Statistics, National Assessment of Educational Progress (NAEP), NAEP 2004 Trends in Academic Progress; unpublished tabulations, NAEP Data Explorer. Rev. March 29, 2010. Available: http://nces.ed.gov/nationsreportcard/nde/

U.S. House Subcommittee on Select Education of the Committee on Education and Labor. *Improving the Education and Achievement of African American Males: Hearing on the Office of Educational Research and Improvement.* 102nd Cong., 1st sess., 1990.

Valenzuela, Angela. *Subtractive Schooling: U.S.-Mexican Youth and the Politics of Caring.* Albany: State University of New York Press, 1999.

Walters, Pamela Barnhouse. "Educational Access and the State: Historical Continuities and Discontinuities in Racial Inequality in American Education." *Sociology of Education* Extra Issue (2001): 35–49.

Waters, Mary. *Black Identities: West Indian Immigrant Dreams and American Realities.* New York: Russell Sage Foundation, 1999.

Welner, Kevin. *Legal Rights, Local Wrongs: When Community Control Collides with Educational Equity.* Albany: State University of New York Press, 2001.

———. "Ability Tracking: What Role for the Courts." *Education Law Reporter* 163 (2002): 565–571.

Wells, Amy Stuart, and Jeannie Oakes. "Potential Pitfalls of Systemic Reform: Early Lessons for Research on Detracking." *Sociology of Education* Extra Issue 69 (1996): 135–143.

———. "Tracking, Detracking and the Politics of Educational Reform: A Sociological Perspective." In *Sociology of Education: Emerging Perspectives*, ed. C. A. Torres and T. R. Mitchell, 155–180. Albany: State University of New York Press, 1998.

Wells, Amy Stuart, and Irene Serna. "The Politics of Culture: Understanding Local Political Resistance to Detracking in Racially Mixed Schools." *Harvard Educational Review* 66 (1996): 93–118.

West, Kimberly. "A Desegregation Tool That Backfired: Magnet Schools and Classroom Segregation." *Yale Law Review* 103 (1994): 2567–2592.

Williams, Terry, and William Kornblum. *Growing Up Poor.* Lexington, MA: Lexington Books, 1985.

Willie, Sarah. *Acting Black: College Identity and the Performance of Race.* New York: Routledge, 2003.

Willis, Paul E. *Learning to Labor: How Working-Class Kids Get Working-Class Jobs.* Farnborough, UK: Saxon House, 1977.

Wittrock, Merlin. "Teachers' Thought Processes." In *Handbook of Research on Teaching*, ed. Merlin Wittrock, 297–314. New York: Macmillan, 1986.

Young, Alford, Jr. "Navigating Race: Getting Ahead in the Lives of 'Rags to Riches' Young Black Men." In *The Cultural Territories of Race: Black and White Boundaries*, ed. Michele Lamont, 30–62. Chicago: University of Chicago Press, 1999.

Zimmer-Gembeck, Melanie, and W. Andrew Collins. "Autonomy Development during Adolescence." In *Blackwell Handbook of Adolescence*, ed. Gerald Adams and Michael Berzonsky, 175–203. Malden, MA: Blackwell, 2003.

Achievement ideology (*continued*)
meaning-making and, 28–33, 166
meritocracy ideology and,
21–22, 27, 51–53
oppositionality and, 166
prior achievement experiences
and, 21–23, 27
rejection of, 22, 28
social-class status and, 21–28,
30, 172
Achievement/race link, 3–9, 15,
17–18, 72–75, 109, 163–65
Achievement-related ridicule.
See also Acting white slur;
Racialized ridicule/teasing
achievement as arrogance,
52–53, 172
advanced classes selection
and, 128, 161–62
gifted programs and, 46–47
intra-racial, 80, 84, 85, 87,
113–19, 122–23, 172
nerd/geek ridicule, 71, 75–77,
104, 115, 166–67, 189n27
racial identity and, 7–8, 51–53,
79–81, 83–84
secure adolescents and, 83–84,
89, 98
self-perception of ability
and, 148–49, 162
social isolation and, 46–47
status-based resentment, 29,
51–53, 55, 84, 189n18,
192n35
vulnerable adolescents and,
83–84, 106–7, 108–10
Acting white slur. *See also*
Achievement cast as acting
white; Racialized ridicule/
teasing

academic underachievement/
achievement and, 11, 17–18,
32, 34, 36, 46, 67, 70, 75,
77–78, 163
achievement/race link and, 3–9,
15, 17–18, 72–75, 109,
163–65
adolescents and, 4, 36–37,
41–43
casting achievement as acting
white, 16–18, 32, 34, 36, 46,
67, 70, 75, 77–78, 163
consequences of, 164–66,
172–73
misinterpretations of, 3–4,
48–49, 75–78
Oreo slur, 7, 35–36, 84
origin of, 73
preadolescents and, 4, 15,
36–37, 37–41
as response to racialized
tracking, 6, 163–65
as symbolic power/control, 53,
73, 166
Adler, Patricia A., and Peter
Adler, 76
Advanced classes. *See also* Gifted
programs; School experiences
of students
achievement-related teasing
and, 128, 161–62
competence/confidence
development and, 9, 19–21,
139–42, 161, 162, 173
course enrollment patterns
and, 46–51, 127–30
definition of term, 134–35,
188n72, 191n9, 191n10
friendship networks and, 128,
130, 153–58, 161–62

McWhorter, John, 4
Meier, Kenneth, Joseph Stewart Jr.,
    and Robert England, 13,
    176n33
Meritocracy ideology, 21–22,
    27–28, 51–53
Methodology, vii–xiii, 168–69
Mickelson, Roslyn, 14, 98, 119
Mickelson, Roslyn, and Anne
    Velasco, 98
Milliken v. Bradley (1974), 178n41
Mounts, Nina, and Laurence
    Steinberg, 82

Neal-Barnet, Angela M., 123
Newman, Katherine, 28

Oakes, Jeannie, 152
Obama, Barack, 3
O'Connor, Carla, 27
Ogbu, John, 18, 25, 26, 29
Oppositional peer cultures
    academic achievement and, 79,
        120–21, 126, 166–69
    adolescent development and,
        81–83, 124
    anti-intellectualism and, 76–77,
        171–72, 176n13
    attitude-achievement paradox
        and, 119
    development of, 28–30, 32
    individual contextualized
        responses to, 79–81
    intra-racial, 113–19, 122–23
    parental input and, 81
    peer influences and, 15, 80–83,
        120
    pressure to conform to, 9, 15,
        49, 80–81, 90, 119, 124, 126,
        167

rejection of negative peer
    norms, 15, 97–98
responses to, 120, 124
responsibility for change
    and, 171
secure adolescents and, 88,
    96–97, 167
vulnerable adolescents and,
    167–68
Oreo slur, 7, 35–36, 84. *See also*
    Racial authenticity; Racial
    identity; Racialized ridicule/
    teasing
Osborne, Jason, 182n42

Painter, Nell Irvin, 36
Parental influences
    advanced classes and, 152–53
    gender and, 78
    gifted students and, 38, 150–53,
        191n24, 192n26, 192n27
    as motivators, 82, 120, 181n13
    oppositional peer cultures
        and, 81
    parental self-blame for
        educational choices, 23–26
    peer pressure and, 119, 120
    school practices/policies, 33,
        152, 181n26
    secure adolescents and, 81, 120
    vulnerable adolescents and, 81,
        101, 110, 120
Patterson, Orlando, 31
Pattillo-McCoy, Mary, 81, 92
Peer influence. *See also* Friendship
    networks; Secure adolescents;
    Vulnerable adolescents
    on academic achievement, 38–39
    achievement hierarchies and, 99,
        125

Peer influence (*continued*)
adolescence and, 81–83
animosity among students,
51–53
attitude development, 38–39,
124–26
conforming to peer norms,
119
distancing from negative cultural
stereotypes, 57–60
friendship networks and,
81–83
identity development and,
124–26
intra-racial oppositionality,
122–23
intra-racial ridicule, 80, 84, 85,
87, 113–19, 122–23, 172
negative behaviors and, 82–83
oppositional peer cultures
and, 15, 80–83, 120
parental influences, 119, 120
peer pressure and, 81–86,
119–24
positive/negative influences,
81–83
race-based discourse and, 29
secure adolescents and, 90, 167,
189n14, 189n15, 189n16
social-class status and, 121–23
vulnerable adolescents and, 99,
125, 167–68, 189n15
Perry, Pamela, 152, 192n36
Preadolescents
acting white slur and, 4, 15,
36–37, 37–41
attitudes toward school/
achievement and, 38–39
gifted programs and, 37–41,
147, 150–52

Race, Class and Education (Meier,
Stewart, and England), 13
Racial authenticity. *See also* Black
identity/blackness; Racial
identity
identity development and,
35–36, 74, 122–23, 164–66,
187n55
Oreo slur, 7, 35–36, 84
post-desegregation, 74
racialized teasing and, 35–36
social-class status and, 105, 116,
122–23
style of dress and, 23, 46, 54, 88,
108, 122
Racial identity. *See also* Black
identity/blackness; Identity
development; Racial
authenticity
academic achievement and, 75
achievement-related ridicule
and, 7–8, 51–53, 79–81,
83–84
adolescent racial identity
development, 81–83, 164–66
racial authenticity and, 35–36,
72, 74, 122–23, 187n55
social-class status and, 105, 116,
122–23
tracking and, 106
Racialized ridicule/teasing. *See also*
Achievement-related ridicule;
Acting White slur
casting achievement as acting
white, 16–17, 32, 34, 36, 46,
67, 70, 75, 77–78, 163
oreo slur, 7, 35–36, 84
racial diversity in schools and,
7–8, 53, 67, 69, 70–71, 84,
109